CARMELITE STUDIES

EXPERIENCING
ST THÉRÈSE TODAY

John Sullivan, OCD
Editor

ICS Publications
Washington, D.C.
1990

ICS Publications
2131 Lincoln Road, N.E
Washington, DC 20002

Typeset and Produced in the United States of America

Library of Congress Cataloging-in-Publication Data

Experiencing St. Thérèse today / John Sullivan, editor.
  p.   cm. — (Carmelite studies: 5)
  Includes bibliographical references.
  ISBN 0-935216-13-8
  1. Thérèse, de Lisieux, Saint, 1873-1897 — Congresses.
I. Sullivan, John, 1942-   . II. Series.
BX4700.T5E97   1990
282'.092 — dc20

89-28813
                                          CIP

TABLE OF CONTENTS

iii

Contents

ABBREVIATIONS

The full series of English-language translations of the Critical (Centenary) Edition of Thérèse's works is not yet available. We will adopt the following conventional abbreviations for use in this volume of CARMELITE STUDIES:

References will be supplied, first of all, to I.C.S. editions unless the authors of articles decide either to make their own translation or to supply the text of some other published translation.

The opinions or conclusions expressed in articles found in CARMELITE STUDIES are the personal responsibility of the respective authors and do not necessarily reflect the views of the I.C.S.

INTRODUCTION

To mark the centenary of St Thérèse's entrance into Carmel the Carmelites of the Ancient Observance (Province of the Most Pure Heart of Mary) conducted a symposium near Chicago late in 1988. This volume of CARMELITE STUDIES is I.C.S.'s way of collaborating with them by making available texts based on the formal papers given there to explore the theme "St Thérèse, Carmelite: An Experience Today."

Strikingly, Thérèse continues to maintain her appeal to thinkers and readers today: the written reflections assembled here point to it; and I.C.S. has known for some time—through distributing its books—that Thérèse still attracts many devotees. Our sales figures rank her *Story of a Soul* as the best selling Carmelite book we have produced, bar none. After publishing several articles in the first volume of CARMELITE STUDIES on Thérèse, we are happy to include the 1988 symposium papers in our series. Confident that they show how well she offers a fresh approach to the Gospel, we feel they deepen our knowledge of her.

One sign of appreciation for Thérèse—and it is mentioned several times in the eleven essays—was Alain Cavalier's beautiful, though flawed feature-length film, "Thérèse." Exiting from a showing of it here in Washington I heard one woman remark to another, "How would you like to be like her?—so pure, so committed." Those two characteristics of Thérèse are main poles of her up-to-date spirituality. Purity of intent—symbolized in so many vivid ways in her writings, but maybe none better than the words quoted by Graham Greene a while ago in his novella *Monsignor Quixote*, "Before we die by the sword, let us die by pin stabs"—made of Thérèse a selfless, dedicated lover of personified Good. Her deep sense of *commitment* to God and neighbor led her to real sacrifices without turning in on herself. By them both, she smilingly directed her attention to people needing help around her: from Pranzini early on, to obnoxious nuns in the monastery, to those at the "table of sinners," on to will-o'-the-wisp Diana Vaughan who elicited so much of her sympathy. They moved her to deep, adult compliance with the Gospel imperative of touching others by effective love.

vii

Pure and committed: traits sought after by so many of us as we start out toward the other end of this decade, one which will ring in the conclusion of a century and a millennium. Thérèse didn't have even a full decade to work with during her stay in the Lisieux Carmel, but no one doubts she was able to fill the years with great meaning precisely because she pursued purity and commitment in her typically wholehearted (but isn't that the real meaning of "little" for her?) way. She offers us a lot to learn from.

Just a word now about the lovely drawing across from the title page. Thérèse herself assured a young girl that she enjoyed sketching in a small sailboat atop a vacation-time letter (June 27, 1887). A few years earlier she drew a map of North America as a school exercise, and we are privileged to be able to reproduce it for the first time ever in the U.S. The original is a precious relic of Thérèse's juvenile artistic efforts. It now stands in the collection of the Carmelites of Darien, IL where the symposium papers were delivered two years ago. We extend our sincere thanks to our collaborators for their kind authorization to publish it here in CARMELITE STUDIES. For the reader curious to know what the caption at the bottom left corner indicates, it says the following — in the words of Thérèse's sister Pauline — about the authenticity of the sketch: "This map was sketched and written / by St Thérèse of the Child Jesus / at the age of 12 / Sr Agnes [Pauline] of Jesus, Unworthy Carmelite Religious / Carmel of Lisieux."

Our cover shows St Thérèse as a novice nine months after she entered Carmel in 1888. We have used this photo because the essays presented in this book commemorate the hundredth anniversary of that entrance.

John Sullivan, OCD
Editor

ST THÉRÈSE, CARMELITE:
AN EXPERIENCE TODAY

THE SONG OF SONGS AND ST THÉRÈSE

Roland Murphy

Roland Murphy is an emeritus professor of biblical exegesis and is one of the three editors of The New Jerome Biblical Commentary. *Currently he resides at the Carmelite house of studies, Whitefriars Hall, in Washington, DC.*

I would like to present two ways of reading the Song of Songs: one according to the historical-critical methodology which is practiced in biblical scholarship today, and the other according to the traditional (or mystical) tradition in which St Thérèse shared. I hold these two approaches together; one complements and develops the other, as I see it. It is helpful to discuss first the literal historical meaning of the Song, in order the better to appreciate the way Thérèse used it.

Certain basic questions immediately present themselves: what kind of poetry is this, and how many poems are there? What do they have to do with Solomon? How many speakers are there in the poem, and how are the lines to be distributed among them?

It is impossible in one article to justify all the positions that will be suggested, nor can all eight chapters be covered. One may consider the following remarks as challenges to one's own presuppositions in reading the Canticle of Canticles: are they reasonable and convincing or not?[1]

1

AN ANALYSIS OF THE SONG

It is the title which attributes the Song to Solomon. Nowhere in the text is he described as speaking. Doubtless the mention of his name in 1:3; 3:7-11 and 8:11-12 is responsible for the attribution. Indeed, we are unable to give a date to the work, although most scholars consider it postexilic. More important is the question of the speakers in the Song. The Hebrew text makes it clear that a man and a woman are the main speakers in a dialogue that extends through eight chapters, and for more than 90 percent of the verses one can be certain of the identity of the speaker. I am assuming that there is only one man (both shepherd and king; the lover is conceived in these disparate roles), and that there is no question of a real drama here, in which two individuals are wooing the woman. The role of the Daughters of Jerusalem is quite subordinate; they serve as a foil for the woman's statements.

The unity of the work is that of dialogue and mood. Dialogue: the man and woman are speaking to each other. (In some cases, it may not be clear whether the partner is physically present, as in 1:2-4.) Mood: there are poems of yearning (1:2-3; 7:8-9), of praise (2:2; 6:4-10), of description of the physical charms of the other (4:1-7; 5:10-16), of boasting (8:10, 12), of teasing (5:3), of self-description (2:1), reminiscences (2:8-14), etc. It is this constantly moving expression that the attentive reader has to be aware of. There are many allusions which are difficult for us to understand, but the general movement is clear. Let us turn to some examples.

There seems to be only a fragile unity to 2:8-17, since the dialogue does not run smoothly. However, a deliberate "inclusio" ("gazelle or young stag" in vv. 9 and 17) suggests that we are dealing with a unit which is best characterized as a reminiscence of the woman. She describes the speedy approach and arrival of her lover, and records his invitation to a tryst in the famous "Spring" song (notice the inclusion, "Arise . . . and come" in vv. 10 and 13). Verses 14-15 are his request to see and hear her, for she dwells in an inaccessible place—and her enigmatic reply. The words about the little foxes are really a conquettish "tease." She is not referring to real foxes and vineyards—although in real life vineyards were often devastated by wild animals. Rather she is suggesting that she is not as inaccessible as the lover indicated in v. 14. Already young men are laying siege to the young women (herself among them), who are symbolized by the vineyard (cf. Sg. 1:6). She closes her reminiscence with the formula of mutual belonging (cf. 6:3; 7:11), and an invitation to the lover to "roam" on the mountains of Bether (the reference is unknown, but it stands for the woman herself).

The parallelism between the search for the lover in chapters 3 and 5 has long been noted. They are not completely parallel, however, and the episode in 5:2ff. is integrated into a larger unit (5:2-6:3) which is addressed to the Daughters of Jerusalem. The woman begins with a description of a nocturnal experience with her lover, the theme of which is seeking and (not) finding (5:2-8); this is the section that is parallel to 3:1-4, which also ends with an address to the Daughters in 3:5. On this occasion she is unable to find her lover, and she delivers an adjuration to the Daughters to deliver a message if they should find him: she languishes with love (5:8). The Daughters ask for a description of this man, thus providing the woman with an opportunity to launch into a typical *wasf* or description of the physical charms of her lover (5:10-16). The interest of the Daughters is captured by the obviously superlative qualities of this "one among thousands," and they ask for his whereabouts (a momentary lapse of memory that he is lost), "that we may seek him with you" (6:1). At this point the woman delivers her triumphant reply: her lover is not really lost, but has always been with her (6:2-3), for "my lover has come down to his garden, to the beds of spice, to browse in the garden and gather lilies." She, of course, is the garden (cf. 4:12-5:1), and lilies are associated with her (2:1; 4:5).

One of the classic lines in the Song is 8:6,

Place me as a seal on your heart,
   as a seal on your arm.
Strong as death is love,
   intense as Sheol is ardor;
Its shafts are shafts of fire,
   a flame of Yah. (author's translation)

The woman desires to be always united with her lover, to be as present to him as the typical seal, or identity card, worn by the ancient Israelite. (cf. Gn. 38:18) She then compares love to death/

Sheol. What is the point of the comparison? One has to comprehend the significance of death and Sheol. Death and Sheol are
paralleled often in the Hebrew Bible. Sheol is, in the words of
Qoheleth (9:10), the place to which all go at death, where there is no
work, reason, knowledge or wisdom, which Job described as "the
black, disordered land where darkness is the only light." (Jb.
10:22) It is a totally negative condition, and its worst aspect is that there is
no living contact with God (Pss. 6:6; 30:10, etc.). But Sheol-Death
was not simply an inevitable end; it was a power. Sheol is dynamic,
conceived as pursuing human beings while they are still alive. To
the extent that any person experiences non-life in the here and
now, to that extent, they are in the "hand" of Sheol (Ps. 89:49), from
which they beseech the Lord for deliverance. Thus the psalmist
praises God for bringing him up from Sheol (Ps. 30:4). The Song
praises Love for its power; it is as strong as Sheol itself, the greatest
power outside of God that the Israelite was aware of in this life. The
poet goes on to describe human love as a fire—a particular kind of
fire, "the flame of Yah." This phrase is commonly rendered as "a
most vehement flame" (so the Revised Standard Version), in which
"Yah" the short form of the sacred name Yahweh, is taken as a
superlative. However, the New Jerusalem Bible renders more literally and in this case more significantly, "a flame of Yahweh himself." What is the meaning of such a statement? It associates the
sexual love described in the poem with the Lord; the flames of
human love are somehow the flame of God. The relationship is not
described further (a participation in divine love? or is the Lord the
author of love? none of this is explicit). There remains a mysterious
connection between human love and divine love—an association
which is described in 1 Jn. 4:16 as "God is love." If this understanding of 8:6 is correct, the Song itself gives evidence of a deeper
level of understanding the phenomenon of love.

These examples may suffice to illustrate the kind of poetry we
are dealing with, and the movement of thought and emotion in the
poem. Whatever lovers can speak to each other one finds spoken in
the Song. This is the language of make-believe, for such is the
language of love which exalts the lovers. We may conclude that in
the literal historical sense, the poems describe love between the
sexes, a man and a woman, whose mutual love dominates the
poetry from beginning to end. The theme of seeking and finding,

or presence and absence, is a perennial one in love poetry, and so here as well. Moreover, the mutual fidelity should be carefully noted. The generosity in their praise of each other, the frankness of their yearning, the extravagance of their language—all these characteristics will be perceived in a careful reading. Moreover, more lines are to be attributed to the woman than to the man. While this might suggest that the author was a woman, we have no way of ascertaining this.

THE MEANING OF THE SONG

It is clear from the foregoing that the obvious meaning of the Song is that it constitutes love poetry between a man and a woman. It is dealing with human sexual love. But is that the only level of meaning in the Song?[2]

It is an astonishing fact that the Song was commonly interpreted among both the Jewish and Christian traditions on another level. It was understood to refer to the love of God and his people: between the Lord and Israel for the Jewish community; between Christ and the Church for the Christian community. Origen early on (ca. 185-254), was the most important commentator in the Christian community, and his approach set the tone for later mystical understanding, especially as the Song is referred to Christ and the individual soul. The question for us today is: can this traditional understanding be maintained in the light of critical scholarship? I would argue that it can be maintained, for the following reasons. First, the literal historical interpretation of a text (any text!) does not exhaust its meaning. This is a hermeneutical issue which nearly everyone agrees on; there is more than one way to read a text. The only qualification I would add to this is that the literal historical meaning serves as a *negative* criterion. That is to say, it helps one to avoid the vagaries of very subjective readings which can build up around a text. This has happened to the Song in the course of history, as the text was allegorized to death, and the literal meaning was simply snuffed out. But the allegorical fantasies of the tradition are not a necessary part of the meaning which refers the Song to God and humanity. Secondly, a significant fact is the presence within the biblical tradition of the use of the love/marriage symbol to express the relationship between God and humans. This is a commonplace among the Hebrew prophets (Hos. 1-3; Is. 62:5, etc.) and it continues into the New Testament (Eph. 5:22-23). It is not intended as a gridlock on the meaning of the Canticle, but to suggest that when a text deals with love, its applicability is capable of expansion and extension. Thirdly the final reason is the interpretation of Sg. 8:6, which has been already presented. In other words, there seems to be present within the Song a connection between the flames of human love and the love of the Lord.

THÉRÈSE'S USE OF THE SONG

The saint herself has given us a text with which we may profitably begin to assess her knowledge of the Bible and the Song of Songs. In her autobiography she writes:

> Ah! how many lights have I not drawn from the works of our holy Father, St John of the Cross! At the ages of seventeen and eighteen I had no other spiritual nourishment; later on, however, all books left me in aridity and I'm still in that state. If I open a book composed by a spiritual author (even the most beautiful, the most touching book), I feel my heart contract immediately and I read without understanding, so to speak. Or if I do understand, my mind comes to a standstill without the capacity of meditating. In this helplessness, Holy Scripture and the *Imitation* come to my aid; in them I discover a solid and very pure nourishment. But it is especially the *Gospels* which sustain me during my hours of prayer, for in them I find what is necessary for my poor little soul. I am constantly discovering in them new lights, hidden and mysterious meanings.[3]

It is surely significant that this passage follows upon a quotation from the *Spiritual Canticle* of John of the Cross, in which echoes of the biblical Canticle are present (stanzas 26 and 28). Doubtless the approach of John to the Song of Songs and its imagery influenced the Little Flower.[4] Let us try to interpret Thérèse's words in a realistic manner. She was not a bookish person, and the level of her knowledge of the Bible would not be above the average French

Catholic of the turn of the century. It is clear that for her David wrote the psalms, to take but one example of her unsophisticated literary approach.[5] Indeed, her knowledge of the Bible was molded primarily by the use of the Bible in the Divine Office.[6] And here the traditional interpretation of the Song of Songs was paramount. Thérèse inherited her understanding of the Song from the Catholic tradition that reaches back firmly to Origen as its most brilliant proponent. It is well for people of our generation to keep in mind that it was the Vulgate form of the text which Thérèse knew, and that time for private study and reading of the Bible was not as available to her as it is for sisters today (one need only recall the cramped conditions under which she wrote her autobiography!).

We turn now to some examples of Thérèse's use of the Song of Songs. To judge from the frequency of certain quotations, she had her favorite passages—favorite in the sense that they easily came to her mind. Some of these are mere allusions; in others she addresses the text in greater detail. For convenience sake we will follow the sequence of the Song of Songs.

Sg. 1:3: "Draw me, we shall run after you in the odor of your ointments." The mention of the odor of the ointments is an expansion of the Latin text, found in some Vulgate manuscripts. Thérèse of course, is not interested in this; she concentrates on the attraction of Christ: "What is it then to ask to be *'Drawn'* if not to be united in an intimate way to the object which captivates our heart?" At the same time she recognizes that she does not go alone: "I feel that the more the fire of love burns within my heart, the more I shall say: *'Draw me,'* the more also the souls who will approach me (poor little piece of iron, useless if I withdraw from the divine furnace), the more these souls *will run swiftly in the odor of the ointments of their Beloved.*" And again,

> Dear Mother, now I would like to tell you what I understand by the *odor of the ointments* of the Beloved. Since Jesus has reascended into heaven, I can follow him only in the traces he has left; but how luminous these traces are! how perfumed! I have only to cast a glance in the Gospels and immediately I breathe in the perfumes of Jesus' life, and I know on which side to run.[7]

Sg. 1:13 (Vg. 12): "My lover is for me a bundle of myrrh dwelling on my breasts." Thérèse merely alludes to this verse in the course

of encouraging Céline to carry her seemingly heavenly burden—
just as Jesus was a burden for Mary (a light one) and for St Christopher. The myrrh here signifies suffering.[8]

Sg. 2:3: In a letter to Père Roulland, there is an allusion to
"resting in the shade of the one I had desired" (Cf. Vulgate). She
preferred such a resting place even over a journey to Jerusalem![9]

Sg. 3:17: The falling shadows. Thérèse seems to have taken this
phrase in the sense of the transience of the world; it is joined with
1 Cor. 7:31 (the world passes away) especially in letters to Céline.[10]

Sg. 6:11-12 (Vg. vv. 10-11): Verse 12 is the most uncertain in the
poem. The woman speaks of going down to the nut garden to see
the awakening and growth of the plants, and she is (suddenly) disturbed "on account of the chariots of Aminadab"—so the Vulgate
reading of an uncertain text. In a letter to Céline Thérèse quotes
these lines as an image of a soul steeped in dryness and goes on to
say that these verses image our souls. That is to say, whereas one
found nourishment before in fertile fields (of writings), now one is
in a dry desert without light and peace. The cause? The chariots of
Aminadab:

> the chariots, those vain noises which afflict us—are they within us or
> without? We do not know . . . but Jesus does. He sees our sadness and
> suddenly his gentle voice makes itself heard, a voice more gentle than
> the breath of Spring: 'Return, return, my Sulamite, in order that we
> may look at you' (Sg. 7:1; Vg. 6:12).[11]

The Aminadab of the Vulgate has been interpreted in extreme
fashion throughout history: as good and as bad. He apears in the
final strophe of St John's *Spiritual Canticle*, and is explicitly identified
with the devil in John's commentary on the verse.[12]

It is worth noting that references to the Song are particularly
frequent in letters to Céline. In one she sends a catena of texts from
Is. 53 and Sg. 5:1.[13] In another letter, a delicate one to Céline who
has not been understood by her sister Pauline, Thérèse remarks,

> In the Canticle of Canticles there is a passage that fits perfectly poor
> little Céline in exile: "What do you see in the spouse but musical
> choirs in an armed camp" (7:1). O yes! The life of my Céline is truly a
> battlefield . . . Poor little dove, she groans on the banks of the rivers

of Babylon, and how could she sing the songs of the Lord in a strange land? (Ps. 137:1, 4)[14]

We may fittingly close our discussion of Thérèse's use of the Song with her bold and fascinating statement, "If I had the time I would like to comment on the Canticle of Canticles; in this book I have discovered such profound things about the union of the soul with the Beloved."[15] There are many reasons to admire these words: for one thing, the ease with which she accepts and even yearns to comment on a biblical book (to my knowledge, she has said this of no other book in the Bible). Can we make a surmise about the missing commentary? What would it have been like? I would suggest the "Sermons" of Bernard of Clairvaux. He wrote eighty-six sermons for his confreres at Clairvaux over a period of eighteen years (1135-1153) in a century that could count some thirty works dealing solely with the Song of Songs.

The similarity between Bernard and Thérèse consists in the fact that both understand the Song in the traditional sense of Christ and the individual soul, and moreover, each uses the text of the Song in a free and easy way—in a sense, the text becomes a trampoline to propel one into deeper reaches of love. Love of God/Christ is the basic reality for both of them. I am sure that Thérèse would have agreed with these words of Bernard:

> Who is it whom your soul loves, for whom you inqure? Has he no name? Who are you and who is he? I speak like this because of the strange style of speech and extraordinary disregard for names, quite different from the ways of Scripture. But in this marriage song it is affections, not words, that are to be considered. Why is this, except that the holy love which is the subject of the entire Song cannot be expressed by words or language, but only in deed and truth. Here love speaks everywhere! If anyone desires to grasp these writings, let him love! For anyone who does not love it is vain to listen to this song of love, or to read it, for a cold heart cannot catch fire from its eloquence. The one who does not know Greek cannot understand Greek, nor can one ignorant of Latin understand another speaking Latin, etc. So, too, the language of love will be meaningless jangle, like sounding brass or tinkling cymbal, to anyone who does not love.[16]

Yes, on these terms, Thérèse would have been an outstanding commentator on the Song. She loved!

THE WORLD OF THÉRÈSE: FRANCE, CHURCH AND STATE IN THE LATE NINETEENTH CENTURY

Leopold Glueckert

Leopold Glueckert teaches history at Loyola University in Chicago. He recently headed Loyola's summer school program in Rome.

The French church and state which Thérèse Martin knew so well grew out of a complex blend of historical factors. She lived her short life assuming, even taking for granted, a lot of things that never occur to us. There was a huge corpus of political and cultural baggage that made her immediate world what it was. Her writings demonstrate that she knew a great deal about world events, political issues, newspaper editorials, and so forth, both inside and outside of France. But this consciousness of hers completely eludes us today, unless we make an effort to reevoke those issues which were never too far from her own mind. If we, a century later, intend to "put on" the mind of Thérèse, to really learn from her in the manner that her thoughts developed, and to see things as she saw them, then we must tap into that huge category called "background" or "context." In this article, I propose to do just that.[1]

The records tell us that Thérèse was born in 1873, entered Carmel in '88, and died in '97. These years perfectly span the formation time of the Third French Republic, from the first provisional government as far as the Dreyfus case. They present a political crucible of the sort of wrangling and very stormy church-state disputes that were just too big to ignore. Thérèse grew up knowing every detail simply by reading the morning paper, or talking with someone else who had. And yet that same resilient republic which so many good Catholics hated from its inception would eventually turn out to be rugged enough and adaptable enough to survive until the French defeat by Hitler in 1940.

Thérèse certainly found her own age a very exciting time to be alive. French colonies were being founded in Indochina, Africa and the Pacific. Missions were certainly a part of her thought and her prayer. The popular enthusiasm for discovery and conquest in faraway places was matched in the French church of her own day by a vigorous missionary zeal to preach the Gospel of Jesus Christ to the people of those lands—a zeal which Thérèse herself shared. She did not become the patroness of the missions by accident! And finally, most of her life also coincides with the reign of Pope Leo XIII, who adapted the Church so successfully to the modern world, and proved that there was genuinely life after Papal States.

So what I plan to do is to briefly discuss the political conditions within France, relations between the French state and the church, and the French Third Republic seen in the context of the world.

Thérèse was born in 1873, as were such notables as Enrico Caruso and Sergei Rachmaninoff. Pope Pius IX still had five years to live, but they would not be very happy ones for him. Former Emperor Napoleon III died in exile that same year, settling forever the question of his possible return to power in France. There was a provisional president who was elected, and the beginnings of the Third Republic were finally, agonizingly, set into motion. The weather that year was pleasant. The harvest was good. The German armies were finally leaving France after a very bitter occupation following the Franco-Prussian war. And in the faraway United States, the gunsmiths of the Remington company decided to diversify ther manufacturing—they started building typewriters.

It was time for some very hot political debate, and in a great sense, soul-searching, for these people of France, who suddenly found themselves without a government . . . *again*. They asked:

"How should we put it together this time? What will be most acceptable to the majority of French citizens? How should we avoid the mistakes of the past and still preserve the good things which have made France literally the center of Europe for so many centuries?" These were the questions on the minds of nearly everyone. The biggest problem was a built-in conflict, nearly a century old, between the two blocs of ideas which divided and polarized most French citizens in a way that we find difficult to even imagine. In one bloc, we have a union between religion and royalism. In the opposing bloc, we have the republicans, the revolutionaries, the anticlericals: the people who represented (as far as most practicing Catholics were concerned) atheism, anarchy, disorder, persecution, and everything else they wanted to avoid. But before we can understand the time of Thérèse, we must backpedal just a bit to consider the French Revolution itself.

I

Although the big Revolution had occurred nearly a century before, nearly every political dispute of Thérèse's own time had roots there. And even though there had been no major upheaval of the same magnitude since Napoleon's defeat at Waterloo in 1815, there were still many of the same questions of the whole knotty problem of church-state relations which were not yet resolved. These questions were still open wounds, which were festering, and creating great problems for otherwise good people. Before 1789, that is, before the Revolution, both the monarchy and the established church had been considered the two venerable pillars of society. Both were quite distinct institutions, of course, but they tended to blend together in the popular mind: when you thought of one, you were naturally reminded of the other, for better or for worse. So when the members of the National Assembly, at the very beginning of the Revolution, set their sights on reforming the monarchy, the church was the next, obvious thing on their agenda.

From the standpoint of the church and the religious orders in France, many of those who took leadership during the Revolution were very unfriendly to traditional religion. Although many of these people were noble, educated and high-minded individuals, they also tended to follow the thinkers of the Enlightenment. Among the reformers, there were many agnostics, Freemasons and Deists, but very few devout, practicing Catholics. This is the heart of our problem.

Unfortunately, there was very little to admire in the leadership of the French church before the Revolution. Every single one of the bishops in 1789 was from a noble family; there were no commoners, not even one. And some of these were also agnostics, in spite of their offices. Many of these aristocratic prelates—those who were part of the problem—were from specific families where there was a long tradition of church service, mainly in the upper clergy, of course. One such dynasty was the de Rohan family; there was a Cardinal de Rohan at the time who was just the latest in a long line of bishops, prelates, and abbots going back for centuries. Another clan was the Talleyrand-Perigord family. Its latest champion was the famous Maurice de Talleyrand, who would go down in history as one of its most astute politicians, as well as a famous turncoat. He began as bishop of Autun, even though he was one of those agnostics. He was a superb administrator, and very consistently followed what his family expected of him, which was to hold a bishopric or two open for them. He was quite good at that. Preaching, sacraments, liturgy were expendable, because nearly everyone considered them so.

People did not trust the bishops to do those things well in the French church. Bishops were not expected to be theologians, but to create jobs. One had to look elsewhere for most of the holiness, most of the piety, most of the good, hard work which made their church a true "people of God." The virtuous were certainly alive and well—France did not have a dead church by any means. But to find these best people you had to look in convents, in country rectories, in peasant communities. Living in some farming hamlets was almost like growing up in a novitiate, because of the many holy people there. There was certainly no general elitism in these places. Still, many bishops were so far detached from ordinary, good Catholics and their concerns, that they were very much part of the overall problem. They were administrators and princes first, and pastors as a very poor second, if at all. The chasm between them and the lower clergy was immense. So when the crisis finally hit, the church went through the Revolution quite badly, as we will see. One can understand a few reasons why educated people of that time might view their church as an obsolete, dying institution, a block to progress, a refuge for superstition and emotional hysteria.

After all, the Deists of the Enlightenment had very effectively sold their image of the Creator-God as a "Divine Watchmaker": a powerful and intelligent being, who could create this wonderfully complex universe with its interlocking physical laws, but who was likewise completely devoid of any emotion and feeling. In other words, the Deists' God was total intellect. God, literally, didn't care about the world. So why should anyone else care in the slightest about making contact with this aloof, unfeeling Creator-Spirit? Can you imagine anything further from the way Thérèse looked at God? There was only one century of difference, but it was like night and day.

So for Enlightenment partisans, some church institutions had obvious social value, such as hospitals, schools, or work among the poor. Other practices like religious poverty, celibacy, intercessory prayer, penance, and fasting were looked upon as valueless (because God wouldn't care) and possibly even dangerous, insofar as they promoted ignorance and misunderstanding among credulous people about the scientifically perfect universe. Seen in this context, people in a cloistered convent might seem perfectly harmless to those of us who know something about them, but they represented a potent threat to people who were schooled in the Enlightenment. They represented much of what these forward-looking modernizers hated and wanted to destroy. And they almost succeeded. Even a century later, the Lisieux Carmel represented the failure of the anti-clericals' earlier campaign to eliminate religious orders. When the Third Republic was founded, there were at least some of these anti-clericals, a "remnant of Babylon," who felt that they had to try again.

Beginning in the fall of 1789, a series of laws were passed which were intended to smash the political power of the church, and systematically dismantle the fabric of religious life. In October of that year, all church property was seized and sold to pay off the national debt. The original suggestion was made by a bishop (Talleyrand) who was already smelling a change in the political wind. In February of the following year, religious orders and congregations were abolished and all communities suppressed, except for those doing "practical" apostolic work. Their property also went to the state.

In July of 1790, the Civil Constitution of the Clergy was published. According to that law, priests were ordered to take an oath to the state, and became salaried employees in what amounted to a national, state church. Religious vows could be declared null and void if the individual would simply ask for release before a civil magistrate; most religious were aggressively encouraged to do so. There were government commissions which made the rounds of religious houses and insisted on speaking with each individual in the community. They proceeded to explain the great favor which was now being offered by the revolutionary government. (They assumed, of course, that the religious were all there as semi-prisoners, against their will, and not voluntarily.) There were some religious who decided to take advantage of their new liberation, and were released from all legal bonds to their orders; most of these, with their newfound "freedom," then began to look for jobs. But all the rest, those who decided to stay, were still not allowed to live in community, wear religious habits and pray in public. So they could continue, if they wished, in their obscurantism, but the government was not going to make it easy for them.

We know that the Carmelites, as a religious family, were wiped out in the Revolution. This means that eight provinces of the Ancient Observance were eliminated; and there were another six provinces of Discalced friars destroyed. This translates to 130 houses of the Ancient Observance with 721 friars, much diminished from the numbers of just a century before. The Discalced lost seventy-nine houses of friars and sixty-five monasteries of cloistered nuns. Some of the Discalced religious managed to maintain their identity long enough to refound a house here or there, but for the Ancient Observance, the suppression was permanent. There were no successful foundations after the Revolution, and still have not been. For the past two centuries, all French Carmelites have been Discalced.

Some of these refoundations took place because the religious simply went underground to survive. Some communities, in effect, never really died out, even though their houses were gone. In both branches of the Order, there were priests or brothers or sisters who managed to maintain connections with one another. They lived a genuine "catacomb" existence until it was finally safe to reemerge once the political storms had blown over. But such a success did not happen all that quickly or all that often.

We have the horrible image of many priests and religious being killed during the Reign of Terror, and there certainly were large numbers of martyrs. But since it appears that most of those sent to the guillotine were *not* Carmelites, it is fair to assume that most of our evicted religious simply blended back into the general population and attempted to carry on as best they could. In effect, these religious were condemned to the slow death of suppression. We do know of a Carmelite connection to the September Massacres of 1792, which began the bloodbath against the clergy and religious. This first episode of the Reign of Terror began at the Discalced Carmelite house on the Rue de Vaugirard. That house had been allowed to function a bit longer than others, principally because many of the friars of the community had favored many of the good changes enacted by the Revolution. But in time even these friars were turned out and the municipal government promptly turned their house into a prison for members of the "black clergy": diocesan priests who refused to take the oath of loyalty to the government. Quite a number of these were killed in early September when a mob broke in there. Among the victims of the September Massacres (there and elsewhere) were probably some 1400 people, including three bishops and several hundred priests—all killed by people who didn't know their names. It was a frightful example of generic, mindless fear, combined with a certain element of pent-up rage against the church for real and imagined offenses from the past. The revolutionary government was able to document the fact that there were no substantial charges against any of the individuals killed.

When it comes to Carmelite martyrs of the Revolution, we are probably most familiar with the sixteen nuns of Compiègne. The sisters of this particular monastery were steadfast enough to stand against the discriminatory laws, and thus became immortalized in the *Dialogues of the Carmelites* by Bernanos and Poulenc. Both artists do a fine job of highlighting the nuns' heroism, albeit without following much of the details of what really happened to them. It is worth noticing, by the way, that these sixteen very heroic women were executed only ten days before the virtual end of the Reign of Terror. I suspect that the spectacle of these sisters being sent to the guillotine, wearing as much of the Carmelite habit as they could piece together from bits of salvaged clothing, was just too much for public opinion to accept. I have a hunch that there was enough revulsion in even the most bloodthirsty members of the Paris mob, people who had seen thousands of prisoners killed for real and imagined crimes, to see that these were not "enemies of the people" in any sense. Maybe the Reign of Terror had gone on just a bit too long. Within less than two weeks, Maximillian Robespierre, the Jacobin leader who was the heart and soul of the Terror, was himself captured and sent to the guillotine. Once he was dead, the Terror stopped as well.

By the time of Napoleon, only a few years later, one of the first things that the self proclaimed First Consul knew that he *had* to do was finally work out some kind of peace between church and state in France. One of Napoleon's most successful actions was the signing of the Concordat of 1801 between France and Pope Pius VII. In so doing, he restored effective peace with the pope and the French bishops, and they in turn allowed a certain degree of compromise on such issues as the loss of church lands, the long overdue reform of diocesan boundaries, a certain amount of state influence over selection of bishops, and so forth.

But it is important to remember that the Concordat, while it ended the persecutions and the cold war with the church in general, did not help the religious orders one bit. As shown, the religious orders themselves were seen as subversive organizations, as people who were preserving the obscurantism of the Middle Ages, as it was conceived; above all, since the orders were international, they were deemed "agents of a foreign power" (the one in Rome). Even among the bishops, the orders were not a high priority. So it would take quite a while before the religious in France would be able to make any sort of recovery.

At this point, it will help to briefly distinguish two trends within the French church: Gallicanism and Ultramontanism. Gallicanism favored a strongly national church which was relatively independent of Rome, although technically "in communion" with the pope (whatever that actually meant in practice). The other tendency was Ultamontanism, which favored a very close collaboration between France and the papacy. Now in theory these two trends will continue, with a few modifications, all through the next century, until the time of Thérèse. By that time, both of them were beginning to wither and die, or more accurately, blend together and salvage the good points of both. The "good" reason for Ultramontanism in the nineteenth century was the need to respond to the post-revolutionary society with a strongly centralized church, uniform in doctrine, clerical lifestyle, discipline, and governed by an infallible pope and a watchful Roman Curia. The Gallicans, on the other hand, favored a strongly French church with only ceremonial ties to Rome. They believed that the church would lose all influence in modern society unless it had very deep roots in the national character and local institutions, with only a very loose federal, collegial structure.

In practice, this boiled down to something a bit less noble, such as which way money was allowed to flow. Historically, contributions sent from France to Rome were always among the first items to be eliminated whenever this problem came up. Essentially, the bishops were declaring a degree of financial independence from the need to support the papacy beyond what they felt was a properly symbolic level. Likewise, there was a great deal of pride and national sentiment in the Gallican position. They stressed the idea of a "splendid isolation" from foreign tampering, and glorified the concept of totally independent French prince-bishops who were supreme and unfettered in their own sees. They were not too favorable to religious orders, of course, since orders tended to be too international, and governed by the pope or by a Father General who lived somewhere other than France.

Unfortunately for the Gallicans, they discovered only too late that, by the time they nearly eliminated Roman influence (near the middle of the eighteenth century), they had isolated themselves from just the people who could have helped them against the revolutionary government. Ironically, the eighteenth-century Gallicans doomed their church, because they were no longer able to appeal for any sort of international sympathy or aid. Just by way of contrast, we might recall that someone as recent as Titus Brandsma gloried in the idea that he belonged to a universal church which had nothing whatever to do with Dutch nationalism. He was able to speak both in Holland and in Germany with much greater authority, simply because he was not bound to the political policies being promoted in those countries.

By contrast, the Ultramontane position was strong on centralization in Rome and all of the control that its policy implied. But it was also much better at following the global perspective, and not being swept away by national politics which, after all, have a way of changing around very quickly. Above all, the centralized Roman church was always much better at promoting mission activity in foreign lands, which of course weren't strong enough to have national churches. So from the perspective of what the church probably needed, at least in the nineteenth century, the centralized model seemed to work better, when it was allowed to work at all.

II

Now after the fall of Napoleon's Empire and the return of the monarchy in 1815, we have a long, extended period of what is collectively referred to as "the Restoration." I'm joining together several different regimes here because, for our purposes, they are all relatively equivalent to one another. We are going to ignore the differences between the Bourbon monarchy (which lasted for fifteen years) and the Orleanist monarchy (which ruled for the next eighteen years), as well as the very brief Second Republic, followed by the Second Empire (another twenty-two years). Both of these were controlled by the nephew of Napoleon I, Louis Napoleon Bonaparte. He was elected president of the republic, then connived to get himself crowned Emperor Napoleon III. But all three of these regimes, at least in part, restored the principle that the monarchy (or the empire) protected and supported the Catholic Church. All three also went on to restrict the church, too, so it was not an entirely happy marriage. The church was certainly *protected* by these three regimes, but once again, it was not really *helped*.

By "help" I don't necessarily mean financial support—money really had nothing to do with what the French church needed. What I'm referring to is the kind of help that *persecutors* give the Church: reining in some of the normal disorder, making people rethink why they are following the Gospel, forcing discussion and defence of values, and so forth. Persecution is never comfortable for the Church or anyone else, but it has a way of keeping us fairly "lean and mean."

The restored church of 1815 was not the same one that had provoked such hatred in 1789. Although it had been shorn of much of its land and wealth, the Restoration church was much more spiritual and zealous, better disciplined and far more conscious of Gospel values than its predecessor. Most of the old prince-bishops had either died off, or been replaced, or had simply resigned and fled to save themselves. By the end of the nineteenth century, Catholics had regained their confidence and political power, especially in more conservative provinces, such as Thérèse's Normandy.

However, one problem remained. The church (the hierarchy in particular) continued to identify with hopeless royalist causes (even after the Bourbon monarchy had been replaced in 1830), and promote anti-republican sentiment. Unfortunately, they were generally not following the best of their own people. Most of the new prelates, the ones named after the Restoration, were very good bishops. They were generally holy, learned, hard working individuals. But they could not seem to let go of that old idea that royalism was essential to a free church. It was not until the time of the Third Republic, the time of Thérèse, that we begin to see the first glimmers of a new and conciliatory attitude: that maybe a strong, healthy, free-standing church *could* live within a republic. Maybe all would get along. Maybe the mission efforts of the church would work after all . . . even alongside republican institutions. Perhaps if one built in some basic controls within the republican constitution (who would even have thought that a century before?), maybe one might even be able to build the *best* church France ever had.

During the first Restoration of 1815 (the restoration of the ancient Bourbon family which had ruled France for centuries) the church was the most protected ever, but it was also the least effective.

After 1830, we have the Orleanist regime of King Louis Philippe —from a junior branch of the Bourbon family—which was administered largely by ministers rather than the king. The most famous of these was François Guizot who, incidentally, was elected to Parliament from the district which represented Lisieux. This fact tells us something of the Lisieux voters: Guizot was a Protestant, but the voters were still broad-minded enough to go outside their own religious community to elect a deputy with obvious talent. Admittedly Guizot was a strong Conservative, but for the times in which he lived he developed a very good policy for France, and deserves to be remembered for that. One might also note that it was during the Orleanist period that the Carmelites were actually re-established in France. Many of the convents of nuns had actually been restored secretly after the first restoration. It was not as though they were clandestine houses, just that they were "off the record," with no formal permissions. By 1880, when Thérèse herself was already considering religious life, there were 113 monasteries of Discalced nuns in France. But only sixteen of them were "legal"; only sixteen of the total had gone through the red tape of getting the government's authorization, with all of the permits, clearances and legal safeguards to ensure their future as a functioning religious community. All the rest were a bit on thin ice. But the mere fact that nearly a hundred unofficial, illegal monasteries were still alive and flourishing indicates something about the enforcement procedures. Most magistrates, judges and police officials, agnostics or not, Freemasons or not, were certainly able to see that these sisters were doing no harm to the people at large. So when it came to "keeping the peace" in their districts, they nearly always asked "Why bother them?"

By 1839, the Discalced friars were able to begin refounding their community in France, too. And even though they sometimes continued to experience difficulties, the growth was fairly steady through the end of the century. In 1838, the year just preceding that event, the monastery of Lisieux was founded on the Rue de Liverot. The founders were sisters from the monastery of Poitiers. I believe that Lisieux was one of the "illegal" monasteries but once again, in Normandy, people were rather solidly religious. They liked the idea of having sisters nearby, praying for them and their needs, so they could overlook the legal niceties. It was probably a good reaction.

Following the overthrow of the Orleanist monarchy (1848) we have the Second Republic, the one with Louis Napoleon Bonaparte as president; but within four years this folded into the Second Napoleonic Empire, with the same man crowned as Emperor Napoleon III. He certainly was not the military genius that his uncle was, but as a political leader he was, I believe, far more successful. For one thing, he simply lasted longer. Likewise, he was able to keep the French people happy, proud, strong, growing and developing without the constant warfare that had monopolized so much of his uncle's genius for so long. Napoleon III did fight several wars of his own, but they were usually short, and at least at the beginning, successful for France. The one large exception was the final one, the Franco-Prussian war, which was his undoing.

One notes with interest that the same Louis Napoleon, before he got himself a crown and a number, was a wandering exile himself. He had made a couple of pathetic attempts to seize power in France, and also participated in a revolution in the Papal States (1831), of all places. He would have been captured by the police if it had not been for the good graces of the Archbishop of Spoleto, Giovanni Mastai-Feretti (the future Pius IX). So, when the failed revolutionary became Emperor of the French, he made it a point to protect the Papal States and to support the pope's general foreign policy throughout Europe. I'm sure there was an element of gratitude there, but his best motive was just good political sense. Napoleon III was sharp enough to see that support of the French Catholics was crucial to his survival. He was a fairly conservative leader, and realized that all of the more radical forces were firmly against him; so the Catholics were too important to ignore.

III

Following the defeat of that same Second Empire in 1871, Napoleon was sent into exile, and the "dreaded" Third Republic began to emerge. The new regime was crafted, ironically, by about 400 *monarchist* representatives (out of some 650) to the National Assembly. These men knew they wanted a crowned head for France, but were deeply split over who should be chosen. These deputies were Legitimists, Orleanists and a handful of leftover Bonapartists, but they absolutely refused to compromise with one another. The three factions hated one another so totally, that the only compromise possible was suggested by Adolphe Thiers: "A republic divides us least." So, the new provisional republic was born in the shadow of three pretenders: the Legitimist Count of Chambord, the Orleanist Count of Paris, and the now exiled Napoleon III, elderly and sick, but still wanting to return. Each of these wanted to sit on the one throne. But then the Assembly decided that there would be no throne.

The new Republic was fairly conservative, at least at the beginning. But it immediately took on a life of its own as a result of three distinct crises (which neatly match the next three decades: the 1870's, 80's, and 90's). Gradually that regime turned into a somewhat more radical republic, which for us means more anticlerical and anti-church. But in time it also passed through that stage as well.

The first of the crises I referred to was the "16th of May Affair." The new provisional president was one of Napoleon's old marshals, Patrice MacMahon. He was a strong conservative who wanted to keep the throne warm for a king. He didn't care which one, but he knew he didn't want a republic. Eventually, he tried a few too many highhanded tricks to manipulate parliamentary elections. French voters hate being told how to vote, so they kept voting against MacMahon's candidates ever more decisively. He finally accepted the inevitable and resigned, leaving the field open to genuine republican leadership.

The second of the formative crises was the Boulanger Affair, involving the young, very charismatic, intelligent and popular general, Georges Boulanger. It was the classic case of a "man on horseback," who looked like the one to solve all possible problems of the corrupt and self-serving republican monstrosity. There had been an extraordinary number of scandals involving civil servants and unpopular ministers, kickbacks on government contracts, taking care of the family with public money—an all too familiar pattern.

General Boulanger looked like the ideal man to lead a coup. He made all the right political alliances and was elected to Parliament by wide margins in many districts, including one in Paris which had long been a republican stronghold. All of the regiments in the Paris garrison were ready to rise in support of him. But Boulanger decided that, on the night that everyone expected him to seize

power, he would visit his mistress instead. Nobody in France ever
forgot it. He never got another chance. He had to flee the country
in 1889, the centennial of the Revolution, and committed suicide a
few years later. Boulanger was the glorious coup d'état that never
took place.

Finally, in the 1890's, we have the famous and very divisive
Dreyfus case. In France it is still referred to as simply "The Affair."
Tragedy marked the case of Alfred Dreyfus: an army officer of
Jewish family, born and raised in Alsace, a province annexed by
Germany in 1871, and therefore enemy territory. He was falsely
accused of selling military secrets to the Germans. Within a few
years the guilty party became known, but Dreyfus had already
been convicted in 1894 and sentenced to Devil's Island as a scape-
goat, and the army refused to admit the mistake. There had been
evidence suppressed in his trial, and the fraud was exposed in the
newspapers with traumatic results for the army and the Conservatives. This case exploded all over the political landscape very close
to the time of Thérèse's own death. The bitterness of the battle
which followed polarized church and state still one more time, just
when it had appeared that some compromise was possible. Unfortunately, many of the army officers who had railroaded poor
Captain Dreyfus were good, practicing Catholics. Most of them
were also solid Royalists. They saw Dreyfus, the Jew, the Republican, as a symbol of everything which had to be stamped out at all
costs—he represented everything "bad" in the republic.

This final explosion was just enough to spoil the Conservatives'
plans one more time. By the time World War I broke out, many of
the best French generals would be *both* devout Catholics *and* backers
of the republic: Foch, Pétain and others.

The life of Thérèse spans the final years of Pius IX and most of
the reign of Leo XIII. This era saw many laws passed against
church institutions. In 1875, independent universities were founded
by the church to compensate for their exclusion from the Sorbonne
and other venerable institutions. In 1879, there were laws against
the Jesuits; in 1880 came laws against other religious orders, though
not as severe as those of the previous century. By 1882 there was
mandatory secular education for all children. Catholic schools were
still allowed to function in addition to state schools, but not in place
of them.

In this whole web of political wrangling and bitter hard feelings, those who eventually brought about a reconciliation were the Catholics far-sighted enough to know that peace was essential. One person who gets high marks for this, of course, is Leo XIII. He did not share the sense of "hurt" which had paralyzed Pius IX, but still saw the truth of much of what Pius defended. This was the same Leo XIII who was born at Carpinetto Romano, where we find a lovely little cloistered monastery today. This is also the man who named one of the most successful healers in the French hierarchy, Cardinal Lavigerie.

Michael Lavigerie had been trained as a scholar and pastor, with studies in Lebanon, where he came to know firsthand about Moslems and Maronite Christians. He was appointed Archbishop of Algiers, a rather awkward colonial diocese with almost no native Catholics. Still, he turned out to be a wonderful choice: this was the man who founded the White Fathers and White Sisters, who became a first-rate reconciler and missionary. He was also instrumental in the abolition of the slave trade, which was a major block to conversions among black Africans. In 1881, the pope appointed him Vicar Apostolic of the ancient see of Carthage, then made him a Cardinal and named him Primate of all Africa, as rewards for a job well done.

But then he asked something much harder. Leo XIII told Lavigerie that he was the man to facilitate a dialogue with the republic. To do this, he would first have to convince the Royalists to abandon their siege mentality. "Rally to the Republic"—this was the political program known as the *Ralliement*. Convince Catholics to support the good things the republic does, and the church will be fine. Lavigerie was apprehensive, but the pope just nodded wisely and said "I know you'll do the right thing." And he did.

Six weeks later, the French Mediterranean fleet docked in Algiers. The Governor was away, and Lavigerie was the ranking dignitary in the city. He was therefore expected to provide a luncheon for these naval officers, most of whom, naturally, were Royalist Catholics. So he decided to propose a carefully worded toast to the republic. This is what he said:

Union, in view of the past which still bleeds and the future which is always menacing, is at this moment our supreme need. Union is

also—may I say—the first wish of the church and her pastors at all
degrees of the hierarchy. Most certainly the church does not ask us to
dismiss either the memory of France's past glories or those whose
loyalty and services pay tribute both to them and to their country.
But when the will of the people has been clearly stated, when the form
of government they choose has nothing in it contrary to the principles
which alone can give life to Christian and civilized nations and when,
in order to save one's country from the pitfalls which threaten it,
sincere adhesion to this form of government becomes necessary, then
the moment has at last arrived to declare that the period of test and
trial is over and we all must unite, despite sacrifices which arise to
work as one for the future and the salvation of the country.

The toast goes on, but here we have the gist. When these officers
heard these words, one could have heard a pin drop. Then they
silently filed out of the room in protest, at which time a small band
which the Cardinal had organized outside struck up the *Marseillaise*,
the republican anthem. Needless to say, the blast was heard all over
the French empire. Every royalist family felt outraged. Lavigerie
was insulted by countless letters and newspaper articles, and many
of the best contributors to his mission funds told him that he would
get nothing more from them. And he got no support whatever from
the rest of the hierarchy. Perhaps worst of all, even the Republicans
offered no sign of friendship or recognition of his courageous stand.
Lavigerie would eventually die (in 1892) before the storm blew
over, probably feeling very much a failure.

But a few years later, about the time Thérèse was nearing death
herself (could we posit some cause and effect here?) there were two
bishops, then three more, then some major prelates who finally
stood up and declared that they agreed in principle with the efforts
at reconciliation. Leo XIII had already written an encyclical specifically for France called *Au Milieu des Sollicitudes* in which he also
supported the *Ralliement*: the partnership with the republic in all
things which did not go against Christian truth. Within another
decade, virtual peace was at hand.

This whole series of bitter memories, not only of the republics of
the past, but of all the persecutions, the stormy origins of the Third
Republic, France's crushing defeat by the Germans in 1870-71, and
the national pride that had been violated, . . . these were all still

open wounds. We have the "16th of May Affair," the traumatic Boulanger and Dreyfus crises, and all of the name-calling and verbal attacks which were exchanged. But gradually, they began to break down.

Many have seen Alain Cavalier's film "Thérèse." It very accurately reflects these conflicts with its well crafted lines, such as the workman's "Vive la République!" There was also the doctor who said to the mother superior, "This monastery should be torched and burned to the ground." When this film ran in France during 1986, that statement was greeted with sporadic applause. These issues are not dead, even today. Far from it. Not all of the hurts are healed, even now, but we are getting there.

Thérèse's life and work took place in the wake of these events; they were front-page news in the world that she knew and prayed for. If we plan to see what she did in context, then we also, as contemporary believers, *must* be willing to look beneath the surface to appreciate and treasure them as they really were

AN ARTIST AND A SAINT: EDWARD WESTON AND ST THÉRÈSE OF LISIEUX

James Geoghegan

Now pastor in charge of St Cecilia's parish in Stanwood, Washington Father Geoghegan is a member of the recently founded Institute of Spirituality located there. He has published several photographs in newspapers and for Paulist Press; and he serves as photographer for Carmelite Digest *(San Jose, CA).*

I chose this subject for a number of reasons. The theme of our symposium is "St Thérèse, Carmelite: An Experience Today." I wanted to look at Thérèse in relationship to the United States of America today. I have known for many years that here at the Carmelite Center was the map of North America that Thérèse drew when she was twelve years old. Edward Weston was born in this area, and soon a major centennial retrospective of his work will be shown at Northwestern University. Thérèse and Weston and Chicago and our symposium began to knit together.

In 1986 I attended the Weston Centennial Symposium in Carmel, California. While visiting Weston's home on Wildcat Hill, Ruth Bernhard said "He was very simple. His home was simple, so were his lifestyle, food and thought. His room was like a monk's cell." Another close friend of the photographer, Frances Baer (a Secular

28

Carmelite) told me that he was close to the Carmelite nuns. He
lived about two miles from the Carmelite monastery. He has a
famous photograph of the monastery and Point Lobos, one that he
published in "California and the West." This monastery was the
first one in the world dedicated to St Thérèse. When I asked Frances
in what way he was close to the nuns she said that he had the same
spirit as they. Sr Thérèse Newcombe, O.C.D. of the San Rafael
Carmel told me that Weston was remembered in her family for his
graciousness, simplicity and beauty of soul. She gave me a photograph of Weston taken by her father, the artist Warren Newcombe.
Weston's son Brett told me "My Dad died a poor man, leaving only
$300.00, but he was rich in friends and in spirit." Relationships be-
tween the saint and the artist became apparent. He is one of the
most important influences in American art of this century; she is
probably the most influential figure in the modern church. So
many things that we take for granted were pioneered by these two
giants. They introduced new ideas, new ways of looking that are
now considered unexciting and normal. In looking at this American
man and this French woman we may get some insights to help us as
we come to the end of our twentieth century.

EDWARD WESTON

He was born in Highland Park, a suburb of Chicago in 1886, the
year of Thérèse's rebirth, her Christmas conversion when she was
thirteen years old.[1] He was eleven when Thérèse died. Like her,
his mother died while he was quite young and like her, he got
bored with school and dropped out. He began photographing as a
teenager and moved to California when he was twenty. He settled
on being a professional portrait photographer, going from house to
house. Thus he supported his wife and four sons. On the side he
did personal artistic work. He early became internationally known
for his romantic and pictorial work. With one of his sons he went to
Mexico.[2] There a profound change came over him that affected his
whole style of photography. Through Diego Rivera, Siqueiros,
Orozco, Charlot and artists who respected and admired him, he
acquired a new confidence in his creative work. In Mexico he de-

veloped an appreciation of beauty in ordinary things. The beauty was there under his nose in the childrens' toys, in vases, plates, saucers, taverns, jars, and even bathroom fixtures. He saw beauty just by looking around him, and also found that the people had a sense of beauty. When he returned to California he was a changed man. He continued to support his family by portrait work. He could not leave his house lest he lose customers who might come by. In Mexico he had learned to look closely at what was close by. At this period he created his magnificient photographs of cabbages, onions, radishes, apples, pears, peppers, flowers and shells. Weston has taught us to look at the ordinary and see beauty, and without him we might not even think to look.

In Mexico Weston also learned the power of the camera to capture the truth—the essence of a person in an instant. He could capture in a "supreme instant" something that had never happened before and would never happen again. Some of his greatest portraits are from Mexico. We see the concentration of Galván as he pulled the trigger while shooting a tossed coin. We see the tear flowing from the eye of Tina Modotti as she recites poetry. He captured the intensity of Guadalupe Rivera as she shouts at the top of her voice. These photographs are clean, simple, unretouched. They have caught the unique personality of the subject in the luminous moment. As Weston continued his search for truth he realized that everything was getting simpler.[3] He stripped away the carbohydrates. Stripping away is his lifestyle, as he lives in a simple home getting down to essentials as much as possible. His photographic equipment was minimal: his home cost $1000 to build. He wanted nothing that would distract him from his work.

One of the dangers of simplicity is that it can become mere sentimentality or a cliché. Weston is saved from this because as he becomes simpler, he also becomes more profound. He saw in the simple form of a pepper or shell forms that flowed from the very life within. He began to see relationships between all forms in creation as they shared life. In the sand dunes he saw relationships to the form of the nude, not because the shapes of the dune look like a woman's body, but because the patterns, the forms have evolved from life and function, and there is a bond between all living creation. This unity of all creation is reflected in his work. There was

EDWARD WESTON AT CARMEL, 1938
by Warren Newcombe

progress, development in his thinking and interests. Major hu... themes and issues appeared: the relationship of life and death; the place of humans in creation; the power of nature; the relationship of decay and new life and growth. As he got older his work struggled with the reality and meaning of death. He was poor. Fortunately he received a Guggenheim Fellowship in 1937. It was renewed in 1938, allowing him to leave aside his commercial work and go travelling throughout California, the West and the U.S.A.[4] His photographs contain the spirit of a locality whether it is the Oregon Coast or Death Valley, or a Louisiana plantation home. The entrance of the United States into World War II interrupted his photographing of the East Coast. He and his new wife, Charis, came back to Carmel, California. As he got older he had Parkinson's disease. He photographed the great cypresses of Point Lobos. They contain a profound somberness and joy. In them we see the struggle of life and death, light and darkness, new life, mulitiplicity of forms united in a brilliant unifying vision. These photographs have been compared to the great Quartets of Beethoven. Due to the disease he was unable to photograph for the last ten years of his life. Many great photographers (e.g., Ansel Adams) have been strongly influenced by Weston, yet they retain their own vision. He had many disciples, but he did not interfere with their freedom, and did not create a school.[5] On January 1, 1958 he died peacefully, aged seventy-two. His ashes were scattered on the beach of his beloved Point Lobos, near the Carmelite monastery of St Thérèse.

It is important at this stage to suggest familiarity with some photographs of Weston. I highly recommend *Edward Weston: Aperture Masters of Photography*, Number Seven. This was published in 1988 by Aperture and is inexpensive. It has many of Weston's classic images, a brief chronology and an excellent selected bibliography (in which the essential books by, or on, Weston are given).

I think we can already see many relationships with St Thérèse of Lisieux. We see a man who progressed and developed, all the time simplifying his lifestyle and his methods. We see his tremendous devotion to truth, his hatred of hypocrisy, and falsehood. He expressed great truths simply, was humble in the face of reality, worked hard with a single-minded devotion to his life's vocation, made many sacrifices, lived and died poor. He kept his photographs inexpensive so ordinary people could buy them. He saw beauty and universal life forms in all creation, and had a tremendous awareness of beauty in front of him. He respected the uniqueness of each individual and was available to all whenever it was possible.

ST THÉRÈSE OF LISIEUX

As we look at St Thérèse we clearly see stages of *growth and development.* Her Christmas conversion changed her.[6] Her life changed after Céline brought selections from the Hebrew Scriptures into the monastery.[7] There she read "whoever is a little one let him come to me," and Thérèse got a new vision of her relationship to God. Her life is different after she made her Act of Oblation.[8] With her first hemorrhage she began her descent into the dark night.[9] There are clear stages in the growth and development of Thérèse's life and doctrine.

Devotion to Truth

Thérèse expressly states on the day of her death "I never sought anything but the truth."[10] When she was having tremendous desires she asked "Lord is this just fantasy? Tell me because I only want the truth."[11] One example of this is her description of Pope Leo XIII: "He is so old that one would say he is dead. I would never have pictured him like this. He can hardly say anything."[12] When Mother Agnes asked her to say or do something to edify the doctor in whom Thérèse did not have too much trust she said in effect "No way, let him think what he wants."[13] A nun of the Paris Carmel asked her to write a poem.[14] She wrote "The Unpetalled Rose." The poem describes the unpetalling of the rose to make soft the ground for the first steps of the Infant Jesus, and finally for the Lord on his way to Calvary to save his feet from hurt. Thérèse sent off the poem and received in reply a request for a final verse describing how —when Thérèse would die—God would gather up all the petals and restore the rose. Thérèse replied that if sister wanted a last verse she could write it herself. That idea was not true to Thérèse's experience. Heaven itself would continue the unpetalling—she would continue to sacrifice herself to give pleasure to Jesus. When the nuns told her of the visit of the Czar of Russia to Paris she said "Don't be bothering me. Speak to me about God, the example of the saints, about everything that is the truth."[15] One time she was looking out the window admiring the sky, and Marie said "You are looking at the sky with so much love." She responded "No, it's because it is so beautiful."[16] Pauline told her "We want to take your photograph because I want it for Mother Prioress." Thérèse told her "to be truthful, you want it for yourself."[17]

On August 5, 1897 Marie suggested that at her death angels would appear resplendent with light and beauty. Thérèse said "All these images do me no good. I can nourish myself on nothing but truth. That's why I've never wanted any visions. We can't see, here on earth, heaven, the angels etc., just as they are. I prefer to wait till after my death."[18] False images never appealed to, or helped, her. We shall see that true images did. In July 1897 she said "I've never acted like Pilate, who refused to listen to the truth. I've always said to God: 'O my God, I really want to listen to You; I beg you to answer me when I say humbly: what is truth? Make me see things as they really are. Let nothing cause me to be deceived.'"[19]

Ability to LOOK

Thérèse had the ability to see something and really look at it with what we might call a contemplative look. We have a photograph of her holding a lily.[20] In her poems and letters she talks about the lily: its colors, its makeup, its different kinds, and how it is nourished.[21] It is nourished by dewdrops, not by rain or clouds. The dewdrop is formed in the night and in it the image of the sun is reflected in the morning. So Thérèse and Céline are lilies, nourished in the darkness of faith, and reflecting the Divine Sun. From her infirmary bed she sits up and bends in order to look out the window at the trees as the sun hits them. She sees the branches, and the shadows they cast,[22] the leaf caught on a spider's web,[23] the dark spot in the chestnut grove that becomes an image of the darkness of her soul.[24] She looks lovingly at the images of Théophane Vénard[25] and Mary.[26] She sees and feels with pleasure some peaches and admires them because they give their sweetness for others.[27] "Look at the nine pears" she says to her sisters.[28] Her poems are full of memories of creation and reveal a mind that is capable of minute and accurate observation. She describes flowers, which she said she loved so much: roses, pink daisies, forget-me-nots, violets, crocuses. She presents fields of wheat, grass, the skies, the swallows, turtle-doves, nightingales, bees, butterflies, animals, insects, glowworms, stars, moon, sea, wheat, fire, rainbow, rocks. (See her poem for Céline "What I Used to Love") The fields, plains, mountains and valleys of France appear in her poem for the canonization of Joan of Arc. She studied the moth flying into the flame.[29] At first it is a symbol of a worldly soul, later it becomes a sign of Céline sacrificing herself in the fires of Christ's love. She see nature as revealing God:

In Thee, the glorious stars are mine;
And often at the day's decline
I see, as through some veil silken and fine
Beckoning from heaven,
Thy hand. ("What I Used to Love")

Simple images fill her writings—pin pricks, elevators, sand, a tear, a piece of straw, a heating box, a seed, ivy leaves.[30] In describing the fog which surrounds one, penetrates with its dampness and cuts off light with its denseness, she is describing the dark night of faith, but also giving us the feel of what it is to be in a fog.[31] She describes the darkness of the subterranean passage leading to the summit of love. She is full of images, the arms of Jesus,[32] the lap of God,[33] the light from the downcast eyes of Jesus,[34] and especially the image of the child which with its weakness, falls, desires to climb, and with its truth and candor and its confidence in its father.[35] Like Weston, Thérèse uses images that are ordinary and available, taken mainly from everyday experience. Simplicity itself and ordinariness are the reason for Thérèse's love of Mary, who is the model for those who walk in faith. Though Mary is simple, she is a woman of great depth. Thérèse sees heaven as Jesus charming her with the revelations of Mary's greatness.

Profundity in Simplicity

Thérèse asked Abbé Bellière to "be simple with God but also with me." In some of her simple images we find profound truths.

She loved birds, kept them at Les Buissonets, and studied them. She saw the little bird running off pecking at grain, unable to fly because of its damp wings, but desiring to fly. The eagle is powerful, and so the little bird will be borne aloft on eagle wings. In this image of the birds she sees the relationship of the Christian to Christ. We fly to the Father on the wings of Christ.[36] Her theology is that of John the Evangelist, who presents Christ coming from the Father, returning to him and bringing us with him. When she saw the hen protecting its chicks she cried, for the scene revealed to her the tenderness of God's love for her.[37] There is one very beautiful incident that brings out Thérèse's power to see or experience something, reflect on it, and go deeply beyond it to a profound universal truth. She was dying. Mother Agnes was sitting at her bedside writing down every edifying word of her little saint. Thérèse was exhausted after a painful feverous night when a sister came into the infirmary asking her to put the finishing touch to a painting. Thérèse was annoyed and let the sister know. Poor Mother Agnes was shocked at Thérèse's reaction. That night she got a letter from Thérèse that is a masterpiece of spiritual literature.[38] The saint explains that she is delighted that Pauline saw her weakness because now she would believe that Thérèse was an ordinary soul. She was not surprised that Pauline forgave her, for she was a mirror of God's mercy. The other sister was a mirror of God's justice. Meeting her in the garden that day Thérèse expected a reprimand, but instead she received a kiss. In that kiss she penetrated to the mystery of the relationship of God's mercy and justice. In God they are one. If God is just he must be merciful. His justice must take our weakness into account. Very soon afterwards she shared this insight with Abbé Bellière, drawing from her own experience a lesson that applied to him and to all little souls.

Grace of the Moment

As Thérèse saw God's hand in all creation so she saw God's presence in every event, in the supreme moment. She who experienced conversion in a moment knew the grace-bearing power of *every* moment. When unable to receive extreme unction she expressed her disappointment that she would die without the sacrament, but then added that that would be alright because everything is a grace.[39] She did not want to let any moment pass to love the

Lord. She warned her novices not to lose time,[40] and was herself careful not to waste it.[41] She did not fear old age, even though it meant a continuation of her suffering because "I live each moment as it comes along."[42] Every moment bears God in a unique way, and she reminds Céline that each moment is a moment to love God and to experience his love. To Céline she writes "Let us profit from our one moment of suffering. Let us see only each moment. A moment is a treasure. One act of love will make us know Jesus better—it will bring us closer to him during the whole of *eternity*."[43] In her Act of Oblation she says that to live is an act of love, and that God can in one instant prepare her to appear before him.[44] In her poem she asks God for the grace to live "just for today," and looks forward to heaven as the eternal glad today.[45] As with Weston the extraordinary simplicity we find in Thérèse is not a cliché because of the profundity involved. Her life was simple, her prayer became simply "I don't say anything, I just love him."[46] Her reading simplified to the stage where a single word of Scripture opened up infinite horizons.[47] The complexity of her apostolic desires was reduced to being the heart in the Church[48] and finally her life is summed up in her last words on earth "My God I love you."[49]

Respect for the Person

Finally we look at Thérèse's respect for the individual person. She does not think in terms of masses. After the picture of the crucified Christ shedding his blood she decided to devote her life to saving souls. She prayed for Pranzini, a horrible character.[50] Through her prayers he was saved at the point of death. She never forgot him. He always remained her child. She prayed for Fr Hyacinthe, a Carmelite priest who had left the Church.[51] She even offered her last Holy Communion for him. She hoped that children baptized by her missionary brothers would be named Céline and Thérèse.[52] She asked that the money to be spent for flowers for her funeral be used to ransom children in Africa.[53] Her missionary and apostolic sense is directed to individuals. We see how she treated each novice in an individual way, adjusting her teaching and methods to the needs of the different sisters. She did not try to make them clones of herself. She is strong and encouraging to Marie Guérin in her scruples, tender with the old and cranky

Sr St Pierre, patient and smiling to the disturbed Sr Teresa of St Augustine, firm but loving with Céline, tactful and supporting with Mother Gonzague, especially after the devestating election of 1896. Each and every person is unique, a child of God, not just a "nun," a "sinner," or a "pagan."

CONCLUSION

Here is what Thérèse and Weston teach us today.

(1) They teach us to grow and develop, never resting on our laurels, but ever open to new possibilities, adventures and ways of thinking.

(2) Thérèse and Weston died poor, their simplicity of lifestyle calls us to rid ourselves of clutter, consumerism and hedonism.

(3) Love of truth, especially truth in the imagination, respect for art and imagery. To go deeper than the surface of images, and not to be fooled by the manipulating images of political and advertising campaigns.

(4) To be awake, and aware of beauty under our noses, to see it and love it in our daily lives, to stop and smell the roses, to develop a contemplative calmness, to slow down and look.

(5) To be conscious of the bond that unites us to all creation. Instead of destroying or polluting the environment they lead us to cherish, conserve, respect and love God's planet Earth.

(6) Commitment and dedication to the path that God has laid out for each of us, even when this requires sacrifice and unselfishness.

(7) If the saint and the artist have a special gift to offer to cure the nation's deepest ills—it is their respect for the uniqueness and dignity of each individual person no matter who or where that person is. When we look at the *person* we begin to cure the evils of racism, legalism, militarism, and sexism. We are drawn out of selfishness by becoming open to others in a true love of country, Church and world.

I would like to conclude by quoting a letter I received from Frances Baer, O.C.D.S.:

I missed a reference to Edward's (Weston) great sense of humility. No matter who came to that simple room—kings, housewife, hippy, fools, aristocrat, fellow-artists, great and not-so-great—all were welcomed with a simple graciousness, really love. He never judged, not the person or the person's work: the most he would do was tap a photograph on the edge and say very quietly "very nice." He was generous with his time, but very firm about the time set aside for his work. I truly know he was a pure man.[54]

Edward Weston, photographer, and Thérèse Martin, saint, have had an immense influence on the U.S.A. and on the world. They continue to be guiding lights for today.

THE RELIGIOUS PLAYS
OF ST THÉRÈSE OF LISIEUX

John Russell

John Russell is a Carmelite of the Ancient Observance who serves as associate professor of theology at Immaculate Conception Seminary, South Orange, New Jersey.

INTRODUCTION

The centenary of the birth of St Thérèse of Lisieux in 1973 welcomed the beginning of a sequence of critical editions of her writings and last conversations.[1] This movement generated a new outpouring of books and articles on St Thérèse. In the English speaking world, Patricia O'Connor has produced a popular biography of St Thérèse as well as a study of her spirituality.[2] Monica Furlong, known for her biography of Thomas Merton, has offered a feminist perspective on the life of St Thérèse.[3] A spate of articles and chapters in books continues to delve into various aspects of her personality as well as the contours of her spiritual pilgrimage.[4]

Students of St Thérèse's writing continue to discover her personal world of freedom of expression in the midst of her attentiveness to the tradition of her Church and her Carmelite community. Readers of her works are struck by her mature and rather independent thinking within a personal context of littleness and professed weakness. People respect and admire her spirit of confidence and hope

41

in a nineteenth-century spiritual milieu marked by an absorbing awareness of sinfulness and divine judgement and retribution.

The least known portion of St Thérèse's writings are her eight recreational pieces, her plays, written between January 1894 and February 1897, for various liturgical and community feasts.[5] In fact, the definitive French edition of the plays did not appear until 1985. These short skits, which most often combine poetry and prose, offer a modest form of theater in continuity with the intent of St Teresa of Avila. St Teresa, aware of the rigors of cloistered life, saw the need for a balance of festivity and celebration.[6] Special feasts called for a more relaxed schedule. The recreational skit ushered in a joyful mood; songs and edifying dialogue renewed a community's spirit. The festive occasions included Christmas, the feast of the Holy Innocents (December 28) which was the novices' special feast, the feast-day of the prioress of the community, the feast of St Martha (July 29) which honored the lay sisters in the community; and also a golden jubilee of profession was celebrated with a recreational skit.

This article will begin with some general observations on St Thérèse's plays. Secondly, it will focus upon images and themes in the plays which reveal attitudes of St Thérèse as well as her understanding of the Carmelite vocation. Thirdly, the article will provide a theological context for connecting her plays to her overall writing as well as to a larger ecclesial and cultural horizon.

ST THÉRÈSE'S PLAYS: GENERAL OBSERVATIONS

St. Thérèse's first contact with a recreational skit came on June 21, 1888 on the feast day celebration of the prioress, Mother Marie Gonzague. The play, "St Agnes," was written by Pauline, now Sr Agnes of Jesus, and St Thérèse played the lead part. The community was struck by St Thérèse's ability to negotiate the role with conviction. She seemed to radiate the presence of "a heart in love with Christ" (T, 19). She was equally well received in the Christmas play of 1889 in which she played Mary, mother of the Infant Jesus. When Sr Agnes of Jesus was elected prioress on February 20, 1893, St Thérèse took over the task of composing the recreational pieces.

St Thérèse accepted the call of obedience to compose the eight plays just as she had obeyed the request to write the *Story of a Soul.* She had no particular desire to achieve any literary acclaim. The plays do communicate engaging images of commitment, deep faith in God's Providence and heroism. Her poems within the plays reveal a simplicity of style which make them quite adaptable to the popular music chosen to present the plays to the community.

It is through the medium of her plays that St Thérèse continues to come out of the shadows of desired obscurity to translate in palpable form her various convictions about Carmelite life. Most often the plays offer models of spousal relationship to Christ, center on the virtues of humility and charity, embrace the God of merciful love over the God of condemning judgement, highlight the centrality of prayer, not only in fostering union with God but also in serving the redemptive love of God in the world. The critical edition of her plays does not suggest that we learn entirely new information about St Thérèse. Rather the plays enhance our understanding of St Thérèse and offer another perspective on various aspects of her spirituality which appear in her other writings (T, 33).

The plays certainly underscore St Thérèse's attraction to the Incarnation and Passion of Christ, her devotion to Mary as mother, her openness to a world spirited by angels and devils and the resulting human environment of spiritual combat. She celebrates the sanctifying presence of Christ in the Eucharist and urges frequent Communion in a Church still somewhat numbed by the lingering anaesthetic of Jansenism. She sees the saints as models of Christian discipleship exhorting us in this world of exile. The presence of the divine milieu or the world of the supernatural/the world of grace is revealed in each of St Thérèse's plays.

St Thérèse's familiarity with Scripture in an age in which the reading of the Bible was not encouraged is rather astounding. She employs biblical references 270 times in the composition of the eight plays (T, 40). Isaiah the prophet and the Song of Songs are obvious favorites from the Hebrew Scriptures. The Gospels energize all of her plays. Scratch pads which she used and continue to be preserved indicate that she knew many biblical texts from memory.

The recreational skits were always performed by the novices. St Thérèse, who did serve as assistant mistress of novices, played the principal role in five of the eight plays. The well known photo-graph of St Thérèse acting the role of Joan of Arc was provided by Céline who had brought along a camera when she entered the Carmel of Lisieux in September 1894. Since the plays were written during the last three years of St Thérèse's life, it is not surprising to note that when she completed her last play, "St Stanislaus Kostka," she was in too weakened a condition to participate in it.

The French critical edition of her plays covers the history of determining that St Thérèse had actually composed theatrical pieces in the form of prose and poetry. The recreational skits had been placed for the most part without titles within her collection of poetry. Mother Agnes, her sister Pauline, did not initially offer St Thérèse's plays as recreational pieces. Only gradually in the course of the process of beatification (1910) did some of the plays become known for what they truly were (T, 43). While St Thérèse had been canonized on May 17, 1925, only in 1929 did the public know for the first time of the existence of three of the theatrical skits: "St Stanislaus Kostka," "The Mission of Joan of Arc" and "Joan of Arc Fulfilling her Mission" (T, 45-46). Copies had been made by other sisters in the Lisieux community and thus in time all the plays came to light. The critical edition reflects a study of the extant material in order to provide authentic reproductions of the eight plays.[7]

THE PLAYS OF ST THÉRÈSE

Joan of Arc

Two of the early plays center on St Joan of Arc: "The Mission of Joan of Arc or the Shepherd of Domremy Listening to Voices" (RP 1) and "Joan of Arc Accomplishing her Mission" (RP 3). These two plays can be treated together since they form a continuity de-picting the life of Joan of Arc. "The Mission of Joan of Arc . . . ." (RP 1) was staged on January 21, 1894 to celebrate the feastday of the prioress, Mother Agnes of Jesus. "Joan of Arc Accomplish-ing . . . ." (RP 3) took place the following year on the same feastday. Of these two plays Guy Gaucher, O.C.D. has written:

For her first "theatrical" attempt Sister Thérèse had big ideas. There were to be two plays on Joan of Arc and she planned to devote two recreations to them: one on Joan's vocation, the other on her suffering, death and triumph. To this end she made a serious study of Henri Wallon's recently published book (1877), which contained extracts from the trials. As author, producer and actress Sister Thérèse did not spare herself. While keeping to the story, she attributed Carmelite sentiments to her heroine.[8]

The critical French edition discusses St Thérèse's use of Wallon's text and adds that she did feel free to introduce indirectly events in her own life which seemed to coincide with the story of Joan of Arc (T, 289-290). For example, in "The Mission of Joan of Arc" (RP 1) Joan hears the voice of the Archangel Michael telling her that it is God's will that she lead France to victory over England. She will be a defender of the faith in her venture. Joan protests of her weakness and inability to respond to this call, but through the comforting attention of St Catherine and St Margaret, Joan is finally able to proclaim: "What change has been worked within me. O gentle Virgin [Catherine]! Your voice dissolves my fears, I am no longer afraid. . . your sweet melody has touched me with joy and I will obey the will of God!" (T, 67-68). The editors of the critical edition believe that this scene captures the temper of St Thérèse's conversion experience of Christmas 1886, when she was touched by the grace of Christ to move into a new stage of maturity. Dialogues between Joan of Arc and her younger sister Catherine suggest parallels with the confidences between Pauline and Thérèse at Les Buissonets during the summer of 1882.

Both plays deliver various convictions about the Carmelite vocation. Joan is attracted to the quiet life of a shepherdess, to a poor and rather frugal existence. Within that environment Joan develops a sensitive relationship to the Lord which leads to the willingness ultimately to accept God's will in all things. A final conversation between Joan and her younger sister Catherine at the end of the play reflects Joan's spiritual maturity. Catherine is worried that when Joan has done what God asks of her by defending France that God will not allow her to return home again, to Domremy. Joan exclaims:

My dear little sister. We need to leave the future in God's hands. If we should not see each other again here below, we will be found together again in our heavenly home never to be separated. And so you should rejoice with me in the mission that the Lord has confided in me today to preserve the faith of France and to people heaven with numerous elect. . . ! (T, 79)

Catherine then wants to know if there is something special that she can do for God. Joan responds: "Be simple always, be continually united to God and you will do great things for him . . . in heaven you will share happiness similar to mine, for by different routes we are brought along to the same end . . ." (T, 80)

The second play featuring Joan of Arc covers briefly her victories and the crowning of King Charles VII, Joan's imprisonment and martyrdom. St Thérèse wrote that this play reveals everything that she understood about a Christian's death (T, 31). In fact, St Thérèse deals rather passionately with Joan's unjust condemnation, death and triumphant reception in heaven. Sensitive to the truth of Joan's life, St Thérèse allows Joan's fear of death to be somewhat tempered by the triumph of her fidelity in one of the final scenes. First, St Thérèse depicts the burning at the stake as a totally unjust end for the saintly virgin of Orleans. "What crime have I committed?" asks Joan of Arc. Fr Jean Massieu, spokesperson for the bishop of Beauvais, states categorically: "You are accused of being a heretic, an apostate, an idolater . . ." Joan's response is strong and faith-filled: "I have the witness of a good conscience and I am a good Christian obedient to the Church . . ." (T, 141) Secondly, when the Archangel Gabriel comes to console Joan, St Thérèse does not gloss over the fear and the anger which Joan feels. Joan exclaims: "You say that Jesus is near me . . . Why then has he permitted that the priests condemn me? If I were judged by the English I would not suffer such a sentence . . . It's a bishop from my own country who declares me worthy of death." The Archangel Gabriel reminds Joan that Jesus came into a world which judged him unjustly and treated him with disdain. Joan speaks again: "How I am consoled in seeing that my agony is like my Savior's . . . However I don't feel his divine presence and death fills me with fear" (T, 145). This passage seems to provide a glimpse into St Thérèse's own heart as she experiences her own dark days of faith about this time.

In this second play St Thérèse has Joan seeking Holy Communion before her death. "When I would feel the Divine Heart beating next to mine it seems that the fire of his love would give me the courage to face the harsh fire at the stake" (T, 146). The words of Wisdom, chapters three to four, offer a sense of consolation and hope: ". . . the souls of the just are in the hand of God and the torment of death shall not touch them." Joan's own words reveal the buoyancy of her faith: "In an hour all that will be left of me is ashes. No, I am mistaken, my God. My soul will soar up to you . . . I will live, never more to die . . . One day my body will rise up from the earth and be reunited to my soul . . . Why then am I still sad, why does the woodpile make me fearful?" (T, 147)

Before Joan is consumed in the flames there is a scene in which she confronts the local bishop. The issue is truth and justice. The bishop tells Joan that she is going to her death because of her defiance of the Church. She had supported a king who is a heretic. Joan's response stands by the truth. "Bishop, you are the one leading me to death. I am not a heretic, I am a daughter of the Church and the king whom I fought for is a very Christian king . . . If I could have gone to Rome, the Holy Father would have acknowledged my innocence, but I am happy to die for my country and I pray to God not to punish my enemies . . ." (T, 152-153)

St Thérèse devotes a final section of the play to St Joan's triumph in heaven. She receives a crown of roses and the palm of martyrdom. Joan accepts her heavenly role of interceding for France. The glory of a faithful life of discipleship marks the play's conclusion. It registers St Thérèse's own desire to live a life worthy of great glory in heaven.

The Christmas Plays

Two recreational pieces belong to Christmas celebrations: "The Angels at the Manger of Jesus" (RP 2) played in 1894 and "The Small Divine Beggar of Christmas" (RP 5) was the Christmas play of 1895.

"Angels at the Manger . . ." (RP 2) reflects St Thérèse's own discovery in Prv. 9:4: "Whoever is a little one, let that one come to me." This passage, which delighted Thérèse and nurtured her own positive image of God, suggested a related thought that "a God who became so small can only be love and mercy" (T, 90). The first Christmas play fills the stage with angels in dialogue with the Infant Jesus. Before the manger St Thérèse offers the community a meditative reflection on the beauty of God's love in the Divine Child, reveals the Child's awareness of a future passion and final glory, dwells upon the continual loving presence of Jesus in the Eucharist and the immense sweep of God's mercy toward his people (T, 89).

The merciful love of God in Jesus Christ is portrayed in a striking manner in a dialogue between the Angel of the Infant Jesus and the Angel of the Last Judgement. The Last Judgement angel suggests a final confrontation between God and the individual soul. "You will tremble, inhabitants of the earth," says the angel, "you will tremble on your last day. You will not be able to endure the anger of this Child, today the God of love . . ." (T, 102) St Thérèse corrects the severe image through the comforting words of Jesus to the angel of his Infancy: " . . . the smallest soul who loves me becomes Paradise for me . . ." (T, 103) To the angel of Judgement Jesus says: ". . . put down your sword. It is not your task to judge the nature which I have lifted up and which I have wanted to redeem" (T, 108). This play succeeds in presenting loving images of God in Jesus Christ, calls for daily reception of the Eucharist for faithful spouses, and tries to maintain a sense of the mystery of the Incarnation through the presence of the angels.

"The Small Divine Beggar at Christmas" (RP 5) involved the action of the whole community before the manger. St Thérèse composed twenty-six brief poems which have an introduction followed by a response/conclusion for each couplet. One by one the twenty-six Carmelites in the Lisieux community approached the manger. After a brief period of adoration before the Infant each sister removed a slip of paper from a basket at the manger and handed it to a "novice-angel" in the play who sang the couplet before the community. Certain characteristics of the Carmelite vocation are distilled through a variety of images: the call to continual prayer; zeal for the good of others, especially sinners, priests and the other sisters; charity; simplicity and humility; confident faith and abandonment to God's love (T, 186).

Each couplet has an identifying title, e.g., "A Smile," "A Toy," "A Pillow," "A Flower." One poem, entitled "A Small Host," includes the words: "Jesus . . . in order to communicate his life, transforms into himself each morning a small white Host. With still more love he wishes to change you into himself. Your heart is his dear treasure, his happiness and unspeakable joy" (T, 192).

The intimacy of God in Jesus Christ evoked in St Thérèse a consistent flow of spousal or marital images. For St Thérèse Jesus has become the "Divine Beggar" who seeks from us, begs us, to offer our lives to him for the salvation of others. Apart from the title of this Christmas play, her letters to Céline make this conviction clear.[9]

Jesus at Bethany (RP 4)

This play celebrated the feast of St Martha, July 29, 1895, and honored the lay sisters in the community. They were to allow the choir sisters to serve them throughout the day. The lay sisters were not to enter the kitchen. They were presented with small gifts from the community that day, and in the evening the skit took place.

This play centered on the Martha and Mary passage found in Lk. 10:38-42. All the lines were put to music. St Thérèse confused Mary of Bethany with Mary Magdalen and thus the play has the Lord assuring Mary that her past sinful life is totally forgiven.

St Thérèse did not touch upon the scriptural line which says that "Mary has chosen the better part . . ." (Lk. 10:42) Perhaps she sensed that the "Marthas" in the community would feel excluded. Rather she chose to emphasize that our occupations are not the critical element in our relationship to the Lord. Love alone counts (T, 167). Jesus tells Martha: "Work is indeed necessary and I came to make it holy. But it is always essential to accompany work with fervent prayer" (T, 176).

What is the virtue which most contributes fire to charity? According to St Thérèse it is the virtue of humility. She retrieves the sense of humility evident in the writings of St Teresa of Avila. In the *Interior Castle* she wrote:

I'm saying that we should walk in truth before God and people in as many ways as possible. Especially, there should be no desire that others consider us better than we are. And in our works we should attribute to God what is his and to ourselves what is ours and strive to draw out the truth in everything.[10]

St Thérèse writes of the same humility when she has Jesus say to Martha: "You have delighted me from your infancy by your marvelous purity. While you have innocence Magdalen exhibits humility . . ." Martha immediately recognizes the importance of what Jesus has said: "Humility pleases you, Lord. I want to live it out" (T, 178). Thus St Thérèse indicates that the greatest foundation for love is not virginity as such but rather humility.

The most truthful reality of all is a profound relationship to Jesus Christ. Martha exclaims: "Finally, I understand, Jesus, the most captivating beauty: your divine look has penetrated my heart. All my gifts are really so few. It's my soul itself that I ought to offer you, my loving Savior" (T, 177). St Thérèse again emphasizes the importance of self-gift over any scorecard of virtuous actions. God seeks not an accumulation of sacrifices as gifts but the very gift of ourselves. St Thérèse has Jesus proclaim: "Yes, it's your heart that I wish. For this I have come in self-emptying love. I have wished to abandon the heavens and their infinite glory for you . . ." (T, 177)

The Flight into Egypt (RP 6)

This play celebrated the feast day of the prioress, Mother Agnes of Jesus, on January 21, 1896. The dialogues of St Thérèse's second longest play are in prose and verse. The play builds upon a legend that the Holy Family while in flight into Egypt spent one night in a den of thieves. St Thérèse portrays the robbers in a sympathetic manner, viewing them as rather open to God's loving initiative in Jesus. It is reported that Mother Agnes was not too happy with the frivolous spirit of the robbers and their lack of urbane speech (T, 206).

St Thérèse recounts the story of the child Dismas, whose mother is Susanna and whose father, Abram, is the leader of the thieves. Dismas is suffering from leprosy. No hope is offered for his recovery. After Mary bathes Jesus the child Dismas is washed in the same bath water and is cured of his affliction. Of course, the band of thieves and Susanna are overcome with joy and gratitude. All kneel while Mary blesses the gathering with the Infant Jesus.

This play brings out the enormous inequality in economic life between the rich and the poor, a major situation of concern at the end of the nineteenth century. In the figure of St Joseph we see the insecurity of the worker. In the play Susanna tells Mary and Joseph that her husband and his friends rob because it is the only way to seek justice in the midst of dire poverty. St Joseph responds: "We're not fleeing poverty. Happiness does not consist in being wealthy but in humbly submitting one's will to God's will who gives to each one all that is necessary to save one's soul" (T, 225). Mary adds: "You poor woman, how can you be so attached to riches unjustly acquired? Why can you not find your joy in forming the heart of this beautiful child that God has given you?" (T, ibid.) St Thérèse does not contemplate a program of social reform as a measure of response to unjust economic conditions in society. Rather St Joseph puts the issue in the context of a futurist eschatology: "If the present life had to be always, you would have some reason for amassing riches. But this life which passes so quickly is followed by an eternity of happiness for those who serve God faithfully in this passing exile . . ." (T, 233) A final hymn celebrates confidence in the infinite mercy of God, the value of poverty and the hidden life.

The play turned out to be a source of humiliation for St Thérèse. Mother Agnes stopped the play before the performance was completed. St Thérèse's reaction was recorded by Sr Geneviève of the Holy Face (Céline): "I surprised her backstage, secretly wiping away her tears. Then regaining possession of herself she was calm and sweet under the humiliation." Mother Agnes later explained her action with some sense of contrition: "I caused her grief one festive evening . . . in telling her bluntly that these compositions for evening recreation were too long and tired out the community" (T, 206).

The Triumph of Humility (RP 7)

This play, which has been presented in a previous article, celebrated the feast day of the prioress, Mother Marie de Gonzague, on June 21, 1896.[11] *The Triumph of Humility* makes clear several aspects of the Carmelite vocation: the importance of cultivating a spousal relationship to Christ; the spiritual life as combat; the distraction of self-preoccupation; the power of the virtue and grace of humility; the value of the hidden life. As I have stated elsewhere:

In order to appreciate this play it is indeed helpful to consider some factors which influenced St Thérèse in its composition. First, there is the figure of Diana Vaughan; the story of her rather amazing conversion was known at the Carmel of Lisieux through St Thérèse's relatives, the Guérin family, especially through her uncle. In order to comprehend the figure of Diana Vaughan it is necessary to turn to the infamous anticlerical, anti-Catholic writer, well known in France, Leo Taxil. He obtained a vast amount of notoriety by announcing his own conversion to Catholicism in 1885. He repented of all his past inflammatory and derogatory writings and supposedly rejected completely his former positions. The papal nuncio in Paris absolved Taxil of the censure of excommunication. What the authorities and people . . . did not know was that Taxil's self-confessed renewed devotion to the Catholicism of his baptism was a hoax. He had made up the character of Miss Diana Vaughan, who was supposedly the high priestess of 'Palladium,' a very secret Masonic order given to devil worship. Taxil wrote a book using Vaughan's name, elaborating upon her conversion to Catholicism. Her fame became . . . widespread in Europe.[12]

Diana Vaughan appears in conversation in this play as perhaps an apt candidate for the Carmel of Lisieux. However, the major portion of the play focuses upon dialogues among various devils. The Carmelite observers of these conversations are already fortified by their committed spousal relationship to Christ. They notice that the devils' intentions are to destroy the spiritual fervor of all Carmelites. The devils' only hope of carrying out this plot rests in finding Carmelite nuns who are full of self-love. Lucifer states: "I assure you that self-love is the best way to diminish the love of God in the hearts of all his nuns" (T, 254). What can overcome self-focus and pride is the virtue of humility. The play concludes with angels singing: "You are the sisters of the angels and virgins of Carmel . . . You desire, fervent Carmelites, to win hearts for Jesus, your Spouse. Then remain always little for him, for humility throws Hell into a rage" (T, 266).

Stanislaus Kostka (RP 8)

This marks the final play that St Thérèse wrote. It served as part of the celebration honoring the golden anniversary of profession of

Sr St Stanislas. The chronicle of the Carmel of Lisieux noted for this day: "1897: February 8. The community celebrated with joy the golden wedding of our dear Sr St Stanislas . . . In the evening the novices played an episode in the life of St Stanislas which their young Mistress, Sr Thérèse of the Child Jesus authored" (T, 263). The episode refers to St Stanislaus' entrance into the Jesuit novitiate. Once again St Thérèse centers upon an event in the life of one who died young just as St Joan of Arc. This play suggests that it is possible after death to do good upon earth (T, 268). St Stanislaus is portrayed as humble and prayerful; he wants to join the Jesuits in order to become a saint. Because of possible opposition at home he travels to Germany to enter the Jesuit novitiate. St Thérèse recounts basically the known events in St Stanislaus' life up to that time. Soon after his entrance into the Jesuit community he is struck with a devastating illness. St Thérèse provides a slightly changed version of St Stanislaus' vision of angels, accompanied by St Barbara, bringing him communion. St Stanislaus says: ". . . I saw St Barbara entering my room resplendent in glory, accompanied by two beautiful angels. She held the host in her virginal hands and I had the unspeakable consolation of receiving God in the Eucharist from her . . ." Br Augustine, a Jesuit novice, remarks: "St Barbara held the Divine Eucharist in her hands? What a mystery! . . . Why was it not the angels rather who gave you Holy Communion?" St Stanislaus says:

> During my Roman trip an angel gave me Holy Communion, but St Barbara wasn't there. In the Kingdom of God her glory surpasses that of the celestial spirits. For that reason before all of the angels this gentle virgin gave me the Bread of Angels. Perhaps she also had desired on earth to share in the divine function of priests and the Lord wished to satisfy this desire. (T, 281)

St Thérèse appears to include in this passage her own desire for priesthood among other vocations which she records early on in Manuscript B of the *Story of a Soul*. The play concludes with St Stanislaus asking Mary to intercede for him so that he be allowed after his death to return on the earth in order to protect "holy souls" (T, 285).

What the recently deceased Hans Urs von Baltazar has written of St Thérèse's poetry can also be said generally of her religious plays:

> Though her poetry remains, as to form, a prisoner of the taste of her time—where, after all, would she have learned the language of Péguy or of Claudel?—her mind is a bubbling spring of the most pertinent, the most original and the most unforgettable images which, I am not afraid to say, render her the equal of the two great Reformers of Carmel in poetic power.[13]

ST THÉRÈSE'S PLAYS: SOME THEOLOGICAL CONSIDERATIONS

In diverse ways St Thérèse broke through the spiritual culture of her own time to offer a fresh understanding of the relationship between God and us. This portion of the article will concentrate upon that relationship in accord with those dimensions of faith which predominate in the plays: the person of Christ, the role of Mary, the dynamics of grace in the spiritual journey and the place of an eschatological perspective.

To St Thérèse it appeared that some nuns in her community reflected an understanding of God bound by images of fear and severe judgement. God would be exacting in weighing the merits and demerits of each person's life. Therefore, in order to achieve some divine acceptance, a person must amass a chart of good and virtuous deeds. For St Thérèse such striving for perfection in life does not evidence the core of a relationship with God. Rather, coming to know, to accept and to rejoice that we are loved by God who seeks our friendship—"the divine beggar" in St Thérèse's play—provides the most authentic foundation for our relationship with God. Passages of Isaiah such as the following were precious to St Thérèse: "Though the mountains leave their place and hills be shaken, my love shall never leave you, says the Lord who has mercy on you" (Is. 54:10). St Thérèse reveals the loving mercy of God in the dialogues between Mary Magdalen and Christ and between Mary, the Mother of the Lord, and the family in the den of thieves. In fact, God's mercy consistently stands out in St Thérèse's writing. In other words, the relationship between God and us is best described as beginning in God who first loved us. The divine initiative, which Catholic tradition views as the center of an authentic and biblically rooted story of grace, has a prominent place in St Thérèse's plays.

Jesus appears as an infant in the plays although frequent references to his passion occur as well as some mention of his resurrection. St Thérèse reflects the christological understanding of her historical period. This high or descent Christology begins in pre-existence with the eternal Word of God who condescends and becomes one with all humanity in self-emptying love. The prologue of St John's Gospel, for example, provides this scenario. In one of the Christmas plays, "Angels at the Manger," Jesus shows signs even in the manger of some foreknowledge of his future passion. This imagery is consistent with a descent Christology. It is recently reflected in Pope John Paul II's encyclical *Redemptor Hominis.* An earlier Christology which again has found resonance in the experience of the Christian community is called an ascending or low Christology which begins with Jesus on earth in his life and ministry. It leads to the risen Christ now forever with God in glory. The scriptural warrants for this view are the Synoptic Gospels. Sometimes these two Christologies are placed in a quasi-polar relationship—the high Christology presented as other-worldly in orientation and a low Christology as more historically and this-worldly oriented. Theologian Elizabeth Johnson, C.S.J. has written of their mutual complementarity and the ability of both to ground a faith life of engagement in the world or a ministry of social justice. "While descending Christology is more philosophical in character and ascending Christology more historically oriented, not only are they not mutually exclusive, but both are needed for the fullness of the Church's faith confession."[14]

While St Thérèse reflects the more traditionally known Christology, in no way does this understanding create an abstract or idealistic relationship to Christ as viewed in her plays. Images of commitment and strength, suffering and doubt, and particularly a marital or spousal relationship describe the individual's involvement with Christ. Flowing from this loving union with Jesus Christ a person willingly identifies with the self-emptying love of the Savior. Thus, Joan of Arc marches in battle for France, the Carmelite nuns sacrifice and pray for sinners and the needs of the world, St Stanislaus Kostka gives up the security of his wealth and noble birth.

Mary, of course, appears as mother of the Infant Jesus in "The Flight into Egypt" (RP 6) and also as a consoling presence to St Stanislaus Kostka (RP 8) in his illness. Mary tells St Stanislaus that he will be under her mantle of protection. In both plays Mary appears as mother, concerned and willing to become involved with others in their struggles. In fact, it is Mary's motherhood which most nurtured St Thérèse's marian piety. But to cover the depth and breadth of St Thérèse's relationship to Mary one would have to turn to her other writings. Fr John Malley, O.Carm., Prior General, in his letter to Carmelites on the occasion of the Marian Year, recalls the famous poem St Thérèse wrote, "Why I Love You, Mary." He notes particularly Thérèse's words: "Mary is my dear mother and usually daughters resemble their mother."[15] This same poem sings the praises of Mary by reviewing the biblical stories depicting her life. St Thérèse provides a miniature portrait of her own spirituality when she writes of Mary: "I know that at Nazareth . . . you lived very poorly, not desiring anything more—no raptures, miracles, ecstasies adorned your life . . . It is by the ordinary way that you were happy to walk . . ."[16] This conviction remained central in St Thérèse's experience of the spiritual journey.

In reflecting upon St Thérèse's plays it is evident that her beliefs about the spiritual life, the life of faith, are echoed throughout the recreational pieces. The notion of littleness and childlike simplicity, the need for humility, the way of faith, hope and love, abandonment to God and prayer for others find a collaborative and life-giving context within the image of "Spouse of Christ." It seems to me that the spousal metaphor provides a focus for the dynamic of grace in St Thérèse's life. (Remember that she created her own invitation to her marriage to Christ at her profession.) The "Sponsa Christi" or bride of Christ motif has a long history in the Church's tradition and in Western literature. St Thérèse's experience does not simply identify with past expression because she continued to insist upon childlike qualities in her relationship with the Lord. Yet even in her childlike loving, mature insight and behavior blossomed. As the English Dominican Simon Tugwell wrote:

Very early in her life Thérèse discovered her own capacity for love, and she realized how easily it could go astray. In her convent she could see how cloying and unhealthy human affection could become . . . She was far from insensible to human affection—she once said that she could not understand saints who did not love their families—but she realized that only God could satisfy the vastness of her capacity to love and be loved. But she came to see not only that God was the only one who could give her sufficient love, but that God must be both subject and object of all that loving. "I will love you with the very same love with which you loved me, Jesus, eternal Word." Unlike some of the late medieval devotionalists, Thérèse realized that it was not enough simply to transfer our own affections to God. It is by inserting our own loving into his loving . . . that we can safely give free rein to our loving.[17]

The spouse of Christ image is fulfilled in Joan of Arc and marks the identity of the novices in "The Triumph of Humility" (RP 7). The virtue of hope rests upon abandonment to God's loving initiative and confidence in his care for his children. Humility is the practical virtue of the spouse of Christ that provides the best response in spiritual combat. In her plays humility is acceptance of the truth about ourselves, the simple acknowledgement of the inevitable limitations found in the human condition, the need for patient endurance in faith. Given a context of weakness we need not succumb to self-pity and self-defeating responses. Rather, humility enables us to trust in God's guidance and strength. Humility would also have us accept our own strengths as evidence of the truth about our own lives. Thus we are led to great sanctity.

St Thérèse's eschatological perspective is typical of her period in history. Her futurist understanding views the life of heaven as release from exile, fulfillment of faith, hope and love, completion and consummation of the spousal relationship to Christ. Yet the eschatological thrust of God's saving presence involves the Carmelite in active relationship to the pains and groans of our world. For St Thérèse the Carmelite vocation involves prayer and sacrifice for sinners, for priests, for those in need. This perspective appears in the plays centering on Joan of Arc (RP 3); The Triumph of Humility (RP 7) and The Small Divine Beggar at Christmas (RP 5).

Since the Plays of St Thérèse were written in her latter years they convey many of the mature convictions of her faith life. These are revealed in simple stories involving family, friends, community life, nature, struggle, love. In the *Story of a Soul* Thérèse found an opportunity to synthesize her vision:

> Ah, Lord, I know you don't command the impossible. You know better than I do my weakness and imperfection. You know very well that never would I be able to love my sisters as you love them, unless *you*, O my Jesus, *loved them in me*. It is because you wanted to give me this grace that you made your *new* commandment . . . Yes, I feel it, when I am charitable, it is Jesus alone who is acting in me, and the more united I am to him, the more also do I love my sisters.[18]

Thus St Thérèse reveals the heart of every pilgrimage: to unite the love of God and the love of neighbor! Perhaps the most fundamental challenge in every age is to find the path that expresses the same solidarity.

THÉRÈSE'S APPROACH
TO GOSPEL LIVING

Redemptus Valabek

Redemptus Valabek heads the office for the Postulation of Blessed and Saints of the Carmelites of the Ancient Observance in Rome. He has also headed the English-language section of Regina Mundi, a theological in stitute in Rome.

Authenticity is high on our list of priorities. With so much being written and discussed about St Thérèse of Lisieux, especially since the centenary of her birth in 1973, we are tempted to demand: "Will the real St Thérèse of Lisieux step forward?" The request is not an easy one. In the first place, Thérèse was such a positive person who found God everywhere, in the banalities of daily living which most of us look on as neutral or even as obstacles to holiness, that much of what has been said about her would somehow fit into her "way." Thérèse is definitely a maximalist type: sin was the only non-graced reality for her. And so, aspects such as trust, abandonment, littleness, weakness, spiritual childhood, and many others, can be singled out, studied in her writings and be appreciated as authentic dimensions of her wholistic view of holiness.

But even this statement is incomplete. Paradoxically, Thérèse was a sworn enemy of hypocrisy, histrionics, holy hysteria. Truth was sacred to her. How she was able to blend a positive-affirmation approach with an uncompromising choice for truth, even when it hurt, even in its unappealing "hard" aspects, is one of the mysteries of grace for which Thérèse is a "great" among God's little ones. Attention to this paradox is essential if the real Thérèse is to appear.

A second problem surrounding Thérèse flows from the occasional nature of her writings. Thérèse's ambition was to have a lot of time for her beloved Jesus; reading and writing about Jesus were never as good nor as necessary as giving Jesus the person pleasure, and so it was mainly under obedience that Thérèse wrote of her spiritual odyssey. But even these writings under obedience were for specific persons and specific purposes. Her poems, for instance, were by and large written to enliven the feastdays of the other sisters and to be sung at evening recreation (and Thérèse raised some eyebrows among the older nuns when she introduced "modern" secular melodies taken from operas and contemporary sources—once in her later years, she was heard humming a children's nursery melody as she was going to Communion). This means that she never sat down to write a logical, detailed exposé of her "Little Way." She was tremendously person-centered, more than theory or program-centered, which means that her writings without fail reflect the status, the personality, the understanding of the people for whom she is writing. This aspect, again, relativizes her writings and warns us to take them as a whole and against the background of her life and experience.

Thérèse admits that she can barely understand what she has just written. She wrote only at the time allotted for personal things which was an hour a day at the most. At times she was rushed and so her thought is expressed not necessarily in the clearest way; she admits this explicitly. Some notes and letters have remained unfinished—testimonies to her strictness with herself in her respect for the daily schedule.

A third difficulty has to do with Thérèse's style, which to modern tastes appears to be too sweet, gushy, bubbling—indicative of the comfortable bourgeoise lifestyle to which the saint was used in her family circle. Thérèse used the stereotyped images and phrases of her day to describe her pilgrimage of faith; she was no innovator in this area. But too many people have been fooled on this score. The "too-nice-to-be-true" style of Thérèse wishes to express the most crucifying and demanding realities. Only of late has the sharing of Thérèse in the paschal mystery of Christ been studied in depth. It has been shown that while she was writing luminous, "pretty" phrases, she was being eaten away by tuberculosis and plunged into a dark night of spirit that made her wonder why more atheists in like circumstances did not commit suicide. This makes imperative the effort to get beyond mere words to the substantial meaning at which Thérèse aimed. We are aided in our effort to reach the real Thérèse by the recent "centenary" edition of her works, masterfully undertaken by the Discalced friar Guy Gaucher and a team of collaborators. We have now at our fingertips the actual words of Thérèse, before they were touched up by her sisters (who by the way were only doing what Thérèse herself commissioned them to do). The Thérèse who emerges from her original manuscripts is not substantially different from the saint we knew before, but there are so many changes of emphasis and highlighting that we understand better the durability of Thérèse's message and witness. Thérèse emerges as a strong personality, ready and willing to accept joyously — and even to look for — the crucifying demands of true love.

I

The "Little Way" of Thérèse has been synonymous with the "way of spiritual childhood." Pope after pope has referred to this as the kernel of Thérèse's message. Yet today we know that in none of her writings does Thérèse use this phrase; it appears as a saying of St Thérèse, recalled by her sister, Mother Agnes, but which reputable authors appropriate to Agnes herself, as a handy summary of Thérèse's approach. In fact, Thérèse never cites the childhood phrases of Jesus himself in the Gospel. This is not strange when we realize that Thérèse did not find inspiration of her "way" in the Scriptures. She lived out the Gospel values existentially, and was glad to find confirmation of her way in the Scriptures. She found the guarantee of authenticity in the Hebrew Scriptures, especially in the prophet Isaiah, and in Proverbs, because her sister Céline, when entering Carmel, brought with her a notebook of citations from the Hebrew Scriptures which she presented to Thérèse and which the latter made her treasure.

Why do so many modern authors object to the centrality of "spiritual childhood" in Thérèse? Simply put, it is because they are convinced that it vitiates the prime thrust of Thérèse's spiritual "way." The way in which it is usually described, "spiritual childhood" puts paramount stress on the "little, passive" virtues which we are to take on — humility, abandonment, trust, simplicity, etc. Integral dimensions of Thérèse's vision these attitudes are; they are not, however, the prime concern. Thérèse's way does not subscribe to a spirituality that stresses the human collaboration, but rather to the primacy and almost exclusive place of God. For Thérèse God is the ground of all life and existence. Thérèse could never (not even in the awful throes of her own passion) finish marvelling at the wondrous ways in which God effected our holiness.

> If a wild flower could talk, I imagine it would tell us quite candidly about all God has done for it . . . I'm delighted to put on record the favors Our Lord has shown me, all quite undeserved. I fully realize that there is nothing about me which could have claimed his divine attention; anything which is good in me is the effect of his mercy — that and nothing else. It was he who chose the soil I was to grow in . . . So far, I've just been giving a brief summary of the blessings God has granted me.[1]

Thérèse was graced with this experiential knowledge: the real world is not the one we experience around us, but rather the world of God and of the things of God. She was given to understand the transitoriness of all earthly reality; no wonder she longed for heaven and even prayed as a child that her loved ones would die so that they could enjoy the "real thing." In her wholistic Catholicism, she understood all of nature to conspire to lift up her thoughts and above all, her love to God. She longed for heaven not because she was intent on escape from the harsh realities of the real world, nor because she feared responsibility (her promise of a shower of roses from heaven radically shows how much the world and all in it meant to her), but rather because she was possessed by the wisdom that made her strain toward the One who gave meaning to everyone and everything else, who fulfilled the wildest desires and dreams of the human heart, and who personally loved us and expected our love in return. In a letter to her sister Céline[2] Thérèse put it bluntly: "Jesus alone *is*; everything else *is not*. . . There is but one thing to do during the night of this life, this only night that comes *but once*, and that is to love, *to love* Jesus with all the strength of our heart and to save souls for him so that he be loved . . ." This life is "but once"; heaven, which is simply Jesus, is forever. Thérèse wishes to be rid of the obstacles that prevent the floods of divine love from "doing their thing" already during this life (which is night), rather than waiting for eternity in order to know them experientially.

Thérèse strove to "take Jesus by the heart," i.e., let Jesus' heart have his way with us, give pleasure to the good God in a way that he and not she willed. Jesus was the most important person in Thérèse's life and thought and love. Holiness basically consists in allowing oneself to be loved by him just how and just when he wills. "Merit doesn't consist in doing or giving much, but rather in receiving, in loving much . . . Let us allow him to take and give all that he (Jesus) wishes. Perfection consists in doing his will."[3]

For Thérèse holiness comes above all from Jesus' heart, from above, from divine initiative; man's collaboration is an eager acceptance, reception. For Thérèse, love is above all "to receive" from Jesus' heart his undying affection and concern. Holiness is to allow Jesus to give to and to take from, just as he wills. When Sr Agnes complained that she would have to face her Creator with empty hands, Thérèse observed: "Ah well, you are not like baby (NV: "me") and yet I am in the same state . . . Still, if I had accomplished all the works of St Paul, I would still consider myself an 'unprofitable servant.' But that is precisely what gives me joy, because having nothing, I shall receive everything from the good God."[4] "I do not desire to die more than to live; what I want to say is—if I had a choice, I would prefer to die, but because it is the good God who chooses for me, I prefer what he wills. I love whatever he does."[5] This overwhelming realization of God's action in the process of holiness needs much more study; it is too central to Thérèse's thought; it permeates her whole vision of holiness. When Céline reminded Thérèse that with death imminent, her dream of going to Saigon would be frustrated, and that perhaps Céline would be sent to complete Thérèse's work, so that Thérèse from heaven and Céline in Saigon would accomplish a perfect work, Thérèse's reaction was predictable: "If you ever go down there, don't think it's to complete anything. There is no need of that. Everything is good, everything is perfect, accomplished, it is love alone that counts . . . If you go there, it will be a caprice of Jesus and nothing else. Don't think that it will be a *useful* work; it would be a caprice of Jesus . . ."[6] This is Thérèse at her best: the only thing that mattered was to let Jesus have his way with her according to his desires. Everything else is a detail and of relative value. Thérèse would have thrilled to our present-day understanding of the history of salvation. She had intuited its radical meaning a century ago. "What does he (Jesus) reserve for us in heaven, seeing that even here below his love gives us such delightful surprises? More than ever I realize that the smallest happenings of our lives are guided by God; he makes us desire and then grants our desires."[7]

Thérèse envisioned God not in theoretical or doctrinal elaborations, but on a spontaneous, awareness level. For her God is Jesus. She never seems overly concerned with the distinction of persons in the Blessed Trinity. Since she was prone to aim at a felt, experienced reality all through her life, spontaneously she riveted her attention and her love on the Incarnate Word, Jesus the Christ. His whole earthly existence—from his birth and childhood to his passion and death, as her name in religion indicates—fascinated her and became the concretization of the loving-kindness of so wonderful a God. Thérèse felt no hesitation in her writings, even in the most solemn ones, such as her Act of Oblation to Merciful Love, to address God as Trinity and in the same breath speak of the Father, but then preferably glide into addressing him as Jesus. The Holy Spirit appears in her writings infrequently. Being an unquestioning Catholic, Thérèse surely committed herself to the God of revelation, and as such the triune God, but her psychological perception of this fundamental truth centered on the revealer of the true God, Jesus himself. Thérèse surely knew Jesus as the initiator and the completer of our faith.

Until her dying breath, Thérèse would insist that whatever is found worthwhile, good, holy, virtuous in herself, is not her own doing, but the Lord's. When on her deathbed, her sister Agnes admires Thérèse's patience in suffering, Thérèse replies energetically: "I haven't had a minute of patience! It's not my patience! People are always fooled!" Thérèse grew throughout her life as to the deepest meaning of the love of Jesus and in the end her desire became that he no longer allow her to love him in return with the love of her human heart, but that he grant her the very Spirit, the Holy Spirit of love with which to love him. Her aspiration was to love Jesus as he wished to be loved, but he could only wish to be loved infinitely—something that no human endeavor but only the Spirit of Jesus could accomplish. Thus in her Act of Oblation she begged: "I beg you, O my God, that you yourself be my holiness!" In this Act of Oblation, Thérèse recognizes the insignificance of her own activities and so she begs for not a momentary but a constant act of love which will be none other than God's own. Already on her profession day, September 8, 1890, Thérèse had prayed for nothing less than "infinite, unlimited love which is yourself . . . the love which will no longer be myself, but you, my Jesus." True lover that she was, Thérèse searched and searched for ways to express the unique reality of God and the relative reality of everything else: for her durable, definitive, decisive life was simply God; everything else was relative to him and his world. Thérèse's lifelong task was to be assimilated by God, to be so taken up by him that her own unprofitable efforts which were many, constant and simple, even banal—would still leave her with empty hands in the evening of her life, but would be subsumed by the superabundant, redemptive activity of her one love, Jesus. At the end of her autobiography, she exclaims that her love ". . . is something less than a drop of dew lost in the ocean. Love you as you love me? The only way to do that is to come to you for the loan of your own love; I couldn't content myself with less."[8]

If Thérèse had to give a single word synonymous with God, it would have to be love. God is love everlasting, who showered his favor on her from her earliest years. He never changes; he continues to pour out the same love to her always and everywhere, even and especially in the terrible sufferings of her last months on earth. When another sister compassionated with Thérèse over her excruciating, terrible pain, the saint reacted: "No, it's not terrible. A little victim of love cannot consider terrible what her Spouse sends to her out of love."[9] Thérèse describes him as the "burning hearth of uncreated Love" and she glories that she "will be united with him forever."[10] She exults that she "has found the secret of how to appropriate your flame of love to myself."[11] Every other dimension of God's rich simplicity, even his justice, Thérèse sees as resplendent with love. Even when her faith was shaken in her final ordeal, she exclaimed: all that is left is love. And even when heaven appeared to be blocked off from her by a wall, Thérèse never wavered in the final victory of love, as her last audible words attest.

There is one characteristic of God's love which Thérèse appreciated to the point of making it her own characteristic: she often spoke of "the nature of love is to lower itself." Thérèse was not content that God is love: He could be such and still remain alone and alien to human persons, given the inner trinitarian life of God. Instead, God bends down to creatures. Thérèse's insights are close to Eastern theology's description of the "condescension of God." Thérèse is horrified that anyone think that God takes pleasure in man's sufferings; rather she saw God in his loving mercy constantly healing and divinizing the whole human person. For her, merciful love is a synonym for the Incarnate Word. In the concrete person of Jesus, Thérèse saw the extremes to which God would go to overwhelm us with his love. But being an authentic lover, God would not be content "to do it all alone"—to squash man's love by the intensity and immensity of his own. God actually begs for our love. Thérèse uses this bold language to stress the point: Jesus is sick with love; Jesus loves us to folly; Jesus hungers and thirsts for our love. It is in this context that Thérèse offered herself as a victim not to divine justice (as tradition would have it), but to merciful Love. To the extent that her powers allowed, Thérèse was determined to make up for all those who abused God's unbounded love for them, those who think little of it or who voluntarily spurn it. The Act of Oblation resulted from a deeper realization of how Jesus wants to be loved. In other words, Thérèse discovered that Jesus was not all outgoing prodigality, but as a true lover, he is someone who asks for love to be reciprocal.

Thérèse's response to God's initiatives is summed up in one phrase: let God act. Already on her First Communion day Thérèse refers to a "fusion" of herself and Jesus; something like the drop of water lost in the immensity of the ocean. "There were no longer two of us . . . Jesus only was left, my Master, my King . . . Hadn't I begged him to take away my liberty, because I was so afraid of the use I might make of it; hadn't I longed, weak and helpless as I was, to be united once for all with that divine Strength?"[12] To Céline she wrote: "Merit does not consist in doing or in giving much, but rather in receiving, in loving much."[13] For Thérèse "love" and "receive" are synonymous. How close to the vision of St Paul this conviction is! To love is, first of all, the harder thing—to allow oneself to be loved by Jesus, just as he wills, with no reservations or restrictions or dispensations asked for.

This stress on the positive, on love, has left the impression that Thérèse has piloted a less demanding way to holiness. Thérèse would be horrified if her way were presented as an easy "comfy," painless way to get to heaven. Authors blame Céline for a certain tendency to present Thérèse's way as a cross-less way. In fact, Céline went through a period of many years during which she could not accept any form of presenting a God who appeared to will suffering for his creatures. In her anguish she struck from Thérèse's writings anything that might give this impression. In her own writings describing Thérèse's doctrine, Céline mirrored her own conviction that little souls do not have great sufferings to endure. Thérèse's way erroneously came to be described as that of minimum self-renunciation and maximum self-fulfillment. On the contrary. Thérèse's way does not prescind from the cross and self-discipline. Attempts to soften the wholistic surrender of self to the action of God simply adulterate Thérèse's vision. To surrender not one's activities, but all of oneself to another—especially when the other is Jesus—is the supremely purifying process. Thérèse realistically declared that she did not remember ever refusing anything to the good God. She understood this could not be authentic if done with stoic indifference. She knew it as a labor of love and so she begged for the strength to rejoice for everything that he did for her. Her apostolate of the smile became the supreme proof of her greatness, especially as her sufferings mounted both physically and spiritually. This joyful abandonment into the hands of God while with excruciating pain and in the darkest of nights is at the core of her "way." There is nothing infantile, compromising or weak about it. Where Thérèse refused to bank on anything that was not God, she paid the high price of the demands of God's invitations.

II

Thérèse's commitment to truth and strength of character are two characteristics that are part of her core values. Only too often Thérèse has been depicted as "soft," as proposing a luminous, cheery way to heaven. Three episodes from Thérèse's life, among many others, should dispel any such impression. She was on her infirmary bed where she would die when the sister who rubbed Thérèse the wrong way in everything she said and did (Sr Thérèse of St Augustine), naively asked Thérèse: "Tell me, have you had to battle?" St Thérèse: "Ah, have I had to battle! I do not have an easy nature. It may appear so, but I feel it. I can assure you that I've not had a single day without suffering, not a single one!" The sister, who considered Thérèse her best friend, observed: "But people make out as if you had none." Thérèse's spontaneous reaction: "Ah, the judgments of creatures! Because they do not see, they do not believe."[14]

This picture of the real St Thérèse was grounded in her inexorable quest for truth/authenticity, the basis of the humility and simplicity which are the basic attitudes of a person overwhelmed with the contemplative experience of God's active and dominant presence. Some months before she died Thérèse was commenting on a story she had read when she was young. It concerned a woman who tried to make everyone content by agreeing with them. Thérèse observed:

> That teacher should not have been afraid to tell her little girls that they were wrong when that was the case . . . And now I have not changed my mind. I admit I have a lot more trouble, because it's always easy to lay the blame on those who are absent and that immediately calms down the person doing the complaining. Yes, but . . . that is just the opposite of what I do. If I am not loved so much the worse. I tell the whole truth. A person should not come to me if she does not want to know it."[15]

This option for the truth was no last-minute resolution formulated when Thérèse was faced with eternity. She confesses: "I have never acted, like Pilate, who refused to listen to the truth. I have always said to the good God: 'O my God, I wish to hear you attentively, I beg you to answer me when I humbly ask you, What is the truth? Make me see things exactly as they are, that nothing may throw sand in my eyes.'"[16]

Thérèse was not theorizing with these statements. Her service as unofficial novice mistress is a good case in point. When Thérèse saw one of the novices too attached to Mother Gonzague to the detriment of her spiritual growth, Thérèse resolved to tell the novice of the danger of her misplaced affection. Thérèse's sister, Agnes, warned her not to do so for fear that the novice would relate everything to Mother Gonzague and Thérèse might be sent off to another monastery (like Saigon where volunteers were being sought) or at least be in the bad books of the prioress. Thérèse's reply: "I know that very well, but since now I know it is my duty to speak, I cannot consider the consequences."[17] Thérèse understood that true charity demanded that at times it meant telling others things they did not want or like to hear. True charity for Thérèse too is the whole and true good.

> Goodness should not degenerate into weakness. When a person has justly scolded someone, she should leave it at that, without allowing herself to become tender to the point of tormenting herself for having hurt the other person, of seeing her suffer or be in tears. To run after the afflicted person in order to console her is to do her more harm than good. To leave her alone is to force her to have recourse to God, to see her misdeeds and to humiliate herself. Otherwise, accustomed to consolation after a deserved scolding, she will always act, in those same circumstances, like a pampered child, who stamps her feet and cries until her mother comes to wipe her tears away.[18]

In fact, Thérèse regarded her role as unofficial novice mistress as the role of a warrior, even to her last breath. Even when the novices did not appreciate her, avoided her and snubbed her, she resolutely remained anchored in her conviction that true charity never compromises with the truth. "I am not a warrior who fights with earthly weapons but with the 'sword of the Spirit which is the Word of

God.' So, this sickness could not beat me and it was only last night that I used my sword on a novice. I have said: 'I shall die weapons in hand.'"[19] Several novices have left accounts of how Thérèse relentlessly campaigned to let God's grace triumph in their lives as they surrendered completely to his merciful Love. Her cousin Marie Guérin (Sr Marie of the Eucharist) recalled: "How many times she said to me: 'I beg you, pay less attention to yourself and pay attention to loving the good God, leave yourself aside. All your scruples are so much self-seeking. Your fretfulness, your difficulties, all that revolves around yourself; it always revolves around the same pivot. I beg you, forget yourself, think about saving souls.'"[20]

Thérèse, a free spirit, often described as unstructured in her spirituality, actually had her cousin make careful notations on her rosary of the number of daily failures. She kept after her even to the point of snapping her fingers when the novice could not restrain her curiosity and raised her eyes constantly. Thérèse's regime was certainly not a unanimous success. Even Thérèse's favorite novice, Sr Marie of the Trinity, resisted Thérèse's recommendations. Thérèse confessed that she felt the tension. She wrote to Céline: "You want news about my daughter (Marie of the Trinity), I think she will stay. She was not brought up like us. That's unfortunate for her; her education is the cause of manners which are unattractive, but she is basically good. Now she loves me well enough, but I try not to touch her except with white silk gloves."[21] For the consolation of all those in formation work, Thérèse during her lifetime never succeeded in winning over or taming young Sr Mary Magdalene, a gloomy personality who had had a very poor family background. The young novice was reluctant and recalcitrant in Thérèse's regard. And the fact was known throughout the convent and even outside. Mother Agnes wrote to her Aunt Guérin: "I had not told you and I really couldn't make you understand to what extent Sr Mary Magdalene is alienated from Sr Thérèse of the Child Jesus, because she feels that she is known to the depths of her soul and thus is obliged to wage war on her nature."[22] This novice was scheduled to have a weekly meeting with Thérèse every Sunday; she invariably would run off to hide in some far corner of the monastery rather than face Thérèse. She later confessed: "She went to look for me and when she couldn't find me, and finally later on met me, she would say, 'I was looking for you,' I would reply coldly, 'I was busy.' In this situation she preserved her calm and her smile."[23]

Thérèse would not give up on this most troublesome of sisters and paid so much attention to them even in recreation that her blood sisters over and again complained that Thérèse was paying more attention to "strangers" than to her own flesh and blood. Thérèse paid special attention to this ornery novice because she was convinced that Jesus included everyone in his love and if Thérèse asked to love not with her own but with his love, then she must emulate him. Thérèse wrote the poem to mark the profession of Sr Mary Magdalene; it is one of her more inspired ones. For her theme, Thérèse chose the traditional one of a grand personage taking an insignificant person to self: a king who makes a shepherdess his queen. Sr Magdalene had been a shepherdess in her youth. Thérèse shows how Jesus spared nothing to seduce this bride by his kindness.[24]

And in the end, after her death, St Thérèse's persevering love won out. The testimony of Sr Magdalene is one of the most beautiful in the whole beatification process.

> Formerly I was not in condition to profit by her advice, but since her entrance into heaven, I have committed the care of my soul to her and how she has changed me! It's incredible. I am all peaceful and confident. I don't recognize myself . . . I don't think I was ever a source of comfort to her. Still, she did not desert me, but showed me a lot of kindness. Whenever I was depressed, she went out of her way to distract me and cheer me up. She never stopped trying to help me, but she was very discreet about it. When it was my turn to wash up, she often arranged things so that she could work beside me and chat with me. She showed trust in me, in an effort to enable me to trust her.[25]

Even her sister Céline found Thérèse's novitiate regime too difficult. It was in this context of difficulty and lack of success that the following battle cry of Thérèse was uttered:

> May the sword of the Spirit which is the Word of God be constantly on your lips and in your heart. If you are coming to grips with a disagreeable person, do not get discouraged, never give up. Always

have "the sword of the Spirit" on your lips to reprove her faults even
without hope of winning the battle. What importance does success
have? What God asks of us is that we don't stop because of the wear
and tear of the struggle, that we are not discouraged, saying "What's
the use? There's nothing to do, just leave her be!" That is real
cowardice; we have to do our duty until the end."[26]

Here you have the real Thérèse. Her innate tendency to see the
positive side of things and to affirm goodness did not blind her to
the real situation in which human imperfections often prevailed:

Ah, there are so few perfect religious, who do nothing any old way
and who say of themselves, "after all, I'm not bound to that . . . It's no
great evil to speak here, to give in to myself in that . . ." How rare are
they who do everything in the best possible way! And still they are
often the happiest. So, in the case of silence, how good it is for the
soul, how many failings against charity it prevents and how many
difficulties of all sorts. I speak above all about silence because it's in
this that we fail the most. How little silence there is here. It's upsetting
to see it so lacking.[27]

For Thérèse, not just in her work with the novices but in all
circumstances, truth was not an abstraction; it was Jesus himself.
Strength was not her own prowess, but the loan of Jesus' strength in
suffering and distress. Thérèse had been confounded in the way of
the saints—by the fact that Jesus, goodness in person, with no malice
in him, could have been made to suffer so much when he walked
our lands. Thérèse intuited that if Jesus trod this path, his disciple
must do the same. For Thérèse this was not doctrine or teaching; it
was experience. For her, suffering was born when the sacred face of
the Man of Sorrows cast a glance on someone. This glance left an
imprint of the sorrowful Redeemer on his disciple. Thérèse experienced this excruciatingly during the mental illness of her father;
she knew that those outside the cloister blamed her entrance for the
mental breakdown of Mr Martin. Her blood sisters were so agitated
by his state that they would miss community exercises; their gentle,
loving father was carrying a gun; in his confused state, the family
was afraid that he would use the gun on himself or on someone
else.[28] Mr Guérin, the uncle, had to have him forcibly disarmed.

Thérèse, in this whole trial, never missed a community exercise. Only two small happenings hint at the suffering she experienced. In one of her letters written at the time in another context, she simply states: the greatest suffering here on earth is to see a loved one suffer and be unable to do anything about it. In recreation she would converse smilingly about her father; involuntary tears indicated her immense sorrow. For her this trial was a *glorious* choice explicitly made by Jesus. "If I have nothing but pure suffering, if the heavens are so black that I see no break in the clouds, well, I make this my joy! I revel in it! I did this during Papa's trials which made me more glorious than a queen."[29] That is the real Thérèse.

Thérèse will not ask to be dispensed from battle. She saw Jesus her Beloved endure atrocious sufferings in order to break the sway of the Evil One; Thérèse would choose no other path. She will not accept suffering for its own sake, but for Jesus' sake and in this way it becomes her joy. This is why she refers to Jesus as "my little divine brother"—because she felt she was a member of God's family, called on to share in Jesus' mission to save all humans. Because they meant so much to Jesus, they must mean much to Thérèse. She would take on her own cross without complaint and with a joyful smile, hoping for one thing: to give pleasure to Jesus, i.e., to make him glad. She had put it so in a prayer: "O little infant! my only Treasure, I abandon myself to your divine whims. I want no other joy than to make you smile";[30] and in a poem: "My joy is to battle ceaselessly / in order to give birth to the elect . . . / For you my divine little Brother / I am happy to suffer / My only joy on this earth / is to be able to make you happy."[31]

One of Thérèse's last battlegrounds was to leave the mode of her final combat in the Lord's hands—to let him decide when she was to die. Life and death are not her choice, but his. "I prefer what he (God) wills. It's what he does that I love."[32] Again, in the same poem she remarked: "Lord, if such be your desire / I want to live for a long time still. / I would like to follow you to heaven / if that would give you pleasure. / Love, this fire of our native land / does not cease to consume me, / What will life or death do to me? / Jesus, my joy is to love you."[33]

Among several other poems on the theme, Thérèse penned one called *My Weapons*. She sums up her courageous surrender to merciful Love. "If I had the powerful weapons of the Warrior / if I imitate him and battle courageously, / like the Virgin I also wish to sing / for all the ravishing graces while in combat. / You make the cords of this lyre vibrate / and that lyre, O Jesus, is my heart! / And so I can chant / about the power and kindliness of your mercies, / smiling, I defy the volley of fire / and in your arms, O divine Spouse, / I will die singing on the field of battle / Weapons in hand."[34]

III

This image of the staunch and uncompromising warrior might be accepted congenially as just one other component of Thérèse's rich personality. But I submit that this would be a mistake. It actually is one of the foundational attitudes that permeate her personality to a degree that all other virtues are marked by it. This combative element rescued her from being a dreamy-eyed, pretty Norman product of the upper middle-class, and made her the apt co-patroness of all Catholic missions. (It was Pope Pius IX, a no-nonsense, unsentimental pontiff who named her such against the advice of his counsellors.)

Some might object that much of Thérèse's writing is lightsome, upbeat (we would say), sentimental and even sugary; and so they would conclude that at the most this combative aspect in Thérèse is ambivalent. They aver that she was a spoiled youngster who had illusions of grandeur, which were expressed in warrior language. For these critics Thérèse remains a pipe-dreamer. But this opinion is voided only because its subscribers have not gotten beyond the word to the substance of her message. Without getting too far afield and being diffuse, I would like to show that Thérèse's wholesome, strong, ready-for-battle personality lies solidly beneath her pretty expressions. I take but one example: her name "the Little Flower." I have been surprised to discover recently that this is a favorite nickname among English speakers. I work with a group of French-speaking lay missionaries, our tertiaries, whose connection with Carmel is their devotion for St Thérèse. They use the Act of Oblation to Merciful Love as their definitive commitment to their missionary family. Yet they are not in the habit of calling St Thérèse the "Little Flower."

Flowers appeared throughout Thérèse's life; they held a special value for her. They were a radiant trace of God's glory, apt symbols for our earthly lives, full of God's goodness, glory and grandeur, yet so fragile and fleeting. Thérèse could hardly find a more apt symbol for the transitoriness of this pilgrimage of faith. The gratuitous beauty of flowers spontaneously made Thérèse take them as symbols of herself; thus she entitled the first part of her autobiography (Ms. A) "the Springtime Story of a Little White Flower." Thérèse picked up much of her appreciation for flowers from the artistic, sensitive soul of her father. She had been moved by his gesture on the day she fearfully asked his permission to enter Carmel. Thérèse describes the

. . . *symbolic* action my dear King performed not realizing its full meaning. Going to a low wall, he pointed to some *little white flowers*, like lilies in miniature, and plucking one of them, he gave it to me, explaining the care with which God had brought it into being and preserved it to that very day. While I listened I believed I was hearing my own story, so great was the resemblance between what Jesus had done for the *little flower* and *little Thérèse*. I accepted it as a relic and noticed that, in gathering it, Papa had pulled all its roots out without breaking them. It seemed destined to live in another soil more fertile than the tender moss where it had spent its first days. This was really the same action Papa had performed a few moments before when he allowed me to climb Mount Carmel and leave the sweet valley which had witnessed my first steps in this life. I placed the little white flower in my copy of the *Imitation* at the chapter entitled "One must love Jesus above all else" (II, 7) and there it is still, only its stem has broken, close to the roots, and God seems to be saying by this that he'll soon break the bonds of his little Flower, not allowing her to fade away on this earth.[35]

Thérèse had a knack for saying the most crucifying things in such optimistic, picturesque, radiant and loving tones that often the underlying, sacrificial dimension leading even to complete immolation came to be overlooked. Thérèse resolutely refused to feel sorry for herself, but only willed to give pleasure to the good God just as he willed. This inevitably included suffering, but

Thérèse saw beyond the immediate to the mercy God was showing her even through it. Her own miseries, imperfections and even atrocious sufferings, to her mind, were not worth recording, because she realized that God was lavishing his loving-kindness on her. Love came to be appreciated more and more as sacrificial.

Two typically Thérèsian poems on flowers go a long way to cleanse Thérèse's image from any tinge of saccharine childishness or sentimentality. She was being ravaged by tuberculosis and plunged into the darkest of spiritual nights. This did not matter to Thérèse, so long as the Lord Jesus who had ravished her heart was pleased. She had written: "A flower is the smile of God."[36] God is naturally good—all that comes from his hand reflects this nature of his; it is for our good whether we realize it or not. A flower is a concrete embodiment of this reality.

It seems to me that if a little flower could speak, it would simply tell what God has done for it without trying to hide its blessings. It would not say, under the pretext of false humility, that it is not beautiful or without perfume, that the sun has taken away its splendor and the storm has broken its stem when it knows that all this is untrue. The flower about to tell her story rejoices at having to publish the totally gratuitous gifts of Jesus. She knows that nothing in herself was capable of attracting the divine glances, and his mercy alone brought about everything that is good in her.[37]

The first poem, *Jeter les fleurs* ("To Scatter Flowers"—PN 34), refers to the concrete act of devotion by the novices, of which we even have a photograph. Each evening the young religious gathered in the monastery courtyard. They would gather wilted roses from the abundant rose bushes and throw the petals toward the crucified Lord in order to console him. This occurred in silence at 8 P.M. On the occasion of Mother Agnes' feast-day, June 28, 1891, Thérèse composed the poem to describe the meaning of this simple rite, so dear to Mother Agnes. Even an unassuming banality was filled with love by Thérèse; it gave her occasion to externalize some of her deepest convictions.

Like a faithful bride, Thérèse wishes to offer her Spouse the most pleasing and beautiful objects. As she sees him suffering on the cross in atrocious pain, she does whatever she can to dry his tears.

"Jesus, my only Love, at the feet of your Calvary / how I love to scatter flowers each evening! / In plucking the petals of the spring-time rose for you / I would like to dry your tears."[38] Thérèse describes what these flowers symbolize: "To scatter flowers is to offer as first fruits the slightest sighs, the greatest sufferings, / my sorrows and my joys, my little sacrifices. / These are my flowers."[39] In fact Thérèse preferred not to unpetal withered roses for her Lord; she wished to give him the best, the very first fruits, marking her own youthful, total surrender to Jesus. To add "joy" in this context is vintage Thérèse. Fr Faber in the same vein speaks only of pain and suffering. Thérèse's catholic sense allows her to recognize grace everywhere: in cross-bearing and in festive celebration. She would vote in the idea that saints are not sad.

She is most explicit on this point in her letter to her sister Marie which has become the second part (Ms. B) of her autobiography:

Yes, my Beloved, this is how my life will be consumed. I have no other means of proving my love for you other than that of strewing flowers, that is, of not allowing one little sacrifice to escape, not one look, one word, profitting by all the smallest things and doing them through love. I desire to suffer for love and even to rejoice through love; and in this way I shall strew flowers before your throne. I shall not come upon one without *unpetalling* it for You. While I am strewing my flowers, I shall sing, for could one cry while doing such a joyous action? I shall sing even when I must gather my flowers in the midst of thorns, and my song will be all the more melodious to the length and sharpness of the thorns. O Jesus, of what use will my flowers be to you? Ah! I know very well that this fragrant shower of these fragile, worthless petals, these songs of love from the littlest of hearts, will charm you. Yes, these nothings will please you. They will bring a smile to the Churth Triumphant. She will gather up my flowers unpetalled *through love* and have them pass through your own divine hands, O Jesus. And this Church in heaven, desirous of playing with her little child, will cast these flowers, which are now infinitely valuable because of your divine touch, upon the Church Suffering in order to extinguish its flames and upon the Church Militant in order to gain the victory for it.[40]

The idyllic tone of Thérèse's language has often fooled people. Yet she speaks from the beginning of being consumed, immolated.

Thérèse adopts the traditional practice of *fioretti*; little sacrifices offered to Jesus to show her appreciation for his immense love for her. Her possibilities are limited, but she will accept all that happens to her joyfully—in the persons she has to live with, in the monastery schedule, in the minutest statutes of the house, in her tasks. Thérèse's ideal is to sing most happily and act most joyfully when the going is toughest and the thorns are the sharpest. This is what has fooled many about Thérèse, as if she taught a carefree way to eternity. Actually it is one of the most crucifying paths because it takes as its *materia* everything that happens and sees it shot through with the divine milieu. Anyone who has continued to sing and smile out of spiritual motives, while being calumniated, misjudged, condemned, would attest that it is a rugged climb of Mount Carmel, as did Thérèse. Immediately, she would add: this is all too little to repay Jesus' goodness and love for me, immediately taking stress off of herself and her rights, and pointing to the summit of Carmel which is Christ.

In this ascent, Thérèse's ecclesial awareness is sharp. In scattering flowers she proposes no intimistic spirituality but, rather, she actualizes her wildest dreams: to be a missionary, preacher, priest, teacher in order to populate heaven with those for whom Jesus has shed his blood. It must not be all in vain. When she promised to send a shower of roses from heaven once she reached her goal, Thérèse was affirming her conviction that no follower of Christ stands alone, but is a family-member. Thérèse understood that the most precious gift she could share with others was her knowledge and love of Jesus. She was willing to throw her flowers into the breeze, allowing the Holy Spirit to use them to touch and inflame hearts just as he willed. This is the contents of her second verse: "Lord, my soul has fallen in love with your Beauty / I want to lavish my perfume and my flowers upon you / as I cast them on the wings of the breeze for you / I would want to enflame hearts."[41]

Perfumes, for Thérèse, were the aspirations of her heart. The excess of love which Thérèse experienced could not be hoarded up for herself—she must share, so that many inflamed and grateful and eucharistic hearts could make her meagre paean of praise into a mighty symphony. The object was uniquely to repay the love of him who deserves so much love in return for his.

Especially during her last year on earth Thérèse realized that she was being invited to tread the same sorrowful way of the cross as did her Jesus, and so her devotion for the sacred face predominated over that for the Child Jesus. In this poem she beings to use the verb *lutter* (to struggle, battle) always in the context of souls to be saved, sinners to be redeemed, priests to be protected from evil. "To scatter flowers, Jesus, that is my weapon / When I want to fight to save sinners. / Victory is mine . . . I always disarm you / with my flowers."[42] Though still positive in approach, Thérèse shows her combative spirit as she enters her road to calvary. She considers herself a seasoned warrior.

Jesus knows all things; he knows that her heart is his without reserve. Her language is that typical of lovers. For the latter, the mosty banal, even insipid phrases are fraught with meaning and reality. "The flower petals, caressing your face / tell you that my heart is unremittingly yours. / You understand the language of my unpetalled rose / and you smile on my love."

Four months before her death, Thérèse took up her favorite imagery in the poem *Une rose effeuillé*—The Unpetalled Rose. The occasion was the debilitating illness of the ex-prioress of Paris Carmel, who did not know how to accept her infirmity well. She feared death, was immersed in spiritual dryness and was discouraged. When told of Thérèse who was in similar circumstances, she found it hard to believe, and asked for some proof of the authenticity of Thérèse's attitude. Thérèse composed one of her most inspired poems. Though she could no longer join the novices in the courtyard, still she used the image of scattering flowers in order to describe her ever deeper share in the passion aspect of Christ's paschal mystery. Through months of smiling through indiscribable pain, and humiliated to the extent that some sisters believed that she was being mollycoddled by her blood sisters, Thérèse had grown into a mystical state of self-surrender. She saw more clearly how the unpetalled rose was an apt symbol for herself. Such a rose is simply destroyed in the act of having its petals plucked off one by one. But this is *not* the important thing: what does matter is that God is pleased at being shown gratitude for so much goodness toward us. If he tries us, this too is out of his love, as will be our final dwelling place in him. The unpetalled rose depicted sacrificial love, ready to become "nothing," if need be, out of love for the Beloved.

Interestingly, Jesus in the poem is not the Man of Sorrows, but the Child Jesus. Helplessness and total dependence on others are the child's lot, and Thérèse's too. As soon as Jesus begins walking our earth, Thérèse saw that he has but one destination: Calvary and death. Thérèse wishes to empathize with Jesus, share his sorrows, since she now experientially is living out the passion. "Jesus, when I see you held by your Mother, / Leave her arms, / trembling, *testing your first steps* / on this sorry earth of ours, / I would like to *unpetal a rose* in all its freshness / before you / so that your little foot might tread with delicacy / on a flower."[43]

For Thérèse this was not theory but experience. Consummation, immolation: these meant that she must be willing to give up what was most precious to her in religious life. As she was overcome by immense fevers, by interminable coughing spells, by sleepless nights, by taut nerves, by painful vomitting, one by one she had to give up the community acts which had been the everyday way she had of proving her self-surrender and her unreserved acceptance of the Will of God. They were her best proof of affection for Jesus; now she had to be detached from the divine office, from work in the sacristy and in the linen-closet, from regular meetings with the novices, from recreation and from the refectory. Thérèse did not grumble; her rights meant nothing. God, and not she, knew what was best for her. She realized more clearly that it was not isolated *acts*, but her whole *being*, that must be rooted in God's loving Will. "The unpetalled rose is the faithful image, / O divine Child, / of the heart which wishes to immolate itself for you unreservedly / at every instant. / Lord, more than a fresh rose upon your altars / loves to sparkle, / she gives herself to you; but I dream of something else: / to be unpetalled."[44]

Thérèse sees that a full-blooming rose provides joy and beauty for celebration. It is attractive and attention-prone. An unpetalled rose, thrown to the wind, is devoid of interest or beauty—it is no more. The depths of self-surrender could hardly be better described by an artistic, sensitive soul. What impresses is that this debilitating and crucifying status was borne by Thérèse without complaint, and even smilingly. "The rose in its brilliance can adorn your feast, / O loveable Child, / but *an unpetalled rose* is simply thrown / to the caprice of the wind. / An *unpetalled rose* gives itself without self-seeking / *so as to cease existing*. / Likewise, I happily abandon myself to you / little Jesus."[45]

An unpetalled rose is considered debris, to be trampled upon without scruple. Thérèse is content to be such by her early death, so long as God's good pleasure is served. "People step on *rose petals* without regret / and this debris / is a simple adornment which one arranges artlessly. / That I've understood. / Jesus, for love of you, I've poured out (*prodigué*) my life, / my future. / In the eyes of men I must die, / a rose faded forever."[46]

Thérèse had a good memory; she recalled how God had spoiled her in her youth—and she counted all the ways. Now she must appreciate the privilege of following Jesus to Calvary. And he had cried out: "My God, my God, why have you forsaken me?" "Child, Beauty supreme, *I must die for you. /* What a fortunate destiny! / I want to prove that I love you by being unpetalled, / O my Treasure. / Here below I want to live in a mysterious way / beneath your *childhood steps* / and I still would like to lighten (*adoucir*) your last steps / to Calvary."[47]

Flowers are but one example of how Thérèse found grace everywhere. Holy pictures, personality quirks, smiles, frowns, letters, poems—and especially the persons who touched her life—were all epiphanies of the divine breaking-through out of the immense love the good God/Jesus bore her. Rare is a more faithful disciple of St John of the Cross. St John, her spiritual father, uses the *nada*; St Thérèse chooses the *todo*. But the spirituality is the same. It is the radical option for Jesus as the center of one's existence, as the most important person in one's life with no exceptions or reservations. It is sheer faith in this one Love of one's life—faith buttressed by the memory of so much of Jesus' love lavished on oneself. This memory becomes the bulwark of faith in the darkest night. While Thérèse confessed in her last days that she never thought it would be possible to suffer so much, she hastily added, and with vigor (as Mother Agnes attests): "I never regret having surrendered myself to love." This love of Jesus is forever, even on those occasions when it means a personal sharing in the sorrowful and painful dimension of Jesus' paschal mystery. Thérèse, in her final agony, kept repeating the words of Psalm 91:5: "Lord, you give me *joy* in *all* you do." She wrote these words on the inside cover of the Gospels which were constantly by her heart. As was her custom, she underscored the most significant words (and she did so several times): "joy" and "all."

THÉRÈSE AND
THE MOTHER OF GOD

Eamon Carroll

A world-renowned Carmelite expert in Mariology, Eamon Carroll is a professor of theology at Chicago's Loyola University. He has already contributed an article to volume 3 of CARMELITE STUDIES ("The Saving Role of the Human Christ for St Teresa").

The month before her death St Thérèse said to her sister Pauline (Mother Agnes):

How I would have loved to be a priest in order to preach about the Blessed Virgin! One sermon would be sufficient to say everything I think about this subject. I'd first make people understand how little is known about her life. We shouldn't say unlikely things or things we don't know anything about! For example, that when she was very little, at the age of three, the Blessed Virgin went up to the Temple to offer herself to God, burning with sentiments of love and extraordinary fervor. While perhaps she went there very simply out of obedience to her parents. Again, why say, with reference to the aged Simeon's prophetic words, that the Blessed Virgin had the passion of Jesus constantly before her mind from that moment onward? "And a sword will pierce through your soul also," the old man said. It wasn't for the present, you see, little Mother; it was a general prediction for the future. For a sermon on the Blessed Virgin to please me and do me any good, I must see her real life, not her imagined life. I'm sure that her real life was very simple. They show her to us as unapproachable, but they should present her as imitable, bringing out her virtues, saying that she lived by faith just like ourselves, giving proofs of this from the gospel, where we read: "And they did not understand the words which He spoke to them." . . . We know very well that the Blessed Virgin is Queen of heaven and earth, but she is more Mother than Queen . . .[1]

It is our good fortune that Thérèse has left us a fairly complete outline of what her one sermon on the Blessed Virgin would have contained, what she would have said in that single sermon. She has done so in a double sense: first, in her life of love and suffering and joy in union with Jesus, the Son of Mary; second, in her writings, especially the poem of her last days, "Why I love you, Mary," about which she said to Pauline on August 21, 1897, "In my poem . . . I have said everything I would preach about her."[2] This article has two main sections, though they are not sharply divided from each other. The first section is the influence of the Blessed Virgin on the life and holiness of Thérèse; the second is her formal teaching, as expressed in her writings, the last conversations, and, above all, in the final poem, "Why I love you Mary."

That last poem on our Lady, written during the month of May, 1897, is a compendium of Thérèse's relationship to the Mother of Jesus as her beloved spiritual mother. She wrote in in the throes of her final illness, while undergoing intense physical suffering and tormented by terrible, unimaginable temptations against faith. It is no wonder that Pope St Pius X called her "the greatest saint of modern times"; that Pius XI, over the objections of his counsellors, named her patroness of the Church's universal missions; and the present Holy Father, John Paul II, said of her at Lisieux that the saints hardly ever grow old. She is indeed a saint for a faithless age, and the more we learn about her, and from her, the better we realize the goodness of God in sending us St Thérèse of the Child Jesus and the Holy Face.

THE BLESSED VIRGIN IN
THE LIFE OF THÉRÈSE MARTIN

The Martin household in which Thérèse grew up was filled with devotion to Mary. All nine children, including the two boys who died soon after birth, were given Mary as their first name. The child just before Thérèse was a girl who died in infancy, and another girl lived only to the age of five. The last child was baptized Mary Thérèse. Her mother died when she was only four and a half years old, and the small girl turned to our Lady to replace her, although the mother's death left a deep wound that even the affection of her father and big sisters could not completely cure.

At six Thérèse made her first confession. In those days she was not yet permitted to receive Holy Communion. At her first confession when the priest urged her to be devoted to our Lady, she resolved: "I promised myself to redouble my tenderness for her."[3] It was to the Blessed Virgin Thérèse turned when preparing for her First Communion at the age of eleven on May 8, 1884. Because she was orphaned of her mother she was chosen that day to recite the act of consecration to our Lady in the name of all the girls.

The previous year, when she was ten, she suffered a strange illness, which had begun at the end of 1882 and worsened by Easter, 1883. Her well-meaning uncle had spoken to her of his sister, her dead mother; and his daughter, Thérèse's cousin, with childish heartlessness, had told Thérèse not to call her aunt "Maman," because her own mother was dead. The illness baffled the doctors; her uncle suspected the enmity of Satan, a diagnosis Thérèse herself was subsequently to second. The distraught father had masses offered for her at the Paris shrine of Our Lady of Victories. During that novena of masses, on May 13, 1884, her sister Marie was in the garden, Léonie was with Thérèse and all three were praying to our Lady for healing; when in place of the statue at the foot of the bed Thérèse saw our Lady smiling, "a ravishing smile" she subsequently affirmed in her autobiography,[4] and she alluded to our Lady's favor also in the final stanza of the poem, "Why I love you, Mary."

There is much evidence of the power of Thérèse's own smile, so constant in her cloistered life, even under straitened circumstances, and especially to the more difficult sisters in the community, as Sr Thérèse of St Augustine, for whom Thérèse had a strong natural antipathy, but who was so conquered by the smiling young nun that she asked her one day what attracted so gracious a smile. As Thérèse wrote in the autobiography, "A word, an amiable smile, often suffice to make a sad soul bloom . . ."[5] One recalls the Spanish proverb: one kind word can warm three winter months.

In 1887 Thérèse accompanied her father and sister Céline on a pilgrimage to Rome, to satisfy her desire to appeal directly to Pope Leo XIII for permission to enter Carmel at the age of fifteen. Two of her sisters, Pauline and Marie, had already become nuns there. We know from the autobiography that she received special graces on her pilgrimage, visiting Marian shrines along the way, particularly Our Lady of Victories in Paris and Loreto in Italy, resulting in an intensification of her love of Mary as her "maman," not just as her "mère."

Opposition was overcome and Thérèse was permitted to enter Carmel—a favor she attributed to our Lady. She entered on April 9, 1888 and took the habit January 10, 1889.

In a letter to Céline (Sr Geneviève), April 26, 1894, when their beloved father was mentally very ill, she wrote of "Mary, who is hiding you also under her veil!"[6] It would seem Thérèse was recalling an experience she had in July 1889, when (as she put it subsequently to Pauline on July 11, 1897): "It was as though a veil had been cast over all the things of this earth for me . . . I was entirely hidden under the Blessed Virgin's veil."[7] There is a connection here to the Holy Face, the part of her religious name that came to mean more and more to Thérèse as she entered the last stages of her life, and which recalled also the veiled face of her mentally deranged father.[8]

Thérèse saw more than coincidence in the fact that her own special days, especially in Carmel, fell on Mary's feasts. She entered the monastery on the feast of the Annunciation, April 9, 1888; the feast had been transferred because of Lent. Her profession was on September 8, 1890, Mary's birthday. In 1896 she wrote to her spiritual brother, the missionary priest Adolphe Roulland in China, that on the day of her profession his vocation had been saved by Mary, queen of apostles and martyrs, a circumstance later verified by Fr Roulland in the process of her beatification. He was ordained in 1896, visited and said mass at Lisieux and talked to Thérèse (July 3, 1896). He died in 1934.

As novice-mistress (Thérèse had the job without the title) she would astonish her charges by knowing what was bothering them before they told her; she attributed this to her prayers to Mary for guidance, and was in the habit of leading her novices to our Lady's statue when they were troubled. When Céline entered the convent the statue of Mary from the Martin home was brought with her, the statue associated with our Lady's smile in Thérèse's childhood. When she began her autobiography, "Before taking up my pen, I knelt before the statue of Mary (the one which has given so many proofs of the maternal preferences of heaven's Queen for our family), and I begged her to guide my hand that it trace no line displeasing to her."[9]

The autobiography in all three parts, the letters, the poems, the dramatic pieces and the last conversations are filled with the Blessed Virgin. In a letter of October 19, 1892 to Céline for her feast-day (October 21) Thérèse wrote,

> With regard to the Blessed Virgin, I must confide to you one of my simple ways with her. I surprise myself at times by saying to her: But good Blessed Virgin, I find I am more blessed than you, for I have you for Mother, and you do not have a *Blessed Virgin to love* . . . It is true you are the Mother of Jesus, but this Jesus you have given entirely to us . . . and he, on the cross, he gave you to us as Mother. Thus we are richer than you since we possess Jesus and since you are ours also.[10]

A bit further in the same letter: "No doubt, the Blessed Virgin must laugh at my simplicity, and nevertheless what I am telling her is really true!"

On May 30, 1889, she wrote to her cousin Marie Guérin, who would enter Carmel in 1895 as Sr Marie of the Eucharist, "Have no fear of loving the Blessed Virgin *too much,* you will *never* love her enough, and Jesus will be pleased since the Blessed Virgin is his Mother."[11] This was the letter in which Thérèse urged her cousin to put aside the scruples that were keeping her from Communion: "Dear little sister, *receive Communion often,* very often . . . That is the *only remedy* if you want to be healed, and Jesus hasn't placed this attraction in your soul for nothing." When this letter was read to Pope Pius X in 1910, he cried out, "This is most opportune! It's a great joy for me," and he told the vice-postulator of the cause, Msgr de Teil, "We must hurry this cause."[12]

August 19, 1897, was the last day she was able to receive Communion. She was unable to retain food, even the detestable milk diet nauseated her. On September 4 she was too weak to join in the Angelus. Mother Agnes (Pauline) said to her, "Simply say, 'Virgin Mary,'" and Thérèse said, "Virgin Mary, I love you with all my heart," and when Sr Geneviève (Céline) said, "Tell her that you love her for me, too," Thérèse whispered, "For 'Mlle. Lili' [Céline herself], for Mamma [Pauline], for godmother [Marie], for Léonie, for little Marie [Sr Marie of the Eucharist, her cousin Marie Guérin], Uncle, Aunt [the Guérins], Jeanne, Francis [Dr and Mrs LaNéele; Jeanne was a cousin-in-law], 'Maurice' [her spiritual brother Abbé Bellière], 'little Roulland,' [Father Roulland, a missionary spiritual brother] and all whom I love."[13]

Among the strange and difficult sisters in the convent was Mother Marie de Gonzague, the superior (d. 1904). On one occasion Thérèse, who had a strong sense of both justice and truth (she said one time, "I tell the whole truth . . ."[14]) was ordered to prepare the night light for some relatives of the superior. The request was unreasonable but Thérèse took it in stride, resisting her rebellious feelings by calling on our Lady for help. Yet St Thérèse was most grateful to Mother Marie de Gonzague, as we can tell from the final section of her autobiography, written at Mother Marie de Gonzague's request in the form of a long letter to her.

In the autobiography Thérèse calls herself simply "the little flower of the holy Virgin." In her last illness she asked our Lady to help her not cough at night so as not to disturb the others. Among her last words were, "Virgin Mary come to my aid." The last lines she wrote were on the Nativity of Mary, September 8. She wrote on the back of a holy card of Our Lady of Victories, to which was fastened the small white flower her father had plucked from the garden wall, roots and all, and given her when he gave his permission to enter Carmel.[15] The words were: "O Mary, if I were the Queen of Heaven and you were Thérèse, I should want to be Thérèse that you might be the Queen of Heaven."[16]

It would be an easy and pleasant task to multiply examples of the place of our Lady in the life of St Thérèse. Several studies explore that theme in greater depth.[17]

THÉRÈSE'S TEACHING
ABOUT THE BLESSED VIRGIN

This second half of the article centers on the poem, "Why I love you, Mary," which Thérèse wrote the last May of her life on earth. Here she set forth what Mary meant to her and gave us a powerful lesson on the Blessed Virgin as the great Gospel woman of faith, our model in suffering and in ordinary life. There is an apparent anomaly here, for Thérèse had received several extraordinary graces through our Lady, favors of which she was well aware and for which she was most grateful. But perhaps even more than her mentor St John of the Cross she did not seek, much less boast, of such special gifts. Instead she made a capital point of the truth that Mary, our spiritual mother, walked the human road of suffering and ordinary life. I venture the opinion that the special signs of Mary's loving care that Thérèse experienced as a child and as a young nun prepared her for the great trials, both physical and spiritual, she was to undergo before her short life ended.

A dossier of Thérèsian teaching on our Lady might be compiled from all her writings, but the focus here is on her masterpiece, the twenty-five stanza poem, "Why I love you, Mary," which expresses everything she would have preached had she been a priest. Guy Gaucher calls the poem "verses she wrote with her heart's blood."[18] On August 23, 1897, she said to Mother Agnes that all she had heard preached about Mary had not moved her.

> Let the priests, then, show us practicable virtues! It's good to speak of her privileges, but it's necessary above all that we can imitate her. She prefers imitation to admiration, and her life was so simple! However good a sermon is on the Blessed Virgin, if we are obliged all the time to say: Ah! . . . Ah! . . . we grow tired. How I like singing to her (And then she quoted two lines from her poem: "The narrow road to heaven you have made visible [Pauline wrote in here: "she said: easy"] / When practising always the most humble virtues."[19]

To Sr Marie of the Sacred Heart (her sister Marie) Thérèse said of her poem: "My little Canticle expresses all I think about the

Blessed Virgin and all I would preach about her if I were a priest."[20] The poem was appended to the first editions of the autobiography, *The Story of a Soul*, beginning in 1898. As first published, along with others, the poem had been considerably retouched by Pauline. Some of the changes were stylistic. Thérèse was a poor speller, as she admitted in the autobiography: "my terrible scrawl and my spelling, which was nothing less than original."[21] Many of Pauline's alterations, however, modified Thérèse's thought; for one thing, her underscoring was completely passed over in the first printed versions. It was only when the critical edition of the poetry was finally published in 1979 that the complete poems in their original authentic form became available.

After some hesitation, Thérèse chose the title, "Why I love you, Mary," for she wrote out of experience, to express her sense of our Lady's love, rather than to present a set of thoughts about her. Her goal was to set forth the reasons that led her to love Mary as her mother. Quite deliberately she passes over the extraordinary interventions of Mary in her life, to concentrate instead on our Lady's ordinary life and her sufferings. The single exception is an allusion at the end of the poem to the smile of the Blessed Virgin which she had experienced as a sick child: "Soon I shall see you in the beautiful heavens / you who came and smiled on my life's morning / come and smile on me again . . . Mother . . . for it is evening!"[22]

When she began the poem in the spring of 1897 she was already very ill. The immediate occasion was the request of her sister Marie, but she had already thought of such a testimony before Marie asked her. She confided to Céline, "I still have something to do before I die. I have always dreamed of expressing in song to the Blessed Virgin all I think of her."[23] Since Easter of 1896 Thérèse had been subject to great temptations against faith. In her last illness when Sr Marie of the Trinity, one of her novices, wondered how her poems could be so buoyant in the circumstances of her suffering, Thérèse told her, "I sing what I wish to believe, but it is without sentiment . . . I would not even wish to tell you how dark the night is in my soul for fear of making you share my temptations . . ."[24] In the third and last portion of her autobiography, when she was already seriously ill (June, 1897), she wrote, "I sing simply WHAT I WANT TO BELIEVE."[25]

The books about our Lady that Thérèse was familiar with are known. The tendency of the time was emphasis on Mary's privileges and glories. Bible studies among Catholics were in a sad state, so little notice was taken of Gospel insights about Mary's faith. Thérèse had little patience with the widely disseminated imaginative accounts of Mary's life, as in Catherine Emmerich and the Spanish nun Maria d'Agreda. On May 15, 1897, she said, when she was completing her own poem, "As for me, with the exception of the Gospels, I no longer find anything in books. The Gospels are enough. I listen with delight to these words of Jesus which tell me all I must do: 'Learn of me for I am meek and humble of heart'; then I'm at peace, according to his sweet promise: 'and you will find rest for your souls.'"[26] On another occasion she said: "Only reality suits me." We might recall that the novices at Lisieux did not have copies of the entire Bible, and even Thérèse lacked the full text of the Song of Songs.[27]

She was only fourteen when, as she tells us, she learned that God grants miracles to strengthen the faith which is the grain of mustard seed, but for those who are close to him, like his mother, he works no miracles before having tried their faith. December 25 of 1887 was a sad day for Thérèse. She had hoped to enter Carmel in time for Christmas, but her entry was put off. She comments in her autobiography:

> . . . *the One whose heart watches even when he sleeps* made me understand that to those whose faith is like that of a *mustard seed* he grants *miracles* and moves mountains in order to strengthen this faith which is *still small*; but for his *intimate friends,* for his *Mother,* he works no miracles *before having tried their faith* . . . At the wedding of Cana when the Blessed Virgin asked Jesus to come to the help of the head of the house, didn't he answer her that his hour had not yet come? But after the trial what a reward! The water was changed into wine . . .[28]

Now for the poem itself: composed in May, 1897, it is number fifty-four in the French centenary edition of Thérèse's writings, published 1979, and has twenty-five stanzas. According to Abbé Combes' analysis it has a double axis in the Gospel portrait of Mary: her sufferings and her ordinary life. On both levels Thérèse finds a community with the Mother of Jesus as her spiritual mother; she experiences a sharing with the Blessed Virgin. Her sense of Mary as mother as recorded in this valedictory poem surpasses all her earlier experiences—as a child, as a schoolgirl, as pilgrim to Paris and Loreto and Rome, even as a younger nun.

In the first stanza the poet poses a three-fold "why," illustrative of the poem's title. She writes: "O Mary, I should like to sing why I love you," then "why your sweet name makes my heart thrill," and finally, "why the thought of your supreme grandeur / will not be able to inspire fright in my soul." At the start of the second stanza Thérèse delineates the direction of her poem: "For a child to love the mother / it is necessary that they share sorrows." Where did she learn this? The Gospel taught her: "to believe that I am your child is not difficult / for I see you are mortal and suffering like me."

The month before her death (August 23), in conversation with Pauline, Thérèse spoke about a letter from a priest who said the Blessed Virgin had not experienced physical suffering. Her comment was: "When I was looking at the statue of the Blessed Virgin this evening, I understood this wasn't true. I understood that she suffered not only in soul but also in body. She suffered a lot on her journeys—from the cold, the heat, and from fatigue. She fasted very frequently. Yes, she knew what it was to suffer." Then, tenderly, she continued: "But it's bad perhaps to wish that the Blessed Virgin suffered? I, especially, who love her so much!"[29]

The following stanzas trace our Lady's life according to the Gospels. This author was reminded of the recent book by Walter T. Brennan, O.S.M., *The Sacred Memory of Mary* (1988), which shows how the Church does not simply offer recollections about the Mother of Jesus, does not just seek to *know about her*, but seeks to *know her*, to know first of all Jesus her Son and with him his mother Mary, in their living presence in the Scriptures and the liturgy. For Thérèse too the Blessed Virgin was vividly present in the Gospel scenes: the Bible episodes were not just events of the sacred past.

From the Annunciation Thérèse considers the indwelling of the Holy Trinity in Mary, and then her spiritual motherhood, for her divine Son is the first-born of the great number of his sinner brothers and sisters. The visit to Elizabeth teaches Thérèse charity, and she learns from Mary's Magnificat to glorify God the Savior. Stanza eight considers the perplexity of St Joseph before Mary's pregnancy, and our Lady's "eloquent silence," a silence that for Thérèse was a sweet concert of the greatness of confidence in God alone, a melody no less enchanting than the Magnificat.

The birth of Jesus in the poverty of Bethlehem is described, and Mary's treasuring in her heart the visits of the shepherds and magi. The presentation of Jesus in the Temple moves from joy to sadness with the prophet Simeon's sword of sorrow. Sorrows come quickly with the flight into Egypt, but Mary had the consolation of the presence of Jesus.

Stanzas 13, 14, 15 and 16 are the high point of the poem. They were written at a most painful stage of Thérèse's suffering, when her trial of faith was at its most harrowing, mid-May, 1897. She writes of the loss of the twelve-year old Jesus in the temple (stanza 14). In stanza 15 she says, "Now I understand the mystery of the Temple / the hidden words of my loving King. / Mother your beloved Child wants you to be the example / of the soul who searches for him in the night of faith."

It is worth noting that Pope John Paul II in his Marian Year encyclical, *Redemptoris Mater* (March 25, 1987), applied to our Lady the teaching of St John of the Cross on the dark night of faith (no. 14, "the dim light of faith"). Thérèse continues (stanza 16): "For the King of heaven wished that his Mother / be plunged into the night, in anguish of heart. / Mary, is it therefore a good thing to suffer on earth? / Yes, to suffer and love at the same time, that is the greatest happiness." She finishes the stanza with this most personal testimony from the dreadful days of May: "Everything that he has given me Jesus can take back. Tell him that he need not stand on ceremony with me . . . He can freely hide himself, I am willing to wait until the day without end when there will be no more need for faith." In the same vein she would say on June 10: "I tell the Blessed Virgin very often: 'Tell him never to put himself out on my account.' He has heard this, and this is exactly what he's doing."[30] In intense pain on July 11 she quoted stanza 16 with its lines: "He can freely hide himself, / I am content to wait . . ."[31] On August 23 when Pauline quoted to Thérèse that statement to our Lady from her poem, "All He has given to me Jesus can take back; tell him not to be shy with me," Pauline added her own comment, "She told him this, and he's taking you at your word." Thérèse answered: "I'm content and I do not repent."[32]

Stanza 17 notes that there were no miracles, no ecstasies, no raptures in the daily hidden life at Nazareth. Hence, the poet continues, "the little ones can raise their eyes" to our Lady "without fear," for "it is by the ordinary way (*la voie commune*), incomparable Mother / that it pleased you to walk in order to guide us to heaven." In the heart of her beloved Mother (stanza 18) Thérèse discovers ever new depths of love. The motherly glance of Mary banishes all her fears and teaches her to both weep and rejoice. Even in the torment of her suffering Thérèse can say that our Lady shared in pure and holy joys and blessed them. Stanza 19 is the wedding feast of Cana. It follows the Gospel closely, and Thérèse adds her interpretation that even though Jesus seemed to refuse at first his Mother's compassionate request, "from the depths of his heart he calls you his Mother / and works his first miracle for you." Unhesitatingly Thérèse looks into the hearts of both Mary and her Son Jesus.

Three stanzas are devoted to the incident from the public life where Mary comes with the relatives of Jesus—the episode known as "the coming of the mother and the brethren" or as "the true kinsmen" (Mark 3, Matthew 11, Luke 8). This was a favorite Gospel story for Thérèse; she returns to it in her writings almost more than to any other event (six times). It is further evidence of the depth of Thérèse's spiritual understanding that decades before these words captured the attention of exegetes and found their way into papal, conciliar and episcopal documents, Thérèse, like St Augustine centuries before, appreciated the significance of the "true kinsmen" story for Mary's faith and spiritual motherhood. "My mother and my brothers are those who hear the word of God and act upon it" (Lk. 8:21). *Lumen gentium* from the Vatican Council, Pope John Paul II's *Redemptoris Mater* and the joint pastoral of the U.S. bishops, *Behold Your Mother: Woman of Faith* (November 21, 1973) all interpret the Gospel incident thus.

Three stanzas develop Thérèse's thought that the Mother of Jesus was willing to be publicly separated from her Son to show that blood ties must give way to deeper bonds. Jesus showed the greatness of his love for us when he said, "Who is my brother and my sister and my mother, unless it is the one who does my will?" "Immaculate Virgin," writes Thérèse, "You are not saddened when you hear the words of Jesus. / Rather you rejoice that we are his family here below. / You are happy that he gives us the treasures of his divinity." Stanza 22 continues: "You love us, Mary, as Jesus loves us / and you consent for our sake to be separated from him. / *To love is to give all and to surrender one's very self.* / The Savior knew your great tenderness / he knew the secrets of your mother's heart. / The Savior gave us to you as the refuge of sinners / when he died on the cross to await us in heaven."

Stanza 23 speaks of Mary's agony on Calvary, as queen of martyrs, like a priest offering sacrifice at the altar. It was prophesied, "There is no sorrow like unto your sorrow, oh Mother of Sorrows." Stanza 24 takes leave of Mary of the Gospels in the care of St John. Beyond that there is silence, but it is again an "eloquent silence." "Oh my beloved Mother / does it not reveal that *the Eternal Word / himself desires to chant the secrets of your life* / in order to charm *your children,* all the elect of heaven?" We note the play on Word and silence. Thérèse offers us the paradoxical reminder that the profound silence of the Gospels about Mary's life after Calvary reveals to us that the Eternal Word intends himself to describe to us the secrets of his blessed Mother's life, to the joy of all the elect.

The final stanza (no. 25) looks to the company of Mary in the joy of heaven. "Soon I will hear this sweet harmony [of Jesus' praise of his Mother] / soon I shall see you in the beauty of heaven. / You smiled on me in the morning of my life / come to smile on me again, Mother, it is now evening. / No longer do I fear the radiance of your supreme glory / I have suffered with you and now I desire / to sing on your lap, Mary, why I love you / and to repeat for ever that I am your child."

At her death they found in Thérèse's book of the Gospels her Act of Oblation to God's merciful love. The inspiration to make this offering came to her on Trinity Sunday, June 9, 1895, as she says at the end of Manuscript A, the first third of her autobiography: "I received the grace to understand more than ever before how much Jesus desires to be loved."[33] Together with Céline Thérèse made this offering of love to the Holy Trinity on June 11, 1895, before the statue of "Our Lady of the Smile." Céline had entered Carmel the previous September and received the habit in February, 1895. The Act of Oblation begins:

> O my God, most Blessed Trinity, I desire to love you and make you loved, to work for the glory of Holy Church by saving souls on earth and liberating those suffering in purgatory. I desire to accomplish your will perfectly and to reach the degree of glory you have prepared for me in your kingdom. I desire in a word to be a saint . . .

A bit further on these words occur: "I offer you, O Blessed Trinity, the love and merits of the Blessed Virgin, my dear Mother. It is to her I entrust my offering, begging her to present it to you."[34]

POSTSCRIPT: THÉRÈSE AND OUR LADY OF MOUNT CARMEL

Another full article might be written on the special relationship of Thérèse to the Blessed Virgin under the title of Our Lady of Mt Carmel. The reader is invited to consult some of the studies that have appeared on this aspect of St Thérèse's Carmelite and spiritual life.[35] By way of conclusion of the present article here are two examples from many possible ones.

In her autobiography Thérèse wrote of her consoling visit to the shrine of Our Lady of Victories in Paris and the assurance she received that our Lady's smile had really occurred, the smile that turned the tide in her mysterious childhood illness.

> How fervently I begged her to protect me always, to bring to fruition as quickly as possible my dream of hiding *beneath the shadow of her virginal mantle*. This was one of my first desires as a child. When growing up, I understood it was at Carmel I would truly find the Blessed Virgin's mantle, and towards this fertile mount I directed all my desires."[36]

In a letter to a friend from childhood, Céline Pottier (née Maudelonde)—they regarded each other as cousins, since they had an aunt and uncle in common, although they were not blood relatives—Thérèse rejoices that Céline's husband had returned to the practise of his religion, a grace Thérèse had promised to pray for before they were married (letter of July 16, 1894). The wedding had been June 19; an earlier letter from Thérèse shared the joy of the impending marriage.[37] The July 16 letter (it was the feast of Our Lady of Mt Carmel) runs: "I had asked for you, dear Céline from Our Lady of Mt Carmel the grace you have obtained at Lourdes. How happy I am that you are clothed in the holy scapular. It is a sure sign of predestination, and besides are you not more intimately united by means of it to your little sisters in Carmel?"[38] Thérèse continues affectionately: "I am asking Our Lord to be as generous in your regard as he was formerly to the spouses at the wedding of Cana. May he always change water into wine!"[39]

THÉRÈSE, A LATTER-DAY INTERPRETER OF JOHN OF THE CROSS

Margaret Dorgan

Margaret Dorgan lives as a Carmelite hermit in Maine. She has published several casette tape series on prayer and Carmelite topics.

St John of the Cross and St Thérèse of the Child Jesus are like two brilliant stars in the sky of Carmelite spirituality. Both light up the apophatic way, the via negativa, a journey in darkness. The substance of their doctrine is the same, though so often people are astonished to think of them together. What does the Ascent of Mount Carmel while in the Dark Night of the Soul have in common with the Little Way? We'll see how much.

First of all, however, we'll note a few differences. John writes for beginners and proficients, but his beginners are not at the first stage of wanting God. They have spent a long time in meditative prayer and John addresses them at the point where God gradually draws them out of the state of beginners to place them in the dark night of contemplation. These are advanced beginners, then, who are experiencing a simplification of their praying with diminishing activity on their part and more quiet listening to God. The onset of a passive, infused mode of prayer is taking place. This is the audience John is addressing. If John were to speak on this kind of prayer to a parish gathering, some of his listeners would feel that springs of water were being released for their parched thirst. I suspect these would usually be a minority of the people in the pews. Most of his parish audience would be puzzled, because for the majority of them, to pray means to say something to God. And since a conversation with the Almighty has many people tongue-tied, they have relied on prayers composed by others. They need vocal prayer that gives the mind something to think about. All very, very good but not the kind of pray-ers who find John of the Cross comprehensible. On the other hand, if St Thérèse were to speak to a parish gathering, probably everyone would find some nourishment to feed his or her desire for God. Why the difference if these two—John and Thérèse—are so alike?

First of all, John of the Cross speaks specifically on the *process of contemplative development.* His words are aimed at those who start to feel dissatisfaction with the prayer of words and thoughts that up till then has given them sure access to God. Now their God seems to be in hiding—although at times sweeter and closer than ever. Such pray-ers are confused and John gives their confusion an explanation which comes like manna from heaven. Thérèse, on the other hand, has little to say about prayer as such but everything about who this God is we pray to, who we are who dare to pray, and how much God longs for our love.

John and Thérèse speak the same language when they tell of the detachment necessary for anyone who is serious about striving for holiness. Both want the journey to be accomplished quickly with as little baggage as possible. Both sing with lyrical joy of the goal, union with the Beloved, and also of the blessedness of the journey itself.

John communicates as a poet well trained in Scholastic theory. At times the lyricism sings to us but often the ponderousness of philosophic formulations weighs down the text. We are centuries away from the superb education John received at the University of Salamanca, and few of us today turn to the traditions of Aristotle and Plato that he relied on so often. But John also drew on experience and Scripture, and the legacy of Western Christian mysticism. All this is far more important in his message than the philosophic systems he used. If you yourself have the experience John speaks of, his explanation may serve you well. His words can inflame you.

At the same time, many spiritual directors recognize that few people in our contemporary culture are able to fathom John entirely on their own. The majority of his readers need some guidance, especially in pondering those instructions of his that seem not only absolutist but also profoundly negative.

In the prologue to the *Spiritual Canticle,* addressed to Anne of Jesus who was the great collaborator of Teresa of Avila, John could declare, "It is better to explain the utterances of love in their broadest sense so that each one may derive profit from them according to the mode and capacity of his/her spirit."[1] This statement of John's is most true of the *Canticle*—more so than of his other major works. In that same prologue, he goes on to say to Anne of Jesus,

> I hope that, although some Scholastic theology is used here in reference to the soul's interior converse with God, it will not prove vain to speak in such a manner to the pure of spirit. Even though Your Reverence lacks training in Scholastic theology by which the divine truths are understood, you are not wanting in mystical theology which is known through love and by which one not only knows but at the same time experiences."[2]

St Thérèse, like Anne of Jesus, knew by experience, and found in John a mentor to guide her. The French school of spirituality puts such strong emphasis on the role of the priest-director that it is surprising to many readers of Thérèse to see her statements that Jesus alone is her director. Actually, a cloistered contemplative community could be severely restricted in its contacts with priests, even though Teresa of Avila insisted that her nuns have good spiritual directors available to them. Part of Teresa of Avila's reason for founding the Discalced friars was to provide such directors for her daughters. But Thérèse never mentions an encounter with a Carmelite friar during her years as a nun. However, she had the writings of John of the Cross, and over and over again, she draws on him to support her own insights into the spiritual journey.

She tells us, "Ah! how many lights have I not drawn from the works of our holy father, St John of the Cross. At the ages of seventeen and eighteen I had no other spiritual nourishment."[3] She feeds especially on the *Spiritual Canticle*: the poem and its commentary.

Judged by our standards, Thérèse's education was very incomplete. She tells us she had a great thirst for knowledge but decided to mortify her appetite. In the highly charged anti-clerical atmosphere of France's Third Republic, a devout Catholic middle-class family like Thérèse's would avoid the secular education fostered by the government. Its decrees were often targeted at religious orders and their right to own property or conduct schools. Academies run by nuns had to cling to the shadows, away from public scrutiny, and emphasize especially instruction in Catholic doctrine. Thérèse was well grounded in the nineteenth-century French theology available. Popular preaching would have warned her against materialism and the treacheries of scientific progress.

It's not surprising her understanding of secular subjects was so limited, but she has less excuse for the many errors in her written French. Yet this eager teenager could find in John of the Cross what he declared he offered: sound and substantial fare.

The well-educated John gives us a systematic presentation of his spiritual doctrine. Thérèse, on the other hand, teaches us by telling the story of her life. With John, each chapter builds on the preceding one. Even in the *Spiritual Canticle,* you can see the framework he used when he composed the *Ascent* and the *Dark Night,* which are really one work. Behind the outpourings of the enamored soul of the *Canticle* is the carefully crafted instruction of the *Ascent-Night.* Sometimes it is explicitly repeated, at other times it is woven into the account of the bride/soul's search for the Divine Bridegroom.

Thérèse moves chronologically, recalling the episodes of childhood, adolescence, and young womanhood to reflect on the merciful love that shaped her ongoing years. She knows nothing of Aristotle's hylomorphic theory (the theory of form and matter) which John uses so often to elucidate his presentation. Thérèse turns to what she sees around her, the stuff of human living, to make her point. Flowers, sky, birds, toys, an elevator, the grain of sand—all are put to use to proclaim the wonders of God's dealing with her. She has the observant instinct of a born naturalist as she delights in plants and cyclical phenomena—the sight of them, their smell and sound, the tactile impressions.

The doctrine of Divine Providence is expressed in Thérèse's simple analogy when she writes, "Just as in nature all the seasons are arranged in such a way as to make the humblest daisy bloom on a set day, in the same way, everything works out for the good of each soul."[4]

Thérèse's story is a paean of praise for what God has accomplished in her. She says, "It seems to me that if a little flower could speak, it would tell simply what God has done for it without trying to hide its blessings."[5]

In telling the tale of her life, she is writing a personal treatise on grace, on the longing of God to share divine life in its fulness with human beings. She wrote to her sister Marie,

> . . . the same God who declares he *has no need to tell us when he is hungry* did not fear *to beg* for a little water from the Samaritan woman. He was thirsty. But when he said: *Give me to drink*, it was the *love* of his poor creature the Creator of the universe was seeking. He was thirsty for love. Ah! I feel it more than ever before. Jesus is *parched* . . . He finds few hearts who surrender to him without reservations, who understand the real tenderness of his infinite love.[6]

Thérèse's autobiography is her attempt to express the tenderness of infinite love poured into her twenty-four years of earthly existence. As she drew closer to the end of those years, she realized that her personal story could enlighten others and arouse in them something of her desire for divine union.

The purpose of John of the Cross in his major treatises is also to give his readers understanding and to awaken in them a yearning to draw closer to God. He says in the Prologue of the *Ascent of Mount Carmel*, "God gives many souls the talent and grace for advancing, and should they desire to make the effort they would arrive at this high state (of union). And so it is sad to see them continue in their lowly method of communion with God because they do not *want* or *know how* to advance."[7] In that passage John gives the two reasons for not making spiritual progress. One is a reason of the mind: we don't know how to advance, we are ignorant of the way. The other reason is based on the will. We don't want to advance at the cost required. The price is too high.

With some effort on our part, through John and Thérèse we will find clear doctrine to illumine the ignorance of our minds and fire to inflame our hearts. But each will explain the path to divine union in a language of spirituality that springs from a culture distinct from ours. In John, a Spaniard of the sixteenth century, the difficulty of the language is often long, pedantic sentences with an absolutist phraseology in the didactic sections. The stumbling block in the writing style of the nineteenth-century French nun, Thérèse, lies in her overuse (to our ears) of diminutives and endearing phrases. Her extended metaphors can also seem sentimental to some readers, while others delight in their fresh unsophisticated quality.

Take the example of the very small Thérèse being offered a basket of toys from which she was to choose one. She paused to consider the selection and then said, "I choose all." Off she went with the whole basket. Thérèse writes,

> This little incident of my childhood is a summary of my whole life. Later when perfection was set before me, I understood that to become *a saint* one had to suffer much, seek out always the most perfect thing to do, and forget self. I understood, too, there were many degrees of perfection and each soul was free to respond to the advances of Our Lord, to do little or much for him.

Then she repeats the childhood choice, "*'I choose all!'* I don't want to be a *saint by halves.* I'm not afraid to suffer for you. I fear only one thing: to keep my *own will*; so take it, for *'I choose all'* that you will."[8]

Thérèse will not be a saint by halves. What she expresses through the charm of a childhood anecdote, John of the Cross says in much more solemn words, but the message is the same. John writes in the *Ascent,* "God communicates himself more to the soul more advanced in love, that is, more conformed to his will. A person who has reached complete conformity and likeness of will has attained total supernatural union and transformation in God."[9] John is telling us this is the person who chooses all, whose will is one with God's.

The childhood stories of Thérèse can be disconcerting in revealing so unswerving a commitment to God. In her last illness, her cousin Marie Guérin asked her, "Did you sometimes refuse God anything?" Thérèse replied, "No, I don't remember refusing him anything. Even when I was very little, at the age of three, I began to refuse God nothing he was asking from me."[10] Yet letters of her mother give us a picture of an intelligent and lively toddler, whose thoughts and words were often about God but who also could be very stubborn. After her mother's death when Thérèse was four and a half, she lost the strength of character Madame Martin had noted and did not regain it until just before her fourteenth birthday. She describes herself at the age of thirteen,

> I really made a big fuss over *everything*! I was just the opposite of what I am now, for God has given me the grace not to be downcast at any passing thing. When I think of the past, my soul overflows with gratitude when I see the favors I received from heaven. They have made such a change in me that I don't recognize myself. It is true that I desired the grace of having absolute control over my actions . . . but I had to buy, so to speak, this inestimable grace through my desires.[11]

Never refusing God anything described an attitude of spirit in Thérèse, not a strong will able to overcome every obstacle. Look at the picture she gives us of herself before the Christmas grace which transformed her just before her fourteenth birthday. That picture portrays a deeply religious teenager, very prone to bursting into tears, unable to mix well with her contemporaries, awkward and shy in society, and most happy in the company of her immediate family. When Thérèse talks about her weakness and her need for God's strength to empower her, we should take her words literally.

Sometimes Thérèse has been depicted as a spiritual amazon with a will iron-strong for any battle, earthly or heavenly. This is far from the portrait she draws. A few months before her death, she still affirms her weakness. To her sister Pauline Martin, who was Mother Agnes in Lisieux Carmel, she said,

> I have my weaknesses, but I rejoice in them. I don't always succeed in rising above the nothings of this earth. For example, I will be tormented by a foolish thing I said or did. Then I enter into myself and I say, 'Alas, I'm still at the same place I was formerly! But I tell myself this with great gentleness and without any sadness. It's so good to feel one is weak and little.[12]

In Thérèse, we see a will surrendered to God. When on the Christmas night before her fourteenth birthday, Thérèse regained the stability of character she had lost at her mother's death, she did not claim the victory as her doing. She wrote, "On that *night*, when he (Jesus) made himself subject to *weakness* and suffering for love of me, he made me *strong* and courageous, arming me with his weapons."[13]

The strength in Thérèse is God's gift to her. The Little Way is more than acknowledging our weakness. That alone could be a willingness to settle into mediocrity. On the Little Way, we cry from the heart to God to give all that we need to move forward in sanctity—and then we actively exercise ourselves in detachment and virtue. John of the Cross explains how to ascend Mount Carmel. The Little Way is a route of ascent, too. Nowhere does it wind around on a level plateau. It is always climbing upward.

All Carmelite spirituality urges us to stretch ourselves, to keep moving forward, not to settle on a comfortable flatland in our relationship with God. Comtemplative nuns in far-eastern countries have told me that the motivation to keep advancing—so strong a characteristic in Carmel's saints—that motivation can hit a cultural impasse in areas of the world where a much more static view of spirituality has prevailed for centuries. The moral demand of Christianity, the "Be ye perfect as my Heavenly Father is perfect,"[14] comes up against a willingness to be absorbed in contemplative repose and stay there. The repose of Carmel is far different. The enkindling of love is for the sake of setting us more and more on fire—not for rejoicing in its heat and staying where we are in our relationship with God. Thérèse's asceticism in the Little Way is as total as what John delineates in the First Book of the *Ascent* and it echoes his poverty of spirit. Mother Agnes asked her to explain what she meant by remaining a little child before God," Thérèse answered,

> It is to recognize our nothingness, and to expect everything from God as a little child expects everything from its father; it is to be disquieted about nothing, and not to be set on gaining our living . . . I've always remained little, having no other occupation but to gather flowers, the flowers of love and sacrifice, and of offering them to God in order to please him.

She went on,

> To be little is not attributing to oneself the virtues that one practices, believing oneself capable of anything, but to recognize that God places this treasure in the hands of his little child to be used when necessary, but it always remains God's treasure. Finally, it is not to become discouraged over one's faults, for children fall often, but they are too little to hurt themselves much.[15]

John says in one of his counsels, "He is humble who hides in his own nothingness and knows how to abandon himself to God"[16]; and in Book 1 of the *Ascent*, "Only those who set aside their own knowledge and walk in God's service like unlearned children receive wisdom from God."[17]

Thérèse in answering Mother Agnes spoke of God placing the treasure of virtues in the hands of his little child. Then she added the clause "to be used when necessary." Virtues are for the sake of virtuous activity. In her autobiography Thérèse explains how her life will be consumed. She says it will be

> by not allowing one little sacrifice to escape, not one look, one word, profiting by all the smallest things and doing them through love . . . O Jesus, of what use will my flowers be to you? Ah! I know very well that this fragrant shower, these fragile, worthless petals, these songs of love from the littlest of hearts will charm you. Yes, these nothings will please you.[18]

Notice her words: Not allowing one little sacrifice to escape.

John of the Cross says in the *Ascent*, "(A person) . . . has only one will, which, if encumbered or occupied by anything, will not possess the freedom, solitude, and purity requisite for the divine transformation."[19]

The Little Way is no invitation to seek holiness by a more comfortable, less demanding route. The diminutives are not to reduce the energy required but to gather in everything that might otherwise be overlooked. Thérèse certainly echoes these words of John's in the *Ascent*, "I should not consider any spirituality worthwhile that would walk in sweetness and ease and run from the imitation of Christ."[20]

Thérèse is not scaling down human life to a miniature size to make it more manageable. She is simply telling us to examine it closely and understand how much we miss by overlooking the opportunities for encountering God in everything.

She didn't lack appreciation for magnificence and greatness. She describes how moved she was by the sight of the ocean as a child; she was enraptured in her journey through Switzerland by the mountain peaks, the ravines that seemed ready to engulf the travelers, a huge lake. She wrote,

> When I saw all these beauties . . . I seemed to understand already the grandeur of God and the marvels of heaven. The religious life appeared to me *exactly as it is* with its *subjections,* its small sacrifices carried out in the shadows. I understood how easy it is to become all wrapped up in self.

She determines, she says, to "forget my own little interests . . . I shall not have the misfortune of snatching after straws."[21]

Thérèse has her sense of proportion in perspective. She knows the small things in our life can entrap us, wrapping us up in their demands for satisfaction. We snatch after these straws, because they are close at hand and have that much more power to engross us.

Thérèse will work a transformation on these straws, the small pettinesses that use up so much of our energy. In the Little Way, she will perform a spiritual transmutation by making them the very matter of her offering, sweeping them up into the holocaust. This is a very active asceticism—"not allowing one little sacrifice to escape."

At the same time, we can't permit Thérèse's words to lead us to a kind of microscopic focus on minutiae, and absorption in trivia. The purpose of detachment is to free my attention from what is less than God in order to fix it on God in inner recollectedness. John writes in the *Ascent*, "Oh, if people knew how much spiritual good and abundance they lose by not attempting to raise their appetites above childish things, and if they knew to what extent, by not desiring the taste of these trifles, they would discover . . . the savor of them all."[22]

In a section of the autobiography addressed to Mother Marie de Gonzague, Thérèse tells of her temptation as a postulant to find a few crumbs of consolation in her affection for Mother Marie by devising some excuse for knocking at her door.

> There came into my mind a crowd of permissions to seek . . . a thousand reasons for pleasing my nature. How happy I am now for having deprived myself from the beginning of my religious life! . . . I no longer feel the necessity of refusing all human consolations, for my soul is strengthened by him whom I wanted to love uniquely. I can see with joy that in loving him the heart expands and can give to those who are dear to it incomparably more tenderness than if it had concentrated upon one egotistical and unfruitful love.[23]

Ultimately the reward of detachment is all that John lists in Book III of the *Ascent*: "Liberty of spirit, clarity of reason, rest, tranquillity, peaceful confidence in God." John goes on, "A person obtains more joy and recreation in creatures through the dispossession of them. He cannot rejoice in them if he beholds them with possessiveness, for this is a care which, like a bond, fastens the spirit to earth and does not allow it freedom of heart."[24]

While detachment gives so high a return in serenity of spirit, Thérèse sees it primarily as an expression of love. She writes to her sister Céline,

> Directors . . . bring souls forward in the way of perfection by having them make a great many acts of virtue and they are right, but my director, Jesus, does not teach me to count my acts, but to do *everything* for love, to refuse him nothing, to be pleased when he gives me a chance to prove to him that I love him—but all this in peace, *in abandonment*. Jesus does everything, I nothing.[25]

The detachment of the Little Way has nothing numerical about it. We don't add up our sacrifices. That would make self-forgetfulness turn right around to take hold of how forgetful of self it was. Thérèse is too little to bother with counting. The detachment of the Little Way is not simply a program for developing discipline and obtaining moral mastery over what could enslave us. It achieves all that.

But for Thérèse—as for John—the whole motivation of detachment is to attach us to what is infinitely more worthy of our desire: to God. Remember her words, "My director Jesus does not teach me to count my acts, but to do everything for love." Love is the moving force for detachment, and we can only increase our detachment according to our love. A director cannot ask more detachment of a person than he or she is capable of. John makes that clear in Book I of the *Ascent* when he writes, "A love of pleasure and attachment to it, usually fires the will toward the enjoyment of things that give pleasure. A more intense enkindling of another, better love (love of one's heavenly Bridegroom) is necessary for the vanquishing of the appetites and the denial of this pleasure."[26]

The Little Way—a way of love, "very straight, very short"[27]—are the words Thérèse used. It doesn't provide detours or side trips for relaxation. But it guarantees that anyone can walk this route. "My way is all confidence and love,"[28] Thérèse wrote. Trust in the possibility of the journey is the only prerequisite. This is not a trek for experienced travelers only, for people especially favored. In Thérèse's perspective, everyone is especially favored. All it takes is the willingness to begin, taking the first step from wherever we are.

Thérèse's God is a God of Merciful Love, of infinite loving kindness. This is simply an echo of the Gospel message. "Come to me all you who labor and are heavily burdened"[29] was the cry of Jesus Christ. What human being doesn't feel the labor and the heavy burden of human existence? Who doesn't need a God of infinite loving kindness to make the journey through his or her particular life not only bearable but worth celebrating? To be human is to take on the weight of suffering, failures, separations, and the ultimate price we pay in death. To be human is also to rejoice and live in wonder. The Little Way takes hold of all of this, and sees it linked to the divine/human life of Christ. Then everything is possible, anything is possible.

Thérèse declares "I considered that I was born for glory." We are all born for this glory. Thérèse goes on, "God alone, content with my weak efforts, will raise me to himself and make me a *saint*, clothing me in his infinite merits."[30]

She isn't reserving a unique privilege for herself. She writes,

Why do I desire to communicate your secrets of love, O Jesus, for was
it not you alone who taught them to me, and can you not reveal them
to others? Yes, I know it, and beg you to do it. I beg you to cast your
Divine Glance upon a great number of *little* souls. I beg you to choose
a legion of *little* victims worthy of your love![31]

Thérèse's originality is striking, when we consider the atmosphere
of her French Carmel at the close of the nineteenth century. The
justice of God was paramount in the consciousness of Catholics who
saw their Christian traditions blasphemed and ridiculed. Devout
Catholics looked at their world under the government of France's
Third Republic and judged themselves under attack. By whom? By
just about everybody else: the scientists with their atheistic materialism, the libertines in the arts with their exuberant hedonism,
and the liberals with their political malice. French Catholics drew
closer together into a spiritual and cultural ghetto in which their
God was served as one who deserved reparation from the faithful.
Their perception that they were under attack in this fin de siècle
era was accurate; and their response to make up to an outraged
deity through their own sacrifice is admirable. The offering to
divine justice for the sake of holding back the wrath of God was familiar to Thérèse. Nuns in Lisieux Carmel had made such a personal oblation—including the saintly Mother Geneviève whom
Thérèse esteemed so highly.

But she will not imitate their generosity. She tells us, "I was
thinking about the souls who offer themselves as victims of God's
justice in order to draw away the punishments reserved to sinners,
drawing them upon themselves." She says she was far from feeling
attracted to such an act. "O my God! Will your Justice alone find
souls willing to immolate themselves as victims. Does not your
Merciful Love need them too? On every side this love is unknown,
rejected . . . Is your disdained Love going to remain closed up
within your Heart?"

"You permitted me, dear Mother,"—she is addressing Mother
Agnes—"to offer myself in this way to God . . . Ah! since that happy
day, it seems to me that *Love* penetrates and surrounds me, that at

each moment this *Merciful Love* renews me, purifying my soul . . ."[32]

Some days after her offering Thérèse was making the way of the cross privately when she was seized by an inflowing of love so strong that she felt wholly plunged into fire. She related it to Mother Agnes but made no mention of it in her autobiography. "I was on fire with love and I felt that one moment, one second more, and I would not have been able to bear this burning without dying.[33] Thérèse believed this high mystical favor, granted to her at the age of twenty-two was God's answer to her offering.

John of the Cross in his commentary on Stanza 2 of the *Living Flame of Love*, writes,

Oh, the great glory of you who have merited this supreme fire! It is certain that, though it does not destroy you . . . it does consume you immensely in glory. Do not wonder that God brings some souls to this high peak . . . Few persons have reached these heights. Some have, however; especially those whose virtue and spirit was to be diffused among their descendants. For God accords to founders, with respect to the first fruits of the spirit, wealth and value commensurate with the greater or lesser following they will have in their doctrine and spirituality.[34]

For Thérèse, the assault of love was not repeated. "I experienced it only once and for one single instant, falling back immediately into my habitual state of dryness,"[35] she said.

She told her prioress, Mother Agnes of other mystical graces in her life. At fourteen, she experienced transports of love. In Carmel during the great silence of the summer evenings, she had what Teresa of Avila describes as flight of the spirit. When she was sixteen she passed a week in extended quietude during which everything earthly seemed remote.

No account of such exceptional favors appears in the *Story of a Soul*. Instead, Thérèse describes her ongoing aridity, her lack of consolation, her continual falling asleep in prayer. But she always concludes these passages with words that affirm her peace and happiness. "Spiritual aridity was my daily bread and deprived of all consolation, I was still the happiest of creatures since all my desires had been satisfied."[36] In another place, she writes, "I can't say that I frequently received consolations when making my thanksgivings after mass; perhaps it is the time when I receive the least." Then she mentions her distractions and sleepiness but adds, "I always find a way of being happy and of profiting from my miseries."[37] She does not cite sections of Book II in the *Dark Night* which could explain her helplessness in prayer.

John of the Cross writes, "The soul must . . . be set in emptiness and poverty of spirit and purged of every natural support, consolation, and apprehension, earthly and heavenly. Thus empty, it is truly poor in spirit."[38]

"The memory must be abstracted from all agreeable and peaceful knowledge and feel interiorly alien to all things, in which it will seem that all things are different from before."[39] This is the purification of the Second Night.

John goes on to delineate that absorption Thérèse experienced when she was sixteen. John says, "At other times, a person wonders if he is not being charmed, and he goes about with wonderment over what he sees and hears. Everything seems so very strange even though he is the same as always. The reason is that he is being made a stranger to his usual knowledge and experience of things."[40]

Thérèse expresses this phenomenon in an image related to our Lady,

> It was as though a veil had been cast over all the things of this earth for me. I was entirely hidden under the Blessed Virgin's veil. At this time, I was placed in charge of the refectory, and I recall doing things as though not doing them. It was as if someone had lent me a body. I remained this way for one whole week.[41]

The sense of being alien to ordinary existence is a characteristic of contemplative prayer even at the early stages. A person's whole perceptual range is being very subtly interiorized and deepened. Everything is perceived in a very general, all inclusive manner that does not want to particularize. Pray-ers then are drawn to more solitude in order to savor this all-embracing awareness. They are reluctant to read and actively choose not to be stimulated. Their perceptual powers are engulfed in what holds them. As contemplative prayer develops, this process moves to a deeper and deeper level, but the pray-er learns to accomodate it to his or her ordinary life and finds the commonplace impregnated with a transformed sense of God's presence. Then possessing a new freedom in dealing with day-to-day duties, the pray-er can sell used cars—maybe more than before—install electrical wiring, teach a class of unruly youngsters, do whatever is required.

What I've described is not the gripping absorption of Thérèse hidden under the Blessed Virgin's veil, but it is of the same order— only nowhere near so pronounced. It is quantitatively different but has something of the same quality.

Thérèse in her quietude had to fulfill the requirements of the refectory. A touch of mysticism would never excuse the assigned nun in Carmel from making sure the community's meal was served according to schedule.

Thérèse leaves the description of such mystical states—even when she has experienced them—to other Carmelite writers.

Her autobiography doesn't take us up to the glory peaks of contemplative illumination. But she gives us good advice for the desert stretches of arid contemplation. She says, "It is especially the Gospels which sustain me during my hours of prayer."[42] Thérèse also tells us she will not allow herself to become discouraged. She doesn't force herself in her aridity but recites a prayer such as the Our Father very slowly. In praying for others, she uses the simple imperative, "Draw me" and knows that everyone she loves is drawn along with her.[43] She never uses force in her attempt to pray. "I say very simply to God what I wish to say . . . and he always understands me. For me, *prayer* is an aspiration of the heart, it is a simple glance directed to heaven, it is a cry of gratitude and love in the midst of trial as well as joy,"[44] she says. Notice her words: a glance, a cry, a movement of the heart. Contemplative prayer in the arid mode can do no more, but it must do this much at least. These very simple acts direct the inner attention to God. They are like small chips of wood that keep the embers burning.

During Easter week of 1896, about a year-and-a-half before her death, Thérèse moved into a much deeper darkness. Was this long descent into a spiritual wasteland at the edge of the void—was this the final cleansing of the Night of the Spirit in Thérèse? Certainly what she says echoes John of the Cross's words about the characteristics of that night. She says her soul was invaded by the thickest darkness, that all her delight in an eternal heaven was taken from her. She writes,

> My dear Mother . . . I must appear to you as a soul filled with consolations and one for whom the veil of faith is almost torn aside; and yet it is no longer a veil for me. It is a wall which reaches right up to the heavens. When I sing of the happiness of heaven and of the eternal possession of God, I feel no joy in this, for I sing simply what I WANT TO BELIEVE.[45]

Teresa of Avila speaks in the *Life* (chap. 30) of times of similar anguish which for her lasted eight of fifteen days or even three weeks. She says,

> What it (the soul) suffers at this time is indescribable. It seeks out relief but God doesn't permit it to find any . . . Faith is then deadened and put to sleep as are all the other virtues—although not lost . . . If it (the soul) hears someone speaking about God, it listens as though the truth about him were something it believes to be what it is because the Church does, but there is no memory of what it has experienced within itself . . . In my opinion, the experience is a kind of copy of hell.[46]

John of the Cross writes of "sufferings which neither sleep nor cease to tear the soul to shreds. For these doubts and fears that penetrate the soul are never at rest."[47]

Until this trial, Thérèse declares, "I was enjoying such a living faith, such a clear *faith* that the thought of heaven made up all my happiness." That thought, she says, "up till then so sweet to me" now became "the cause of struggle and torment. This trial was to last not a few days or a few weeks. It was not to be extinguished until the hour set by God himself and this hour has not yet come."[48] John writes of afflictions which are "immense." He says:

> Sometimes these afflictions pierce the soul when it suddenly remembers the evils in which it sees itself immersed, and it becomes uncertain of any remedy. To this pain is added the remembrance of

past prosperity, because usually persons . . . have previously had
many consolations in God and rendered him many services.[49]

Thérèse sees in what she suffers a means of reaching out to those
who have no faith. She will endure *their* experience, allow all her
joy and illumination to turn to bitterness and darkness, in order
that the gift of faith may enter their hearts. She says, "Your child,
. . . O Lord, has understood your divine light and she begs pardon
for her brothers. She is resigned to eat the bread of sorrow as long
as you desire it."[50]

Thérèse does not ask to be relieved of her desolation. She transforms it, as she did everything negative in her life—she transforms
it into something positive. The deprivation becomes fulfillment for
others. Throughout her autobiography, Thérèse witnesses to her
apostolic yearning—the desire that her life may bear fruit for other
lives.

She tells us that as a teenager, "The cry of Jesus on the cross
sounded continually in my heart: I *thirst* . . . I felt myself consumed
with a *thirst for souls.*"[51] At sixteen, she wrote to Céline: "Don't let us
waste the trial Jesus sends us. It is a goldmine we must exploit.
Shall we let the chance slip? The *grain of sand*"—this was a name
Thérèse applied to herself—"the *grain of sand* would set herself
to the task without *joy,* without *courage,* without strength and all
these *conditions* will make the enterprise easier. It wants to work for
love."[52] Later she wrote Céline, "Let us turn our single moment of
suffering to profit, let us see each instant as if there were no other.
An instant is a treasure."[53]

Thérèse's statements about suffering always see pain not as loss
but as coin for spiritual enrichment. When she writes, "I find only
one joy, to suffer for Jesus, but this *unfelt* joy is above every joy,"
she immediately adds, "Life passes . . . eternity comes with great
strides."[54] There is no masochism in her longing for suffering. She
desires it for the work of purification it accomplishes within her,
also because the pain measured in time is exchanged for eternal
delight, and always because through her torment others are led to
God.

The particular horror of her last year-and-a-half of desolation
was the absence of all certitude about the worth of her agony except

in terms of leading unbelievers to faith. Even that realization was a hollow recompense for one who experienced unbelief herself. "Everything hinges on heaven," she cried in the darkness of her last illness.[55]

For a believer to walk through what is experienced as the barren, bleak landscape of nonbelief is not actually to reach the position of the true unbeliever. Faith continues, but the mystical wasteland offers no consolation, and the previous certainties seem to be crumbling. The tormenting questions, "Where is God? Is there a God?" plunge the person into an abyss at the same time that he or she continues to reach out to the God faith has always presented. This God still remains the basis of ontological contact. The heart says its yes to God. Yet empirically everything else is the utter darkness of human existence agonizing in the void of divine absence.

The Night of Faith for Thérèse may have been an extension of anguish far beyond her personal need for purification. In that case, it would not have been the second night of the spirit John describes as necessary for the final transforming union with God. Instead, it must be seen as a response to her longing to serve the Church. Her last suffering, in this interpretation, enters into the redemptive agony of Christ, the innocent Victim. The anguish of her night of faith is not based on what John says are the two determinants of the second night: the first being the person's need for purgation, and the second being the degree of sanctity to which God intends to raise that person. Thérèse's pain was an overflow beyond those conditions. She seems to have reached this judgment herself when on the day she died, she said to her sisters, "Never would I have believed it was possible to suffer so much! Never! Never! I can't explain this except by the ardent desires I have had to save souls."[56]

Thérèse earliest letters and her recollections of herself as a teenager contain many expressions of longing for suffering. They are almost always connected with some aspect of the passion or mystery of the incarnation. Every suffering joins her to Jesus Christ and his Church. She tells us she wanted martyrdom of every kind. She wrote of her desire for martyrdom at a time when France was expanding its colonial interests. The secular decrees against religious orders often exempted missionary congregations. It was recognized, even by atheists, that taking Christian values to alien cultures made it that much easier to establish French economic and political bases. But of course, resistance to the European intrusion occurred often on foreign soil and missionaries were killed. Catholics read the tales of these brave French exiles in distant lands who died with the name of Jesus on their lips. They were inspired as Thérèse was. She wrote, "I would undergo all the tortures inflicted upon the martyrs."[57] This was written before the excruciating physical pain of her last illness, but she testified to Mother Agnes that she would change none of her desires.

Original as Thérèse is, she reflects the spiritual climate of her times. Offering oneself as a victim seems much less attractive to people on a spiritual quest today. Our striving for union with God will find different expressions according to our time and place in history. Thérèse has little sense of systemic economic injustice and the misery of the underprivileged that fires our spiritual aspirations. Yet her utter selflessness and concern for any in need has inspired contemporary social crusaders like Saul Alinsky and Dorothy Day.

Ultimately that selflessness asked for nothing of God except the divine will. All the specifications—the I yearn for this or for that—had given way to what the French call abandonment, complete surrender. Thérèse writes, "Neither do I desire any longer suffering or death . . . it is *love* alone that attracts me . . . Now abandonment alone guides me. I have no other compass!"[58] She quotes a strophe from John's *Spiritual Canticle* which ends, "Now that my every act is love."[59]

The longing to perform deeds of heroic service for the Church are satisfied in the love John describes when he comments on the *Canticle*'s stanza 29, "For a little of this pure love is more precious to God and the soul and more beneficial to the Church, even though it seems one is doing nothing, than all these other works put together."[60]

A month before her death, Thérèse declared to Mother Agnes, "It is incredible how all my hopes have been fulfilled. When I used to read St John of the Cross, I begged God to work out in me what he wrote . . . to consume me rapidly in love." She concluded, "I have been answered."[61]

All of John's works could be considered an explanation of how God leads a human being to that union of likeness where he or she is consumed in love. But Thérèse may have been referring to a line of the *Spiritual Canticle* where the bride-soul asks for "a flame that is consuming." John comments on this phrase,

> The soul . . . in affirming that the Beloved will give her all the things she mentioned in this stanza, and that she will possess them with consummate and perfect love . . . affirms all this in order to reveal the complete perfection of this love . . . Having reached perfection, the soul possesses a love so comforting and conformed to God that, even though God is a consuming fire . . . His is now a consummator and restorer.

The perfection of this love can only be effected in eternity, says John. The flame in this life is, he declares, "somewhat consuming and destructive, acting as fire does on a coal . . . the flame reduced it to ashes."[62] In Thérèse's last days, the image of being reduced to ashes by the consuming fire of love was a fitting portrayal of her condition.

Her blood sisters were looking for a fulfillment of other more glorious descriptions of John of the Cross, and their youngest sister died. But Thérèse's down-to-earth prosaic presentiment that her death would be far from raptures and exalted religious delight, promised her sisters only what so many human beings endure in passing through the painful valley of dying. "Don't be troubled if I suffer very much and if you see in me no sign of joy at the moment of my death . . . Our Lord died on the cross in agony and yet this is the most beautiful death of love. To die of love is not to die in transports."[63] Her last words as she looked at her crucifix were "Oh, I love him. My God, I love you."[64]

Thérèse had delighted in the passages in John of the Cross which spoke of love and especially of a love that existed in hiddenness. Her spiritual message proclaims how the little, the weak, the power-less—and the hidden—attract the infinite loving-kindness of God. A nun who had lived with her for seven years testified, "There was nothing to say about her. She was very kind and very retiring. There was nothing conspicuous about her. I would never have suspected her sanctity." The holiness Thérèse sought was so rooted in the ordinary as to be wholly unnoticed, not attracting any special attention. Like a true apophatic mystic, she turns by preference to a vocabulary that emphasizes what is concealed, veiled, secret, underground.

But after her death, Sr Thérèse of the Child Jesus stepped out of the shadows to shine like a beacon enlightening millions. Pius X called this twenty-four-year-old woman the greatest saint of modern times. Thérèse once wrote to a priest assigned to her as a missionary brother,

> The idea of eternal beatitude scarcely stirs a vibration in my heart . . . What attracts me to the homeland of heaven is the call of Jesus, the hope that I may at last love him as I have so longed to love him, and the thought that I shall bring a multitude of souls to love him, who will bless him for all eternity.[65]

Like John of the Cross who ended the *Ascent of Mount Carmel* in the middle of a sentence, Thérèse concluded the *Story of a Soul* without finishing *her* last sentence. The last words she penned were "confidence and love."[66]

A FEMINIST VIEW OF THÉRÈSE

Joann Wolski Conn

Joann Wolski Conn is professor of religious studies at Neumann College in Aston, Pennsylvania. She frequently contributes articles about St Thérèse and other topics to leading spirituality journals.

I wish I could have enjoyed more the recent film "Thérèse," winner of the Jury Prize at the 1986 Cannes film festival. During the second viewing I was able to suspend some of my disappointment with the superficial portrayal of Thérèse's personality and notice two scenes that hint at a deeper story: the prioress once explicitly adresses Thérèse as an adult, and Thérèse once demonstrates insight into the meaning of the spiritual darkness she suffered during the last eighteen months of her life. Nevertheless, I remain disappointed because the film perpetuates the one-dimensional image too often associated with this saint. Most of all I remain disappointed because my feminist concerns have led me to discover how this image is profoundly distorted.

This essay offers a more adequate vision of Thérèse, a resource for feminist spirituality. In order to accomplish this goal, I will proceed in three phases: (1) explain my feminist perspective and its consequent methodology for studying Thérèse; (2) review briefly the conclusions of two earlier stages of my project of recovering Thérèse for contemporary Christian feminist spirituality; (3) move to a new stage of the project and explain four ways in which Thérèse could be a resource for "a discipleship of equals."[1]

I should like to begin with a biographical sketch. Thérèse Martin, called Thérèse of Lisieux to distinguish her from the sixteenth century Spanish mystic and Doctor of the Church, Teresa of Avila, was born in Alençon, France, the youngest of five daughters (four children had died before Thérèse was born). Thérèse's mother, who ran a lacemaking business from her home, died when Thérèse was four years old. Her father, whose life was centered on the church and his family, then moved the family to Lisieux in order to be near his wife's relatives. At age nine Thérèse lost her "second mother," Pauline, who entered the cloistered Carmelite monastery in Lisieux. This triggered six weeks of nervous illness in Thérèse. Four years later (1886) her oldest sister Marie entered the same Carmel. On Christmas Eve of that year Thérèse experienced what she called her "conversion," a transformation of her from a self-centered child into a person who is concerned about others. The next year she asked for special permission to enter Carmel (at age fourteen), not for any other reason but "for God alone." She was refused at first, but eventually given permission to enter in April, 1888. The next year her father, senile and disoriented, was committed to a mental hospital. Céline, the fourth daughter, stayed near to attend to him until his death, five years later. Then she, too, entered the same Carmel (1894). By this time Thérèse (a nun for six years) had been entrusted with the religious formation of new members, so that Thérèse became Céline's Novice Mistress. Léonie Martin, the only sister not in the Lisieux Carmel, also became a cloistered nun, but in a different order. The following year (1895) Thérèse offered herself formally as a "Victim of Holocaust to God's Merciful Love," and wrote the first of three autobiographical manuscripts. On Good Friday, 1896, she first coughed up blood, the first symptom of her death from tuberculosis, and within a few days she entered into the "thickest darkness" of a trial of faith. In September she wrote a letter to Marie describing her vocation to "be Love" in the heart of the Church (Manuscript B). In June, 1897, severely ill, she wrote more about her spiritual insights (Manuscript C). On September 30, 1897 she died at age twenty-four. All of her sisters lived into their seventies or older. Thérèse was canonized a saint in 1925.[2]

FEMINIST PERSPECTIVE
AND METHODOLOGY

I agree with the conclusion that "feminist perspective" is an ambiguous and unstable category and that the most productive method is to admit the illusion of "a consistent, coherent theory accepted by all feminists" and proceed to use the instability as a resource for thinking and practice.[3] Therefore, I will clarify, as best I can, what I want to say at the moment and acknowledge its limitations.

My feminist perspective includes the following convictions and goals. Feminism affirms and promotes women's equal value and possibilities in society and religious institutions. It requires a critical awareness of the history and effects of women's oppression, especially the story of how and why religion both oppressed and liberated women. I am committed to a "reformist" position in religion, namely to the "loyal opposition" in the Roman Catholic tradition which now seeks to recover a "usable past" for women and reconstruct a nonsexist Christian tradition and present practice. I seek hermeneutical categories and methods which allow me to approach classical texts, images, and persons in Christian spirituality with feminist questions and allow these texts, images, and persons to question me.

Among the most significant questions to address to the text (assume, also, the image or person) are these. Can this text promote equality of women and men? That is, can it promote the relationships of mutuality and non-domination that are essential to a "discipleship of equals?" Does this religious text reveal that women's spiritual development necessarily involves a struggle for autonomy and self-direction as much as a desire for relationship and loving union with God and others? Are the relationships characterized more by mutuality and reciprocity or by domination? What is recovered in this text when it is approached from a perspective that pays as much attention to women's experience as it does to men's? Or what is noticed when it is approached from a totally women-centered perspective? Does this text grasp women's experience as an agent as well as a subject of androcentric religious institutions? Some questions that the text could ask me include the following: "Why do you resist certain beliefs and images in this text and what does that tell you about your self and your relationship to the religious perspective of this text?" "Does the experience of God communicated in this text resemble your own?" "Do the religious desires of the person(s) in this text resemble your own?" Hermeneutics of a text involves a genuine dialogue, a two-way process of questioning.

All of these questions are part of my ongoing project of dialogue with the texts and images of Thérèse of Lisieux, but they are more comprehensive than the limited focus of this essay. Here I wish to focus simply on two issues: the process of spiritual development and the appropriate feminist method for studying it. Regarding the first, I am interested in whether the texts reveal that Thérèse attained a spiritual maturity which included autonomy and self-direction as well as relationships of mutuality rather than control or hierarchical status. Regarding the methodological issue, I wonder what is uncovered when Thérèse is approached from a feminist perspective, that is, one which pays as much attention to women's experience as it does to men's. A feminist perspective on these issues — method and spiritual development — deserves some further explanation.

Women's Spiritual Development

As I explain elsewhere[4] contemporary women's spiritual development is perplexing and difficult because Christian spirituality includes every dimension of human life. Once this view is accepted, women's spiritual development begins to be recognized as problematic for several reasons.

(1) For women, the possibilities for mature humanity/spirituality are restricted. Models of human development universally recognized that movement away from conformity and predetermined role expectations and toward greater autonomy (i.e., self-direction, self-affirmation, self-reliance) is necessary for maturity. Yet women's experience shows that too many women are arrested at the threshold of autonomy. To make matters worse, the most prevalent psychological models of human development assume that maturity aims at autonomy, at differentiation. Yet women's experience convinces them that maturity must include not only autonomy but also relationship; indeed it must value belonging as much as independence.

Thus, women's experience makes them suspicious of autonomy as the goal of maturity even as they struggle against social pressure to reach that ambiguous goal.

(2) Christian teaching and practice, instead of promoting women's maturity, has significantly contributed to its restriction. Women have been taught to value primarily one type of religious development: self-denial and sacrifice of one's own needs and interests. While men have been taught to couple self-denial with courage to resist unjust authority, women have been taught to assume all legitimate authority is vested in males who determine the criteria of appropriate self-denial for women. A common criterion is, of course, that assertion of women's own desires is a sign of selfishness.

Recognizing these problems has led me to seek resources in Christian tradition that will assist women (and men) to correct these distortions of human and religious maturity. Thirteen years ago I began a long-term project to study whether Thérèse of Lisieux could be one of these resources for promoting religious and human development that takes account of the feminist issues described above.

Method

My Catholic theological perspective regarding grace and nature assumes that God's grace works in and through nature, that they can be distinguished theologically but cannot be, in concrete human life, separated. Everything is "graced." But everything cannot be "reduced" to grace, nor can anything be "reduced" to nature.[5] What this implies for the study of Thérèse is that I assume that human and religious maturity are mutually compatible. Indeed they must have the same general characteristics; otherwise, religion would be detrimental to one's mental and emotional health and, conversely, human maturity would prevent religious "perfection" or maturity.

There is no doubt that the primary characteristic of human and religious maturity is relationship. Religious maturity has always been described this way in biblical and systematic theology. Union with God and loving relationships with all are the two aspects of the one goal of Christian life. There is doubt, however, about whether autonomy or self-direction can be claimed as a characteristic of religious maturity. This looks, at first glance, too much like the classical description of sin, and it is particulary suspicious as a characteristic of a holy woman.

Yet every psychological model of adulthood has given primacy to having one's own identity, in the sense of directing one's own life independently of the wishes of others. That is until recently, when feminist psychologists (women and men) questioned this model of maturity for several reasons. It is rooted primarily in the experience of men. Its bias toward autonomy causes it to lose sight of the fact that adaptation is equally about integration and attachment. The result of this bias has been that differentiation (the stereotypical overemphasis of males) is favored with the language of growth and development, while attachment (the stereotypical female overemphasis) gets referred to in terms of dependency and immaturity. This doubt about the adequacy of most models of human maturity led me[6] to adopt the model developed by Robert Kegan.[7]

For the purposes of this essay it is sufficient to say that Kegan's model of human development is more compatible with study of religious development than other models I know for two reasons.

First, it demonstrates that both attachment/relationship and independence/autonomy are integral to *every* state of development. Consequently, it defines maturity as the intimacy made possible by moving beyond autonomy to relationship rooted in differentiation-for-the-sake-of-relationship. This is characteristic of religious living. Second, it pays as much attention to women's experience as it does to men's in order to guard against the bias described above. I see this as a bias that not only favors men but also, inevitably, leads to suspicion of religion as "immature" because it gives primacy to attachment and relationship.

This essay will use Kegan's feminist model of development as a primary hermeneutical tool for examining how Thérèse struggled for autonomy and mutual relaltionships as necessary dimensions of her religious maturity.

Reliability of the Texts

In 1976, when I began my scholarly study of Thérèse, I was amused to learn that my devotional study of her, going back as far as 1947, had been based on unreliable sources. To paraphrase Patricia O'Connor's summary of the situation,[8] when the first scholar to probe beneath the editions of Thérèse's autobiography that were published according to her sisters' wishes entered the Carmel Archives in 1945 he found Thérèse's original manuscripts in a shocking state. While correcting Thérèse's grammar, spelling, and style, Pauline had extensively edited and altered the manuscript.

In 1956 a completely reliable facsimile copy of Thérèse's three major autobiographical writings was published. In 1895, as an act of obedience to her sister, Pauline, who was prioress at that time, Thérèse filled a copybook with memories of her childhood and earliest years in Carmel (Manuscript A). During her private retreat in 1896, Thérèse wrote a letter to her sister Marie describing her current darkness and struggle of faith as well as her own unique vision of her religious vocation (Manuscript B). As she was dying in 1897, at the request of Mother Marie de Gonzague, her new prioress, Thérèse filled part of a small notebook with her spiritual insights until her hand was too weak to hold a pencil (Manuscript C). My references are to the Institute of Carmelite Studies English translation (1975) of this reliable manuscript.[9]

Thérèse's letters were withheld from publication by her sisters for many years. Then, under restrictive conditions, many letters were published in French (1948) and English (1949). In 1972-1973 all of Thérèse's letters were published in a two-volume critical French edition that also includes correspondence to Thérèse and about her. This is now available in English.[10]

Only retouched photographs of Thérèse were available until 1961 when François de Sainte-Marie published an album of authentic portraits. Thérèse's poetry has not yet been translated in a critical English edition. Neither of these sources is referred to in this essay.

Following a pious custom of some monasteries, Thérèse's sister Pauline kept a detailed account of Thérèse's last illness and of Thérèse's conversations with her and others during the final months of Thérèse's life. Clarke's English translation of these *Last Conversations* (1977), omits the controversy that surrounded them when they were published in French in 1971. As I explain in more detail in my review of this English translation,[11] the public dialogue of René Laurentin and Jean-François Six held at the Institut Catholique,

Paris (1973), demonstrates divergent scholarly opinion about the reliability of Pauline's notebooks.[12] As Pauline admitted, she edited these notebooks many times before publication, and, as evidence now reveals, she altered Thérèse's autobiographical manuscripts to suit her own image of Thérèse. Can she reliably transmit Thérèse's authentic spirituality? Laurentin answers definitively, yes, and Six strongly disagrees. I concur with Six and, therefore, make no refferences in this essay to these "last conversations."

In summary, I approach these texts from a feminist perspective. Seeking to find in Thérèse a resource for contemporary feminist spirituality, I needed, first, to demonstrate that she went beyond the conventional image and interpretation of her that I had inherited from my Catholic elementary school education. As I became sensitized to feminist issues I wanted to see if I could recover this young woman as a resource for Christian feminist spirituality.

THE BEGINNING OF A FEMINIST PERSPECTIVE ON THÉRÈSE: WAS SHE A CHILD OR A MATURE ADULT?

As I explain in an earlier article,[13] what most people remember about Thérèse, when they are alerted to feminist issues or to the characteristics of adult faith, makes them quite uncomfortable. She is imaged as the epitome of the simple, unquestioning, pious, sentimental, accepting "child-woman." People cannot envision Thérèse dealing with the struggle for adult autonomy as an integral aspect of what she called her "Little Way" to holiness. They can only imagine her from popular holy-cards and stories, where she is portrayed as the Pollyanna-type "good little Sister" who picked up pins for the love of God and let filthy laundry water splash in her face.

The Thérèse I have discovered is quite a different woman from the "Little Flower" I loved years ago. Studying Thérèse from a feminist perspective, I originally discovered two things: first, the central religious experience that Thérèse calls her "conversion" was, basically, a movement into adulthood that developed into deeper human and religious maturity; second, that Thérèse's holiness was the opposite of conventional conformity to the ideals of her family and her Carmelite monastery. On the contrary, Thérèse demonstrates a central feminist value: a developing appropriation of her own original vision of life.

Conversion in Thérèse of Lisieux

Using Bernard Lonergan's definition of conversion as a hermeneutical tool,[14] I noticed several aspects of Thérèse's religious experience. I discovered that the event which Thérèse calls "my complete conversion" is more accurately understood as a moral conversion rather than as a religious conversion, which is its common interpretation. Understanding Thérèse's conversion in this way demonstrates her development into religious and human adulthood; indeed it reveals a movement into authentic maturity. I will summarize my argument here since the appropriate texts are quoted and explained in detail in the earlier article.[15]

Nine years after the event she is describing, and only two years before her death, Thérèse narrates the story of what she calls "my complete conversion."[16] I believe the basic reason why she calls this a conversion is that a dramatic change happens, she says, "in an instant." This permanent change in direction is from being a girl of thirteen who "was really unbearable because of [her] extreme touchiness" to a "strong and courageous" young woman whose "source of tears was dried up and has since reopened rarely and with great difficulty," who "discovered once again the strength of soul which she had lost." She who "wasn't accustomed to doing things for [herself]" now experienced "the need to forget [herself] and to please others." She now had "a great desire to work for the conversion of sinners."

Because this dramatic change occurred after the Midnight Mass of Christmas, Thérèse uses the images and symbols of Christmas to explain the conversion's cause. The following underlining is that of the original text and follows Thérèse's literary device of frequent underlining for emotional emphasis. "Jesus, the gentle, *little* child of only one hour, changed the night of my soul into rays of light. On that *night* when he made himself subject to *weakness* and suffering for love of me, he made me *strong* and courageous, arming me with his weapons."[17]

Although Thérèse gives this conversion a religious interpretation, I believe it is more accurately understood as a moral conversion. This is not to deny genuine religious aspects of the event. Rather, it is to affirm that the basic change of direction described by Thérèse corresponds more closely, in three ways, to that of a moral conversion.

First, Thérèse speaks principally of a change in her criteria of decision from adherence to self-pity and an excessively sensitive desire for attention to an attitude of self-forgetfulness, to a desire to care for others, to convert sinners, and, thus, to do good. This change—from concern for self-satisfaction to desire for a life lived according to value—is the primary characteristic of moral conversion, according to Lonergan.

Second, moral conversion is an experience of more adult decision-making. Children are persuaded or compelled to do what is right. As one's knowledge of reality increases one discovers that one's choosing affects ourselves no less than the object which we choose or reject—we create ourselves through our choices. Thus, we must freely decide what we will be. This movement out of childhood is precisely the process that Thérèse identifies as most characteristic of her own conversion: "God would have to work a little miracle to make me *grow up* in an instant, and this miracle he performed on that unforgettable Christmas day."[18]

This change of direction away from childhood can be more or less independent of parental or social values, that is, more or less critical. Reading the full text one notices that the occasion for Thérèse's conversion, her "growing up," is her father's annoyance at her prolonging a childhood ritual of filling her shoes with Christmas presents. Jean-François Six emphasizes that here Thérèse realizes that, from now on, her father does not want to see her as a child but as an adult.[19] I emphasize that Thérèse stops crying out of a desire somehow to please her father, which would suggest that her conversion, at this time, was uncritical and, thus, typically adolescent. Yet I agree with Six that Thérèse later progresses in detachment from dependence on her father and in steadfast freedom from reliance upon the values of her "second mothers," her older

sisters, Marie and Pauline.[20] That is, her Christmas conversion
became more critical in the following years. A little further on the
next section will present evidence of Thérèse's independent thinking and action.

Third, the qualities of strength and freedom of decision—charac-
teristics of moral conversion and of adulthood—are singled out in
Thérèse's later interpretation of this conversion. In a letter of 1896,
Thérèse interprets her conversion as that of a woman whom
St Teresa of Avila would acknowledge because Teresa wished her
daughters to equal strong men.[21]

In summary, Thérèse describes her conversion as a dramatic
entry into adulthood. She understands it as a change from selfishness to self-forgetfulness. It is a shift from self-satisfaction to a
choice for value. Although this conversion demonstrates a movement into greater maturity it raises the question of adult autonomy.
Is this experience of a young woman of thirteen part of a deeper
movement that reaches authentic autonomy?

Thérèse's Struggle for Autonomy:
An Original Vision of Life

Since automony is a category of contemporary psychology not
that of Thérèse's nineteenth-century milieu, I have searched for the
analogous experience in terms of Thérèse's originality.[22] Do the
texts demonstrate that Thérèse was her own authority? That is, was
she the author of her own distinctive vision of life?

How could Thérèse acquire an original vision of religious life
while living according to the Carmelite Rule which values obedience and conformity to religious customs handed down from the
sixteenth century? She does this in two ways. Principally, Thérèse
trusts her own experience of God and her own insight. Thérèse
calls herself an "explorer" into Scripture, discovering new insights
that she is drawn to because they support her own prior experience
of God. Second, she strengthens her original vision by attempts at
expressing and sharing it with her sisters—three of whom are in the
same Carmel. When she realizes that most often they misunderstand
her, she makes a basic effort to clarify her ideas but does not pursue
the explanation. She does, however, peacefully persevere in acting

according to her own original vision. This originality demonstrates Thérèse's growth beyond the conventional to an autonomous, adult personality who can freely give a mature self to relationships to God and to others. I will explore Thérèse's relationships in the third section of this essay. But first it is necessary to demonstrate her independence in order to affirm that her relationships were more than conformity to role expectations authored by her family or her religious superiors.

In what ways is Thérèse original? One way has always been associated with her: in a Catholic milieu permeated by fear and rigorism Thérèse proclaimed her experience and conviction about a God who is full of tenderness, mercy, and love. There are, in addition, many other aspects of her originality that could only recently be recognized with the help of critical editions of her autobiography and letters, with more thorough studies of nineteenth-century French popular religion in general, and of French Carmelite monasteries in particular. This essay will summarize just one of the three aspects of Thérèse's vision explained in an earlier article:[23] the originality of her vision of spiritual development.

The Nature of Spiritual Development

Thérèse had several motives for communicating her vision of spiritual development with care and precision. First of all, during the first seven years of her religious life Thérèse wanted to share with her dearly-loved sister, Céline (who was at home caring for their sick father), all that she, Thérèse, was discovering about the spiritual life. She did this in letters which gradually reveal the younger sister, Thérèse, as the spiritual director of the older sister. These letters (1888-1894) cease when Céline enters the Lisieux Carmel where Thérèse is, by now, the acting directress of novices. Second, Thérèse's involvement with the religious formation of the novices from 1893 onward, naturally, prompted her meditation upon issues at the core of Christian spirituality. Lastly, during the final three years of her life Thérèse is told to write about her life, a task she interprets as an opportunity to review "the mercies of the Lord" in her life. These texts demonstrate that Thérèse is well aware of the fact that the vision of life she has developed is uncommon and even goes directly against methods for spiritual growth which were habitually used in her culture.

After six years in Carmel, Thérèse, in a letter to Céline, confides that she is not following the most basic pattern of advice adhered to by other religious (and laity) in her day. As late as the 1950s this pattern was a common method of spiritual formation. Thérèse says,

. . . directors have others advance in perfection by having them perform a great number of acts of virtue, and they are right; but my director who is Jesus, teaches me not to count up my acts. . . . to do *all* through love . . . in peace, in *abandonment*, . . .[24]

This affirmation of Jesus as her director is Thérèse's way of saying that she trusts her own religious experience. Her departure from the common practice of "counting one's acts of virtue," was a personal choice for spiritual freedom.

Another ubiquitous presentation of the spiritual life assumed that religious perfection automatically meant a search for the "more difficult." Thérèse breaks with this perspective, also. She conveys this in a letter to her sister, Léonie, whose worries and scruples were generated, in part, by the commonly accepted image of God as being fully satisfied only when humans suffer.[25] Thérèse not only affirms a maternal God, unusual in her time, but also maintains that we can share Jesus' redemptive mission by offering the *joys* of life as well as the sacrifices.

Another original insight into the nature of spiritual development is presented in summary form in this same letter to Léonie. Later on (in Manuscript B) Thérèse will explain her own style of spiritual life to her sister, Marie, as a "Little Way" of love and confidence which differs from the common assumption that one must please God by manifesting "works," that is, by making many acts of virtue. Marie, embedded in the latter assumptions, persists in interpretations of Thérèse's message as one of "works." Here, in this letter, one should note that Thérèse is communicating her "Little Way" for the first time to Léonie, who was considered by the Martin family, as backward and almost a misfit since she was in and out of the convent four different times.[26] For this sister, considered a "poor soul," Thérèse took the initiative to explain her central message, even before she gave it to her Carmelite sister, Marie. Thérèse declares that there are not two classes of souls: on the one side, the great souls capable of heroic abnegation and, on the other, the lesser souls who can do ordinary things. Rather, "the *smallest actions* done out of love are the ones which charm [God's] Heart . . . Jesus allows himself to be enchanted by the *smallest* things."[27]

Ironically, although Thérèse's canonization process was designed to prove that she practiced "heroic virtue" (as is every canonization), Thérèse rejected that ideal of holiness. She was never interested in the extraordinary, in what others could observe and testify about. Only once in Thérèse's autobiography does she use the word heroic.[28] There it refers to her burning desire to do every courageous, daring deed to make Jesus loved. Yet her thoughts move immediately to declare that she was not satisfied to identify herself with any visible organ of the mystical body of Christ (i.e., which did heroic deeds), but could only rest in identity with the heart (love) which is hidden. Thérèse always chooses what is hidden. This term (*caché*) appears forty-six times in her autobiography and represents her own ideal of holiness.

A common misunderstanding of Thérèse's hiddenness is the portrayal of her as practicing "little heroism" rather than great heroism; that is, she is imaged as being heroic in doing little things (e.g., picking up pins for the love of God, allowing dirty laundry water to splash in her face). This influences some people to imagine her as preoccupied with little things, as a typical product of the cloistered milieu where small things take on a disproportionately larger significance. On the contrary, in the context of her autobiography, Thérèse speaks of these small acts with ironic humor, genuinely seeing them as small and candidly admitting that she "often . . . allow(s) these little sacrifices . . . to slip by."[29] For example, she does not describe herself as standing heroically silent to receive the reprimand of a sister who was upset when Thérèse caused a racket which awoke the sick prioress. Rather, knowing that she could not take this reprimand in peace, Thérèse describes her own flight and the angry sister as one who delivered a "heroic oration."[30] For Thérèse, striving for heroism is a misplaced ideal. True holiness is hidden, even from oneself. Love is all that matters.

Lastly, Thérèse's final manuscript reveals that she clearly departs from the ascetic ideal of the nineenth-century Carmel: "the rough stairway of perfection." Rather than use this classical metaphor, which some authors have associated with a Platonic hierarchy of being which has levels to which not everyone can aspire, Thérèse's central image is very modern (for 1897): an elevator. Trusting her own experience of desire for a straight, short way to God, Thérèse searches the Scripture and finds a reinforcing image of God as mother (Is. 66:12,13) which she immediately associates with Jesus. For her, the "elevator" is Jesus' maternal embrace into which she abandons herself and is content to be little and to be lifted up to God.[31]

I have examined some of the evidence which supports the conclusion that Thérèse was the author of her own vision of life, that she manifests genuine originality, and is, in that sense, autonomous. There is a final aspect of maturity that must be explored. What is characteristic of Thérèse's experience of relationship? Does it reflect a desire for mutuality and equality? More significantly, could Thérèse be said to reveal that the closer one comes to God the more one actually experiences equality with others and even with God?

A FEMINIST PERSPECTIVE CONTINUED: MATURE RELATIONSHIPS MANIFEST MUTUALITY, EQUALITY

As I continue to interpret and evaluate Thérèse's religious experience according to a feminist model of maturity, I look for feminist values in her relationships. In a saintly Carmelite nun I expect to find love and concern for others, but the issue here is what *kind* of loving relationship characterizes Thérèse's life? Does she desire and experience true mutuality and equality? Focusing my investigation on the final two years of her life, I see that Thérèse does desire and experience mutuality in four relationships: (1) with her companions in Carmel; (2) with those in the Church; (3) with sinners and unbelievers; (4) with Christ and with God.

Relationship with Her Companions in Carmel

The following examples from her autobiography and letters demonstrate how Thérèse, the youngest nun in the Carmel of Lisieux, relates to her companions in a way that is inclusive and reveals mutuality. She disagrees with others' standards of virtue without being patronizing. Her instinct for mutuality prompts her to approach even her prioress in this way.

In the last year of her life Thérèse summarized, in her autobiography, her experience of charity:

> This year . . . God has given me the grace to understand what charity is; I understood it before, it is true, but in an imperfect way. I had never fathomed the meaning of these words of Jesus: ". . . You shall love your neighbor as yourself." . . . How did Jesus love his disciples and why did he love them? Ah! it was not their natural qualities which could have attracted him since there was between him and them an infinite distance . . . And still Jesus called them his *friends, his brothers* . . . charity which must enlighten and rejoice not only those who are dearest to us but "ALL who are in the house" without distinction.[32]

Thérèse loved and honored all, not favoring her family who were in Carmel with her, but caring especially for the women who were very difficult and neurotic or compulsive. Her desires lead her to notice the way Jesus manifests a desire for mutuality with humanity, for friendship with all. This mutuality, this equality in friendship is her ideal of loving relationship.

Thérèse's instinct for egalitarian relations, in a situation that could foster a condescending attitude, emerges in the following narrative from her autobiography. She recalls the year she entered Carmel and the tension she felt in her relationship to another novice who was eight years her senior. Although these two young women had been given special permission to talk during times ordinarily restricted to silence, Thérèse was uneasy because the conversations were too worldly, the other novice was infatuated with the prioress, and she was doing things Thérèse "would have liked to see her change." This is how Thérèse communicated her disapproval:

The hour we decided upon for coming together arrived; the poor little sister, casting a look at me, saw immediately that I was no longer the same; she sat down beside me, blushing, and I, placing her head upon my heart, told her with tears in my voice *everything I was thinking about her*, but I did this with such tender expressions and showed her such a great affection that very soon her tears were mingled with mine . . . When the time came for us to separate . . . in us was realized this passage from Scripture: "A brother who is helped by a brother is like a strong city."[33]

There is no patronizing self-righteousness here; rather, Thérèse creates an equality in tears and affection. Having no "sister helping sister" passage to quote from the Scripture, Thérèse's sentiment is clear, nevertheless.

A rare example of daring, even bold love is the letter Thérèse wrote to her superior, Mother Marie de Gonzague, who was very upset at the time of her re-election as prioress.[34] She was humiliated because she had been elected only on the the seventh ballot when she finally gained more votes than Thérèse's sister, Pauline. Marie de Gonzague confided her feelings to Thérèse who wrote her a letter to console her. In this letter Thérèse creates a parable of a "Shepherdess" (Marie de Gonzague) and a "lamb" (Thérèse), and Thérèse places herself in the prioress' point of view and tries to encourage the "Shepherdess" to be detached from her self-esteem and be consoled at the good that could be done through this humiliation. This tender letter gives us a glimpse of Thérèse's intuition that mutuality, even between an older prioress and a very young nun, was not only possible but also preferable for the sake of genuine charity.

Relationship to the Church

Although living a secluded life in a cloistered convent, Thérèse desired to be connected with the entire world and to be effective for the good of the world. This desire for completely inclusive love is clearest in her identification with the symbolism of the heart, an experience she recalled vividly in her autobiography.[35]

Considering the mystical body of the Church, I had not recognized
myself in any of the members described by St Paul, or rather I desired
to see myself in them *all*. *Charity* gave me the key to my *vocation* . . . O
Jesus, my Love . . . my *vocation*, at last I have found it . . . MY VOCA-
TION IS LOVE!

Constance FitzGerald, commenting on this text out of her own
experience as a Carmelite contemplative,[36] stresses that in order to
situate this text, it is essential to remember Thérèse is near the end
of her spiritual journey, five months after her first hemorrhage and
only a year before her death and enshrouded in her dark night, the
"trial of faith," she reaches out of a deep prayer presence to Christ,
out of the genuine mystic's refusal to partialize awareness, the contemplative ability to become increasingly present and conscious at
the deepest level. FitzGerald explains the inclusive maturity attained by Thérèse:

> Paradoxically, while experiencing and ultimately surrendering to
> her own fragility, brokenness, limitation and the death-dealing forces
> within her body . . . Thérèse, by awareness or empathy, does break
> through the barriers of human finitude to a presence in spirit, a
> presence of love and compassion, that is universal, all-embracing,
> personal and Christ-centered.[37]

Companionship with Sinners and Unbelievers

An unusual and unexpected experience of mutuality and equality
emerges for Thérèse when she is plunged into a deep darkness
and radical trial of faith. In one of the most moving pieces of
spiritual literature, Thérèse describes her trial and interprets its
meaning.[38] Whereas she once enjoyed a clear, living faith and the
thought of heaven made up all her happiness, now, since the Easter
season of 1896, her soul has been "invaded by the thickest darkness"
and the thought of heaven is no longer anything but the cause of
struggle and torment. Part one of this account concludes with
Thérèse's cry that she experiences a "night of nothingness." Part
two concludes with her interpretation of this night, her new feeling
about the Lord, and her new appreciation of the implications of the
Act of Oblation to God's Merciful Love which she made two years
before writing this (June 9, 1895):

Never have I felt before this . . . how sweet and merciful the Lord really is, for he did not send me this trial until the moment I was capable of bearing it . . . I no longer have any great desires except that of loving to the point of dying of love. June 9.[39]

By writing the date, June 9, at the end of this page of her manuscript Thérèse shows that she interprets her "night of nothingness" to be the way Jesus is leading her to live out the unconditional surrender, the "dying of love" which she intended in her declaration of June 9, 1895. Thérèse's contemplative reception of this dark "nothingness" bears fruit in the paradoxical way of all spiritual darkness; it generates the light of self-knowledge. In this case, it is new insight into her relationship to unbelievers.

First, Thérèse's darkness gives her the capacity to accept the fact of authentic unbelief. Before this time, she says, "I was unable to believe there were really people who had no faith. I believed they were actually speaking against their own inner convictions when they denied the existence of heaven . . ." After being plunged into darkness herself, she reverses her opinion: "Jesus made me feel that there were really souls who have no faith . . ."[40]

Second, not only can she affirm the existence of unbelievers, but she can also rejoice in a relationship of sisterhood with them. In contrast to her maternalistic attitude toward sinners after the conversion of Christmas 1886, when she wanted to convert them or to snatch them from the flames of purgatory,[41] Thérèse now demonstrates a sisterly attitude. She now identifies with them and participates in their experience. She does not view sinners from some purified place above them but, instead, accepts participation at their table. She speaks of her relationship to sinners in imagery that is an inverse analogue of the Eucharistic table.[42]

Your child . . . begs pardon for her brothers. She is resigned to eat the bread of sorrow as long as you desire it; she does not wish to rise up from this table . . . at which poor sinners are eating until the day set by you.[43]

Thérèse who, formerly, was afraid of soiling her baptismal robe,[44] can now peacefully accept her role of solidarity with sinners and be a sister to unbelievers.[45]

In a Relationship of Mutual Intimacy
with God and with Jesus

Not only does Thérèse desire to be in full mutuality with her Carmelite sisters and the whole Church as well as with sinners and unbelievers, but she also is convinced that God and Jesus, the Son of God in the Spirit, desire mutuality with her. She is amazed to realize that the one whom she most desires, desires her. Thérèse's experience of God is an experience of "having the ground of my being desire me," to use the vocabulary of Sebastian Moore.[46] Both her autobiography and her letters reveal this mutuality.

In her autobiography Thérèse speaks of God having "need" in relationship to us. God does not need our works, she maintains, but God does genuinely need us.

> See, then, all that Jesus lays claim to from us; he has no need of our works but only of our *love*, for the same God who declares he *has no need to tell us when he is hungry* did not fear to *beg* for a little water from the Samaritan woman. He was thirsty. But when he said: *"Give me to drink,"* it was *love* of his poor creatures the Creator of the universe was seeking. He was thirsty for love. Ah! I feel it more than ever before, Jesus is *parched* . . .[47]

Thérèse experiences that the One she loves above all is, actually, in need of her love.

In a letter to her sister Léonie, who is feeling powerless and insignificant, Thérèse declares that the God who approaches us is also fragile. God is begging.

> Ah! we who are living in the law of love, how can we not profit by the loving advances our Spouse is making to us . . . how can we fear him who allows himself to be enchained by *a hair* fluttering on our neck.
> . . . understand, then, how to hold him prisoner, this God who becomes the beggar of our love.[48]

Here the issue is not one of collapsing the difference between the status of God and of creatures; rather the focus of Thérèse's message is her experience of relationship. The more deeply she is related to

God, the more Thérèse is amazed to discover that this relationship is an experience of genuine mutuality.

CONCLUSION

Having addressed my feminist concerns to Thérèse's texts, I believe that these texts reveal an adult, in a mature stage of faith, who understands the meaning of her trial of darkness as an experience of profound and mutual relationships. Thérèse's loving response in these relationships is far from immature conformity to role-expectations; indeed, it is the surrender of a mature adult who has struggled to be the author of her own vision of life: freely chosen, completely inclusive Love.

My feminist perspective also continues to make me uncomfortable with some aspects of Thérèse's life. Her preference for sentimental religious art and language are, at times, repugnant. Her literal interpretation of Scripture jars my theological nerves. Her confining bounds of social awareness are disappointing yet expected, given her culture.[49] For example, a primary source of suffering is her self and her family: her father's illness, her own dryness in prayer. There is no expression of concern for the suffering of the Vietnamese under French colonialism, even when she volunteers to go to the Carmelite monastery in Saigon. There is no awareness of oppression caused by the patriarchal church aligned with French monarchists. But these effects of Thérèse's physical and cultural enclosure do not cancel, for me, the benefits of Thérèse's life as a resource for Christian feminist spirituality.

One great benefit of Thérèse's spirituality is its confirmation of the truth that psychological enlargement results from the experience of mutuality, despite its cultural limitations in Thérèse's case. In other words, it is clear that mutuality increases her vitality; it enlarges her ability to act within relationships as well as beyond them; it increases her knowledge of herself and others; it strengthens her self-worth and deepens her desire for more connections beyond her immediate interaction.[50] This ability to make and sustain relationships characterized by mutuality is fundamental to Thérèse and to Christian feminist spirituality.

RELIGIOUS DEVOTION OR MASOCHISM?— A PSYCHOANALYST LOOKS AT THÉRÈSE

Ann Belford Ulanov

Ann Belford Ulanov is Professor of Psychiatry and Religion at Union Theological Seminary in New York. She has her own private practice as a psychoanalyst and is a faculty member of the C. G. Jung Institute of New York.

I

The questions most often directed by the world of depth psychology to the world of religion, and to Thérèse specifically, are: why all the suffering? Is it an essential part of religious life? The recent movie *Thérèse* reawakened this question. Why did she refuse medicine? Why refuse relief from pain? Isn't this masochistic?

A second set of questions follows from the first. If masochism is not true of Thérèse then why do people associate it with her? Why does her kind of religious devotion strike anyone as a masochistic embrace of suffering? These questions will be my focus. What, in sum, are the differences between religious devotion and masochism? And, if Thérèse is not masochistic, then why is she accused of it?

The second question is easier to answer than the first. I will start with that and return to it again at the very end of this article. Thérèse is accused of masochistic sentimentality because of the depth of her feelings, her lavish, all-out loving of Jesus. Loving with all one's heart, mind, soul and body, like Thérèse's, fills most of us with dread. We cancel that dread by accusing the loving one —Thérèse—of groveling sentimentality. But the underside of sentimentality is power. We accuse Thérèse of too much feeling, too much devotion, while keeping for ourselves the power to put her at a safe distance, and to keep her there. We stay in control of our feelings by caricaturing hers. We charge her and her followers with being like a too sweet and sticky icing in order to avoid facing the real achievement—her capacity to love and to feel without any obstacles in the way of her feeling. Thérèse is accused of masochism and of sentimentally seeking suffering because she threatens us with a possibility we fear to make actual.

Thérèse shows us that within our ordinary life—going to work in our cars or on the subway, doing our taxes, getting our children ready for school, fixing meals—we can find the mysterious exchanges between ourselves and God in prayer and meditation, no matter how brief or hurried. She reveals the hidden works of love that go on daily, not in some special precious time, but in ordinary everyday time. Thérèse poses a tremendous threat because she brings hidden mystic life out into the open and says, in effect, here it is for the taking, for all of us, not just the specially gifted, but all of us, each with our own gifts.

Thérèse acts as a perfect complement to our century's huge explosions that force power outward—into bombs, into space, across new frontiers. Thérèse shows us explosions of energy inward, into inner space, and a spirit so powerful it spills over into relationships with others, near and far. She uncovers an energy of tremendous intensity in daily life. We can no longer say, "Oh no, we cannot love like that, we are not members of a religious community; we know nothing of that kind of power." If we are members of Carmel we can no longer say, "We cannot love like that; we do not have Thérèse's genius; her power to love is only for the saints." Thérèse closes all those escape hatches. She says, "Yes you can, any moment of any day; here, now, this afternoon, we can know the mysterious and wonderful exchanges of love."

Another aspect of our century is its horrible denial of the person. As we know, guards even pried the gold fillings out of the teeth of concentration-camp victims. Living breathing persons were treated as objects of medical experiments, or outright sadistic torment. People by the hundreds of thousands have been thrown into prisons, dungeons, gulags, and left there to rot. The mysterious center that makes up the person has been ruthlessly attacked, canceled, obliterated. Even in less dramatic circumstances, the ordinary commerce of everyday life, we suffer nullification of personhood. We know perfectly well we did not buy what the computer printout stubbornly, repetitiously reports we did buy. We write the company; we phone; we write again. The bills keep spitting out of the machines, as if what we wrote or said never was heard, or if heard, made no difference.

In this century, where on every side we feel personhood diminished, questioned, anything but seen, held, and cherished, this young woman, this girl, this wise woman makes us see that each of us is precious as a center of being. She shows us we are held in the sight of God, precious to the Lord, precious to one another. She links through the chain of love our nearest neighbor and our most distant neighbor.

Thérèse's own immediate leaps into spiritual maturity are worth noting. At thirteen, as she was running to look for Christmas gifts that had been put into her slippers, she overheard her father sigh, weary of preparing presents once again. She fled to her room and howled with hurt and disappointment. But quickly she gave up her tears and in a leap recovered "la force d'âme," the strength of mind and soul that she had lost.[1] The summer after that Christmas leap, she leapt again. Starting then with her nearest neighbor, her father, she reached in that summer to her farthest one, the murderer named Pranzini who was about to be executed. She felt herself wounded now, not by another's weariness in meting out pleasures, but with the indifference of the world to its Redeemer. Praying as intercessor for Pranzini, she felt God's love break through. The moment before his execution, he was reported to have seized the crucifix and kissed it. Barry Ulanov describes her intercessory action:

She would gather up the blood that was being wasted. She would give it to those who needed it. She heard her Lord's cry, "I thirst," as if it was addressed to her, and she determined to respond to it by giving him souls for which he thirsted, sinners . . . she longed to save . . .[2]

Thérèse herself summed it up: "It was a true exchange of love. To souls I offered the blood of Jesus; to Jesus I offered the same souls, brought to life again by the dew of his precious blood . . ."[3]

Thérèse recovers for us in our time the mystery of love in person, between persons, between persons and God. That somehow threatens us. Hence the accusations that pile up against her—hers is too much feeling, too much an embrace of suffering. She gives us her gift of self-assurance, of completeness in love, of a courage to act that overflows out of that love. In return, we accuse her of sentimentality and masochism. We look to protect ourselves from the power she puts into our hands.

II

Psychoanalytical theory offers three approaches to what is called masochism. Masochism is not something we do; it is a suffering, an affliction, and a very painful one. Three types of theoretical understanding of masochism act as maps that outline this country of pain. Some of us have ventured into that country and know that the experience is quite different from the maps. Most of us know something about it. We may also know that the great temptation in the psychological, as in the spiritual life, is to rest content with the map and never go into the country that it charts. Then we think we can stay in control. So I will state these theories in ways that may evoke the actual painful experience they describe and its temptations and difficulties.

The first of the three approaches to masochism sees it as a manifestation of the death instinct; the second, as a defensive strategy of the ego; the last, as a means of hiding a missing piece of ourselves and a reflection of our need to venerate something transcendent, beyond ourselves. The first originates with Freud and is shared by

Melanie Klein. They in turn distinguish among an erotogenic masochism, where pleasure is mixed with pain; a feminine masochism where aggression is directed inward; and moral masochism, the one most relevant to my purposes, in which we submit our ego to a sadistically critical superego as our ruling moral authority.[4] In this submission we accept almost gladly what anyone accuses us of; we take unconscious pleasure in confessing to others' sins; we submit to an inner punitive voice that says in effect that we are no good, that we are never enough, that we are fools. The ego cooperates and develops chronic low self-esteem, a habit of excessive self-criticism, and timid behavior.

An extreme example of such behavior can be seen in the willingness of people around Jim Jones in Guyana some years ago to drink poisoned grape juice and die, simply because he had told them to do so. Less extreme examples, and ones that need all our attention to discern whether people are veering toward masochism or moving into real dedication or devotion, are to be found in the vows of obedience we make to a religious or military supervisor, that a young person does in effect to a teacher or a coach, that is shown in a lover's fealty to a beloved.

The second way of mapping the suffering of masochism moves from instinct to defense of the ego, to strategies we develop to protect ourselves. We use masochistic attitudes and actions to protect our ego from the threat of being annihilated. Horney, Berliner and Esther Menaker represent this view. In its terms, we relinquish our self to avoid anxious conflict with the person, usually a parent, on whom we depend for our very life. We accept suffering from the hands of the other as if it were love. We confuse love and hate. Masochism here is an adaptation of the ego into chronic and exaggerated self-critical, self-abasing behavior because we are terrified of being abandoned by someone on whom we depend, without whom we feel we cannot survive. And so we demean ourselves to appease, placate, propitiate the other whom we need so much. We are even willing to give up a center of awareness in ourselves, our place of willing, our capacity to grow independent and use our energy for creative self-expression in the world, in order to preserve our dependent bond on this other before whom we feel so helpless. We will even distort the reality of what we perceive to preserve this bond, confusing unkind and cruel actions of the other with affection and support. Thus we collude in denying our own value as a person. We take into ourselves the disparaging attitude of the other toward us and identify with it. That keeps us mired in frustrating repetitive behavior. The only sound we hear inside us is a same harsh critical voice. Thus our egos cannot develop new and different perceptions of ourselves as achieving, willing, creative.[5] Our ego, stuck in the repeated experiences of feeling small, unable, unworthy, is passively dependent on the other. We conclude we can never accomplish anything. We will accuse ourselves of anything to maintain the illusion of connection to the idealized other. We refuse to recognize the other's flaws and problems.

Somewhere, however, we know this is no good. Somewhere, we see and feel the unkindness and cruelty of the other. We get angry. We want to use our aggression to strike back, all the aggression that is natural to us. All that we have left unconscious and unchannelled is stirred up in fantastic ways because we have developed no weapons of self-assertion or verbal aggression with which to fight or argue our case. Instead of responding positively to the previous aggression, we are afraid and feel guilty. We even feel we deserve punishment for our hostile feelings. Thus our masochistic self-belittlement increases. We give our power away to those who make us angry. Secretly, we hope this maneuver, forcing them into a superior position over us, will also prove a means of obliging them to keep taking care of us.

In this masochistic adaptation of the ego toward other, we are trying to go back to a time when no conflict existed between us. We are trying to reinstate the unambivalent pre-oedipal time when we were young enough so that it was appropriate to depend on others to take care of us, when everything seems sunny and good. We do not want to rebel and strike back. And so our backward yearnings keep us trapped in an age that is too young to fashion relationship with others. We always fear they will leave us. Unconsciously we devise schemes to control others to stay in protective parenting relationships with us. We fasten on to one fantasy version of ourselves as humble, weak, meek, totally devoted to others who hold all the power. We offer this to them. Then they dare not leave us. Thus we also protect ourselves from the anxiety—the dread, really —of abandonment. To preserve a false security, the ego sacrifices its whole independent development.

We can understand how people think religious life fosters such masochistic self-deprecating attitudes. All power and might, all authority and goodness are ascribed to the Almighty. Who are we but miserable offenders? This is what has been called "I-am-a-worm" theology. How often we have heard about the excesses of the flagellants, or other distortions of the sacrament of penance, and that most central appropriation to evidence of masochism in religious devotion, the One who redeems through suffering death upon a cross.

In contradistinction, Erasmus offers humorous criticism of the true groveling tendencies of religious devotees. One will "spill out a hundred bushels of hymns" in praise of God. "Another will show a voice grown hoarse with chanting; "another, a tongue grown dumb under his vow of silence."[6]

In the third approach to masochism, I combine the theories of Masud Khan and Jung. Here masochism is not an instinct, nor really a defensive strategy of the ego. Rather, it is a place of protection where we are hiding something that we cannot quite bring ourselves to find and venerating something that is not big enough for our devotion. We are hiding something painful that happened to us before our egos were developed, before we had developed a real object relation, that is, sturdy relation to another.[7] What is hidden is a part of our true self, something of great value to us and our religious devotion. Such masochism involves chronic low self-esteem and accompanying action of self-abasement. These become routines, whether attitudes or actions, and hold us compulsively. We are afraid to let go, fearing what might happen to us. We become addicted to these routines, having rerouted pleasure into them, having constructed in them elaborate defense systems, hiding within them precious pieces of self that we have lost or never even found. Our masochistic habits both express and mask, try and fail to manage some pain inflicted, some suffering endured and remembered in action rather than words, in behavior rather than idea. Our perversions, such as they are, tell the story of our suffering in the only way we can tell it, through enactments of repetitious self-abasement.

Jung speaks of a religious instinct—an inherent impetus to be conscious of relationship to a Deity, to devote ourselves in that all-out lavish loving that we find so well exemplified in Thérèse of Lisieux.[8] If we do not find a way to live with this religious instinct, it will trouble us just as much as hunger or sexual instincts do if we deny them. We fall prey to disorders of the spirit as costly to us as eating disorders. We burgeon with spiritual repression at least as upsetting as sexual repression. Or we suffer religious perversions, such as masochism, if we cannot find a way to live with our urge to submit and pour ourselves into adoration.

In masochistic rituals and attitudes of self-humiliation hides an unlived religious impulse to venerate.[9] We have fixed the impulse on the wrong object, giving to another what properly belongs to the transcendent. We have blunted the impulse to devotion, mixing it with pain and degradation. We are caught in covert ways of control, of self, of other, of the religious impulse itself, refusing to give over to the source and power of being. Instead, we try to regulate the power, change the purpose of this instinct.

Jung looks at this disorder symbolically, asking what meaning the suffering of masochism bears toward us. We find in masochism a compensatory movement to the cultural picture in Western society of the ego as heroic, striving, mastering.[10] Masochistic tendencies pull us down into our unconscious psyche, where we do not understand but only suffer. We are in the passive mode, where we feel ashamed to be caught in actions and attitudes we cannot understand, master, or change. Masochism pulls us into what Jung calls our shadow, where is to be found all that we would like to repudiate, recover from, or improve upon. We feel sick, humiliated, and stuck. But it may be just here that meaning waits to greet us. Through the shadow we may be put in touch with forces which could and should live through us if we could consent to them. Here we find archetypal energies and images that ask for relationship. The suffering of masochism hides the passion of the psyche to give over the central places of the ego to unconscious relationship to power at the source of being.

III

This brings us to the main question: What is the connection and difference between religious devotion and masochism?[11] This crucial question addresses not only a religious giant like Thérèse but any person of religious sensibility. Are we loving God in our humility, or are we avoiding the rough tasks of psychological development where we have to learn to channel our aggression? Are we devoting ourselves to the glory of God, or are we merely mealy-mouthing around, rejecting God's Will in fact by refusing to become the person God created us to be? Are we trying to give unselfishly in the name of Christ's love, or are we secretly controlling others by appeasement, placation, manipulations for sympathy? Are we listening in our prayers for God's word and our own true words or are we denying them out of fear and pain? Are we really serving the causes of justice and peace, or are we finding a respectable surrogate for sadism and bullying, so that those who reject our particular cause fall under our persecutory eye, all in the name of justice and peace? Are we really helping downtrodden persons, oppressed in foreign countries, or are we condemning whole generations to unemployment, and all that that involves, by insisting our American companies immediately get out of those countries? Are we really praying for the souls of the world or are we hiding out in our churches, our convents, and our monasteries? Are we really experiencing the communal life in church or are we filling an emptiness that we are afraid of with church suppers and community fairs?

These tough questions lie along the frontier between the disciplines of depth psychology and religious faith. We cannot precisely delineate those disciplines. We cannot precisely separate psyche from soul, nor sickness from health. Nor can we answer those questions in a nice neat formula, so that we can conclude, comfortably, "Yes, I am doing the religious thing, not the masochistic thing." Part of the suffering of masochism is that we are never quite sure. We can never guarantee in our most ardent moments of devotion that we are not also a little bit mad. Equally, in our most mad moments there may also lurk religious devotion. The contrasts that I draw now as simple and clear, then, are not like that at all. In real life they are all mixed up. What I offer is a way to think about this fascinating subject, not a replacement for going into the country itself.

When any of us is caught by the pull of moral masochism we suffer the chronic feelings of inadequacy I have been talking about. We try to relate to the other or to the transcendent through appeasement and placation, because unconsciously we feel hostile and then guilty to feel that way. This moral masochism stands in sharp contrast to Thérèse's devotion to Jesus. She does not feel low self-esteem, but loved and loveable. She is not hostile, but alive with curiosity about her divine lover. Throughout her life, she actively exercises her will, her imagination for others and for God, whether in writing poems or drawing pictures or seeking countless ways to please. Why? Because it is so pleasurable; not to appease, but to please. Her pleasure shows in her appealing image of herself as a ball, not an expensive or fancy ball, but an ordinary one for the child Jesus to kick and throw and play with because it is so much fun. Here, then, is the first difference between masochism and religious devotion, the sharp one between feelings of self-abasement, and inferiority on the one hand and experiences of pleasure and love on the other.

The second contrast is between dependency and self-assertion. When we are caught in a masochistic undertow, our ego denies any perceptions of what others are doing to us that is unkind or negative. We deny the painful perception because we cannot give up others. We depend on them for our very survival. We fear abandonment which will bring on us a sense of nonbeing, of nothingness.

Thérèse certainly feels dependent on the divine object, but not in a way that cancels growth. Instead, her dependence emboldens her. She wants to grow and grow up and use her mind, energy, imagination and aggression always to come closer to the center. Thérèse asserts herself in ways aimed at union with Jesus. She wants to enter Carmel early and secures the permission of father, confessor, even the pope! Instead of going unconscious of the way others treat her or of what is painful, she looks to become more conscious through her daily self-examinations. Instead of defending her ego, she wants to expose it again and again to the anxiety of nonbeing which the masochist both avoids and ends up wallowing in.[12] Thérèse works at emptying everything out of her mind which is not God, so that only friendship with the Lord remains, making all her desires into the desire of oneness with Jesus.[13] She does not hold herself back from suffering but embraces it as part of life, not to revel in but as a way to use her aggression to see through the pain to a fundamental truth. She saw, for example, that the other girls at school when she was eleven did not like her very much.[14] She registered the hurt, and suffered it, and used her aggression to see through it to the truth that all affections on earth are transitory. She used her aggression not to protect herself from the blow, but to penetrate to the truth that none of us are permanently part of a group on earth. She asserted her will consciously to choose to respond to each harshness with gentleness. She chose to take the hurt of others' indifference or criticism not as proof of her inadequacy, as a masochist would, but as part of offering her little suffering to Jesus' big suffering.

The third contrast is between sacrifice and give-and-take. When masochism catches us, we disown our negative feelings and drive other people crazy. The masochist sacrifices an independent ego in order to stay passively dependent on another without the conflict of ambivalent feelings. Caught in such a position, we give up our own development for a presumed safety. We disown our aggression, leaving it untamed and unchannelled so it seeps into others. We become the guilt-makers. Hypochondria, for example, offers untold opportunities for the masochist. A hypochondriac phones. We say hello, and we hear a voice sigh in response, "Not so good." Immediately we feel guilty. It is our fault others feel bad. We cannot make them healthy, young, rich, let alone cure them. Masochists manipulate us into double-duty guilt. First, we do not save them from the misery of foul weather, fatigue, illness. We are made to feel guilty that we cannot make them thin without dieting. And then, we feel guilt for the rage their manipulations engender in us. We know all this is nonsense. We are not omnipotent. How can we control the weather? We resolve not to answer the phone the next time, or if we do, will speak out, at least gurgle in protest, maybe even shriek. "Take your symptoms and . . ." But the cry dies in our throats. Our words strangle over new guilt, for all these murderous thoughts. What do we do? We end up staying on the phone twice as long in penance, and even asking, "How do you feel?" a question never to ask a masochist. Masochists arouse our own sadism, but we feel so guilty for our ruthlessly aggressive responses that we end up appeasing and placating, just like masochists.

In contrast, the religious person uses aggression, does not leave it unclaimed to drive others crazy. Thérèse wanted all she could get, all the ego, all the self, in order to offer all to the God she loved. She said, *"I want to be a saint,"* thus not stinting on using her aggression.[15] She actively took everything into herself to give it back to God and gratefully received what God gave back to her. The religious person makes a different kind of sacrifice from that of the masochist who refuses to claim and develop the ego. The religious person develops the ego fully, offers it in love to God, and takes back a fuller self in love. For example, like any good French housewife who sent out betrothal announcements, Thérèse sent announcements of her forthcoming marriage to Jesus and claimed all the merits that belonged to her husband and his family. She offered the Holy Trinity all the merits of Jesus and the Virgin Mary! This is passionate, aggressive, audacious love. When she offered herself as a burnt offering to the work and glory of God, she also took what was given back. Five days later she felt a wounding by the dart of love which plunged her into the fire of mystical union with her divine lover. Thérèse's power lies in this give-and-take. She expects in love not only to yield, but to reap endless grace.

The religious person does not sacrifice to get rid of the ego but to gain the self in God. The religious person does not sacrifice to avoid aggression but to harness it in service to God. The religious person does not empty out the ego in purgation in defense against fullness, but in order to fill up with God's love, which then spills over into intercession for others. Thérèse was full to overflowing.

The fourth contrast centers on pain. Both the masochist and the religious person know a lot about pain and suffering. When masochism captures us, we see pain as an end in itself. The details of pain preoccupy us, even if they concern the most minute changes in bodily symptoms, moods, or the aesthetic accents of a ritual coiled with anguish. We are caught in bondage to suffering. We repetitiously rehearse misery-sharing conversations. We are held fast in self-loathing and degrading ritual. To be enmeshed in any kind of addiction brings great humiliation. We are prisoners of literalism. The punishing attitude or action repeats itself countless times with no meaning shining through. No symbolism beckons through the ritual. It simply grinds us down.

The religious person also knows pain, but only as a by-product of the loving union. In our attempt to reach out to the ones we love, painful things will happen. We all know this about childbirth, for example. But any creative endeavor, whether originating a new meal, a book, a sermon, a prayer, an attitude, a liturgy brings suffering. Any time we try to create a wilderness of feeling chaos and death may attack. Any of us struggling to create know this plunge into nothingness. Sometimes these forces attack us in the body and we actually fall ill.[16] In those moments part of the greatest suffering is not to know if we have fallen into masochism or have really reached what we love. Both may have occurred. Pain is not sought, then, but is not easily avoided. Thérèse tells us simply to accept it.

The more we embrace religious life, the more our defenses wear thin. We become more vulnerable to others' suffering as our devices of tuning out and numbing ourselves in the face of pain weaken. The victims of flood and famine in Bangladesh take on the faces of our own children, our own parents, our own neighbors. We suffer with the person languishing in prison, justly or unjustly. We feel the absence of one who has died, or suddenly been killed, of the baby who should have been born but died in the womb. We can no longer so easily stand aside. We are pulled into a current where everyone's life touches ours. What do we do with this heart full of these persons' unlived lives? Pray, the saint tells us, even though praying brings us more fully to share their suffering.

Thérèse's experience goes further. She wants to join Jesus in his pain, wants to join him precisely where his disciples left him and ran away. She wants to join the women who stayed at the foot of the cross. This crucial point, subtle and decisive for anyone drawn to the religious life, provides the fifth contrast between religious devotion and masochism. Here we look for relationship with what depth psychologists call a whole object, a true other, as against looking for a missing part of ourselves. The religious person, as Thérèse shows us, looks through pain toward the whole object, Jesus, with whom she wants to unite in love. She wants to become her whole self, her biggest self, in union with him, and at the same time to hide her little self in his. She desires this union above all else and will take anything which furthers it. She chooses this. She is free.

When we are pulled by masochistic impulses we are not free, we do not feel whole. We are compelled to look for what is missing in ourselves, the part without which we cannot be whole. We must find it and thus we repeat and repeat the rituals in which the missing part is hiding. We cannot do without this missing piece. It is essential, and yet we cannot find it. We end up substituting rituals of concealment for the whole of ourselves and of others. That substitution enslaves us. We are not free.

Religious persons' relation to suffering is a willing one. If necessary they are willing to enter that place of nothingness, whether brought on by bodily pain or psychological anguish, where we are stripped of every attachment that competes with love of God. Thérèse voluntarily takes nonbeing into herself in a small imitation of Jesus' large redemptive work. Like other religious geniuses, Thérèse chooses to put herself in situations where she will be separated from everything that separates her from God. She chooses the suffering that comes with giving up false crosses for the sake of what shines through, what endures, for the love that is stronger than death.[17] Thérèse says, "MY VOCATION IS LOVE!" Finally, she centered her service there: "my misison [is] making others love God, as I loved him." *"I want to spend my heaven doing good on earth . . ."* She summed it up: "To love, to be loved, and to return to earth to make Love better loved."[18] When we are enmeshed in masochistic attitudes we know nothing of the shelter of love that makes all things possible. Instead, we tangle with will power, either forsaking it or struggling to achieve it. We end up sacrificing what does not belong to us, other people's peace of mind or possessions, sometimes even their lives. We even presume to substitute ourselves in such a place as Isaac's, sacrificing our sanity, our allegiance to right and wrong, to secure and control attachment to the other.

Religious persons know a very different passion, to sacrifice only what is their own. In devotion, we offer our own life for God's work. We do not seek martyrdom, but if it comes, we know we must meet it, not as an end in itself, but for the sake of union with God. We offer what belongs to us into the larger whole of God's life in others. In masochism the reverse happens: we call others and God into our tiny selves and our meaningless rituals.

The last contrast guides us best in differentiating masochism and religious devotion. Here the results tell all. Our masochistic experience produces suffering, in ourselves and in those around us. Full of sighs and our own inferiority, refusing to claim the good given us, we leave a hole in the human circle, where bruising constantly repeats itself and evil jumps in. We act like a magnet, attracting and inflaming aggrieved feeling. Insult piles on injury. We examine every slight, real or imagined, as proof of our inferiority or others' neglect. Our pain causes pain in others. We manipulate and control others, make them feel responsible, helpless to help us, and guilty because they fail. Masochism leaves us stalled in our fruitlessness. We do not live the life given us. Round and round, like the squirrel in the cage, we miss the exit. Sadness clings to us, the sorrow of unlived life. It is not so much that our religion is a neurosis, but rather that our neurosis has become our religion. We are keenly aware how much that costs us and keenly suffer it.

The true religious, as Thérèse shows us so well, knows the opposite experience. Whether in suffering or willing, or in daring imaginative gestures, she always points to the center. She feels loved and grateful, spilling over out of her own little cup into actions and happiness in relationship to others. Joy ensues. If we follow her example, we feel ourselves alive to Love in all things. Intercession is the special result. In it, a religious person reaches to a love which is no longer possessive. Here, religious devotion may resemble masochism, but the substance is different. Here is a love where we lay down our arms, open our arms, put power and pride and self-preoccupation at the other's feet. This is the *agape* of 1 Corinthians 13. Here love is poured out lavishly without obstacles. This is the first commandment and the second too. Love is given. Love gives back. Thérèse was not on a constant high; she did not have an idealized solution to any of life's problems, which is what we seek when masochism ensnares us. She did not expect magical protection from all bad as the masochist does. In masochism we are pulled to dissolve our ego in order to get a fresh start. A true religious wants to offer up the ego, to bring it as a gift of love for love given. In our masochism, we aim to remain safe by getting rid of ourselves. In the religious impulse, we aim to give all of ourselves in union with the other, so that as the eucharistic prayer puts it, "he may dwell in us and we in him."

IV

Thérèse is not a masochist. Why, then, is she accused of being one? Because she threatens with the intensity, power, force and mystery of her loving, makes us conscious of our capacity for that loving which she says is available to all. She makes us conscious of our resistance. We fear what we will have to give up to serve God. Religious institutions, unhappily, abound in examples that inspire our worst fears—when people's gifts are denied in the name of obedience to God. Nuns with contemplative gifts are forced to do administration instead. A socially active monk is set to work in a library. An academic mind is sent to do manual labor for the poor. A nun with originating insight for new patterns of community living is forced to live the old institutional way. Religions can tell people, and has, that they are disobedient if they do not comply. This sort of sadomasochistic behavior brings suspicion on religious life. In reaction, we withdraw.

Thérèse calls us out again with sound and simple directions for the spiritual life. Above all else, we must try to discover God's intention with each individual soul and encourage it. She did that when mistress of novices. We must accept the individual as she or he really is, in the idiosyncratic expression of being, and accept it with love. Barry Ulanov writes, "One must love one's own way no matter how awkward, and in one's own words, no matter how inadequate."[19] Then we choose what God wants for us. This is Thérèse's image of littleness. Our little way in everyday life reveals the great exchanges of love. We find in daily tasks the suffering of having scrubbed off us all the dross, the inessentials, everything that competes with the exchanges of love. Thérèse helps us find images for our own way. She described her way as little, hidden, a plaything of the Divine Child. Her specific work was intercession, a work that still affects us and draws us today. Love plunged her into life. She summed it up by saying she wanted to be with Jesus in all things, to make all exchanges loving ones.

Just before she died, Thérèse could not sleep because she was suffering too much bodily pain. Her sister Céline asked what she was doing and Thérèse answered she was praying. What are you saying to Jesus, Céline asked. Thérèse answered, "I'm saying nothing to him; I'm just loving him."[20] That is the point. That is Thérèse's gift to him and to us.

THÉRÈSE AND
THE MODERN TEMPERAMENT

Barry Ulanov

Barry Ulanov is McIntosh Professor of English Emeritus, Barnard College, Columbia University, and also past Chairman of the English Department, the Program of Fine Arts, the Foreign Areas Program and the Religion Department at Barnard. His personal bibliography is varied and extensive.

A title is not a small thing. It is often what distinguishes us from others, in some way identifies us to our world. And how much a title can convey—a family connection, a professional category, from the stage of preparation, say as student or novice, to accomplishment as professor, doctor, lawyer, nun, priest. A title proclaims authority, inherited or designated by others, such as king, queen, president, general, saint. When we take title, we take possession. We establish our rights of ownership. Titleholders in sports or popular music or films are champions. By their titles they claim our attention if not always our respect. Thérèse's titles hold me, hold us. They are important. They are worthy of more than casual attention. We know them well: Little Flower of the Child Jesus, of the Holy Face. They are not only chosen titles; they are earned titles, titles of accomplishment, lived for, lived through, lived up to. They lead inexorably, I think, to the special title of category I thought it necessary to add to her list: a modern saint. When I called my biographical study *The Making of a Modern Saint*, the adjective "modern" was pivotal. It guided my thinking; it guarded my thinking. And yet, in a sense, I did not really think it out. It came unbidden. This was she, this is she, Thérèse, a modern saint, the modern saint.[1] She is, it seems to me, that saint of our time who speaks to us in words and gestures and movements of the inner life that are particularly clear to us now in this time, in this world, at the end of the century following hers. She speaks to us of us. She makes us understand much, about herself, about ourselves. Her way is simple; it is also complex. It is a little way, but it is also the largest way of all, because there is nothing of consequence to the life of the spirit missing from it.

What does this title mean, really? What does it mean to call her, Thérèse, a modern saint? What does it mean to call anything or anybody modern? Certainly it means more than simply to record of a person or a life or a doctrine that he or she or it is of recent origin, is of today's world, is of this world. Can one ever say of a saint that he or she is simply of this world? And yet we must say of Thérèse, with every emphasis, how much she is of today, for today, in and of this world, this late twentieth-century world about to pass into another century and in the passing to be seen in a new perspective, perhaps to be defined more clearly as it passes.

Thérèse is modern, I think, in many of the same ways that the large figures in the arts who are contemporary with her are modern. She is in her little and large way, her simple and complex way, in the art of the spiritual life what James Joyce is to the novel, what Igor Stravinsky and Arnold Schoenberg are to music, what T.S. Eliot is to poetry and criticism, what Pablo Picasso and Henri Matisse are to painting, what Henrik Ibsen and August Strindberg and Anton Chekhov are to the drama. She is what those imposing figures called the Modernists are, central to our epoch, definitive of it, endlessly exemplary of it. As they do over their long years, their many opportunities in their many worlds, she does in her short life, in her little world, that obscure Carmel, tucked away in a little known part of Normandy. She makes it possible for us, when we come to know her well, to put up with and to survive our world, and does so as the great moderns do, with an extraordinary, with an exemplary tough-mindedness. Hers, like theirs, is a realism that we may not yet, a hundred years later, fully understand or appreciate. It is not a naturalism, confined to surfaces, but a stubborn determined way with ideas and experiences centered on the reality beneath the surfaces. She moves, too, as so many of the moderns in the arts do, with an incomparable economy of words, movements, doctrines. To compare her to the moderns, as I propose to do, is not then to make a trivial comparison, a comparison of surfaces, nor simply to locate people of distinction in the calendar as contemporaries or near-contemporaries, nor do I make these comparisons to decorate the modern saint's name with pleasing associations.

Thérèse in her setting is, of course, like all of us in ours, a product of a particular time and place. Her understanding of God, her religious consciousness, is shaped by the language she is called to speak and the customs she is called to observe in the Lisieux of her time. As we have been made aware only too often by her detractors and even by some of her supporters, she was tutored by her family community, by her religious community, by the lineaments of the life lived in late nineteenth-century Normandy, by the Church of her time, which was in many ways an awkward church, as Paul Claudel makes wonderfully clear in describing the church architecture contemporary with Thérèse as having the appearance of a bad confession. Thérèse came from a France of ugliness and beauty, of criminals as well as of innocents, and knew that for a fact and did not dissociate herself from either the ugliness or the criminals, as we know from her remarkable intervention in the famous Pranzini case.[2] Hers was a world of simple-minded little people but also one lived in the shadows of the giants of Carmel, whose spirituality she knew and understood a great deal more thoroughly, it seems to me, than any of us writing about her has yet been able to establish as clearly as it should be established. No matter what we do, however, to place Thérèse in her setting, large or small, she remains her own wise self, anticipating, adumbrating, prophesying our time, our world, and in that curious way which I associate with the Augustinian tradition, making her substance both its content and the form with which she presents that content.

Thérèse's substance is so elusive, I think, because of this intermingling of form and content, because—as is so often true of love—the boundaries are blurred and it is at least as much in the way it is presented as in what is presented. It is elusive often enough, and

difficult at moments to grasp, but it is the love toward which we all
move and the love, however sought, however identified when found,
toward which the great moderns seem to be drawn and of which
they seem to hope to provide some understanding. It is a love in
which ends and means are inextricably interwoven, this Thérèsian
love, a love in which no matter how clumsily we move, we move
in love as a means, toward love as an end.

The movement betrays the source. In one of her poems, Thérèse
puts it simply enough:

> God asks our all, and we must give
> What he did first bestow . . .[3]

It is a circle that she draws there, that astonishing one that associates
her with Joyce, whose epics, *Ulysses* and *Finnegans Wake,* move in
large circular paths to join beginnings to ends and ends to beginnings; marriages to a new life, in a return to first wooings;
everything that achieves lasting being to its first becoming. Joyce's
Ulysses is an odd everyman, Leopold Bloom. He bears the equipment, the body, the spirit, the substance of a Jewish Irishman who
moves in almost endless circles around himself as he moves around
Dublin. Then, in their turn, his family and hordes of Dubliners
and almost all who touch them come together in their beginnings
and ends, all in one day in June in 1904, Bloomsday. In the *Wake,*
everyman is a kind of godman who rises and falls and rises again,
emerging in and energizing a whole series of "HCE" identifica-
tions, such as Humphrey Chimpden Earwicker and Haveth Childers
Earwicker and, most important, Here Comes Everybody.[4] Each
epic ends with a series of affirmations, *Ulysses* with a string of Yesses
which is much more than a loud acceptance of the sexuality to
which on the surface it may seem only to testify, the *Wake* with a
return to the opening running of the river of time in Dublin and in
all the world with which the book begins. Return, affirmation,
coming together again in the affirmation—this is Joyce's insistent
event. It lights up all his books, brings Bloom and his wife back
together, joins Bloom and Joyce's alter ego, Stephan Dedalus, Plato
with Aristotle, man with woman, body with spirit. Always in Joyce
there is some contemplation of the possibility of a new coming to-

gether, of man and wife, of old and young, of being and becoming, out of a treacherous spiritual and bodily *Exile* in the play of that name, out of the mists of a suppressed consciousness in the long story "The Dead," out of the most trivial events and the largest in the two epics.

Mediation plays an important part in Joyce's work and most often the mediation is by a woman; that earthiest of women, Molly Bloom, in *Ulysses*; that combination of earth and high heaven, Anna Livia Plurabelle, in the *Wake*, a mixture of mother and wife and goddess and saint, of every sort of womanly presence. It is much more than help that Joyce's woman brings, for what in his sometimes rude, often ironic, occasionally sentimental, and always provocative way Joyce is trying to reach is some grasp of understanding of that underlying substance, that enduring love, which he had learned about in his own beginnings. The instruction for Joyce in late nineteenth-century Ireland was not so different from Thérèse's in Normandy just a few years earlier. It was from handbooks in both cases, pious, compendious, perhaps sterner in Thomist terms in Joyce's case, all grounded in some logic and rhetoric of love. Joyce mocks the learning process in *A Portrait of the Artist as a Young Man* and *Ulysses* and the *Wake* and at the same time bends to it, even bows. His brilliant ironies in the service of mockery never altogether efface the awe edged with fear and love with which religious exercises are contemplated in his work.

Awe, fear, and love are differently expressed in Thérèse, but there is a slight mockery in her, too, as she points us to a spirituality of little things, to a systematic recognition of the large things that are contained in the little. In a letter, she plays with a line from The Song of Songs:

> How can we fear him who says: Thou hast wounded my heart, my sister, my spouse . . . with one hair of thy neck? When he speaks of a single hair having such power, he means that the least action done out of love wins his heart. How unhappy would be our lot if great deeds were expected of us, but how fortunate we are to be able to win Jesus by means of such trifles.[5]

Thus Thérèse, in what for her is an admonishing mode; thus Joyce's little people in their least actions, living out what I would call the

Thérèsian metaphysic, a philosophy and theology of being in which least actions reflect large movements of the soul and a single hair may become the occasion of salvation.

In Thérèse as in Joyce, the movement is not only circular but cyclical. She is always returning to the enactments of scriptural metaphor and gospel tale which are so much alive for her in the re-enactments she finds in her own life and the lives of those around her. Joyce says in the *Wake*, "All that has been done has yet to be done and done again."[6] The image is once again circular and cyclical, like Tim Finnegan who will fall again and rise again, like sin again, like love again. The early nurturing which both Joyce and Thérèse had in understanding one's modern self in terms drawn from an ancient instruction made both celebrants of acts of return. Each came from less than perfect backgrounds, but backgrounds that in each case proved to be as nurturing in their limitations as in their advantages. Each draws from individual and collective histories material to turn over again and again, to enlarge with each new doing, which is also an old doing. Each makes the act of writing an act of oblation.[7]

Thérèse's constant return, like Joyce's, is to her family. She has always stirring in her an awareness of her roots and she stirs a matching awareness in us, making us feel somehow in this constant recapitulation of family themes the large movements of the spiritual life when we correspond with the graces offered to us in such an awareness of our roots. It has the inexorability and the majesty of the recapitulations at the ends of movements in the last Schubert piano sonatas. The incredible fact of family for Thérèse is that she could return to it with such certainty and assurance of understanding all through her life and find it again in her last movements in, of all places, the monastery. It may not be the most generally approved pattern for conducting religious life, but there it was and it worked. Would you like your sister with you? Would you like your sisters to continue to be your sisters, in religion as in your family? One? Two? Three? It seems ridiculous even to think of as a modality for religious life, but it proved the making of a modern saint and a modern religiosity. We cannot shorten God's arm with an insistence on rules and probably can do no better by avoiding rules. We can learn from this that there are no rules, made even by the wisest of rule-makers in the religious life, that cannot be broken or stretched or enlarged when the end-product is sanctity. We see in the family gathering here a symbolic regathering of past and present, of old and new families, that transcends rules and traditions and somehow protects both.

This is the kind of gathering of spiritual and psychological resources, across cultural and religious epochs, that T.S. Eliot is so determined upon as he makes his way from *The Waste Land* to the *Four Quartets*. We move with him from a neurotic disposition, articulated with genius but still neurotic, to an authentic posture of contemplation. What we constantly confront in that astonishing career is another loving religious sensibility. He is never entirely free of neurosis, perhaps, but he develops as very few people have been able to do the skill to convert neurosis into devotion and devotion into literature. We live across tenses, he reminds us at the beginning of the *Quartets*:

> Time present and time past
> Are both perhaps present in time future,
> And time future contained in time past.

Though each is present in the others, we cannot conflate them. In the separations of time, in the dying of one to make room for the other, in the retrievals and lettings go, is nothing less than our salvation:

> If time is eternally present
> All time is unredeemable.[8]

Eliot is attempting to reach to the primordial out of the clock time in which we live in the modern world. He has some palpable understanding of the echoes of the past that can still be heard by those who will turn their ears with their eyes to what is present of the past — say in an English country garden, where once centuries ago there was a grand house and a significant life — and in their viewing of the past can anticipate the future. In any world where there are or have been human beings, the imagination can be engaged: speculation brings "perpetual possibility," and the maker of human beings can be found, even if only in echo and anticipation. We may find Eliot's an uncertain road to reconciliation of tenses, of epochs, in his peregrination through religious experiences, in his inherited understanding and misunderstanding of others' literary and religious experiences, in his determination to discover, with whatever difficulty, something that will bring him "a little consciousness." The modes of time "Allow but a little consciousness." It is no small thing to achieve even that, for "To be conscious is not to be in time."[9] But where can we go, how else can we go, except through time? In exalted pages, Eliot paraphrases, reproduces word for word, whole chunks of John of the Cross to make clear that it is only through time that we can go beyond time.[10] Isn't this a kind of commentary on love, the kind made again and again by the suitors of consciousness in their use of The Song of Songs? Isn't this what is to be found in Thérèse's use of the Song? Isn't this the essential quest in the religious life of any modern saint or modern writer of great dimension?

Thomas Stearns Eliot and Thérèse Martin are reasonably quiet in their movements toward consciousness. Ibsen's great figures, the grandly besotted figures of his dramas, charge up mountains to an end they can only glimpse as they fall away, defeated. They are unable to face, some of them, the consequences, say, of a bristling masculinity trapped in a woman's body, like Hedda Gabler. They look to make an inhuman perfection of an all-too-human relationship, as Rebecca West does in *Rosmersholm*. They are never more deformed or deforming than when they attempt to reform the world around them, to reform others and others' worlds, everything and everybody but themselves. And yet, pushing people beyond themselves, making minor disarrangements into major chaos, they bring us consciousness, at the very least of ourselves, guilty creatures sitting at a play, as Bernard Shaw describes the Ibsen audience in *The Quintessence of Ibsenism*. They make us face our own possibilities, positive as well as negative, even the graces of contemplation, in a fullness of consciousness where we must see how much more major currents in our lives, altogether positive ones, survive when they are allowed to stay minor in the way that they do in the graces and disgraces of ordinary family life. How much is to be won, in Thérèse's words, "in the least action done out of love." We are

made to see, and at great length, how much reform, true reform,
rests upon love grown from interior consciousness, as against hate
constructed upon outer cause.

The greatest of modern dramatists, I think, was Ibsen's contemporary and Thérèse's, Strindberg, master in his plays of the violences
of love, inner and outer. No men and women battle more fiercely
against each other, trying, usually in vain, to get through to each
other, than Strindberg's. His symbolic dramas are for some of us
the central texts of the modern theater, allegories of the soul in
torment, seeking solace, finding on rare occasions a little consciousness. His ultimate allegory is in a trilogy called *To Damascus.*[1] The
title says much. In a set of spirals, we accompany a central character,
The Stranger, who is in fact everyone in all three plays, from religious conversion to deconversion to reconversion. We have melo-
drama on the edge of tragedy, tragedy at the edge of comedy, built
upon and against the experience of Paul on the road to Damascus,
modern man and woman experiencing with every intensity a
coming to faith and a loss of faith and a regaining of it. In and out
of what may well be considered a divine presence, The Stranger
and all the other characters who represent various aspects of his
character struggle and lose, struggle and win, fall and rise and fall
and rise again. The Stranger is both protagonist and antagonist,
fighting for love, fighting against it, but always deeply involved in
it. My desire, Thérèse says, is to die of love as Jesus died upon the
cross. One feels the same desire in Strindberg, less ordered, less
accessible to consciousness, but in spirit not as far from the saint's
world as one might think. His characters, filled with the playwright's
own demonic force, are never satisfied with half-measures; they
push through, and even if they fall just at the edge of an all-saving
love, they bring us with them right up to that edge.

Anton Chekhov's characters are exactly the opposite. They are
really quite happy with half-measures. They are masters and mis-
tresses of half-measures. All they want is to be heard. They sit
around waiting to talk, or waiting for others to stop talking so that
they can pounce and start talking themselves. They are funny, they
are desolate, they are nagging, they are eloquent, they are rude,
they are courtly, they are long-winded, they are curt and never
quite clear about what it is they have waited so long and so impa-

tiently to say. When they finally take center stage, they are lo-
quacious sometimes beyond endurance. But they and their human
failings and spiritual longings hold us when they are well acted and
decently directed. And like so many of the other products of the
moderns whose musings about failing and whose longings for a
deepened or heightened consciousness I would compare with
Thérèse's, they send us back to look in upon ourselves with greater
courage and understanding. They make us, if we are attentive,
either stop talking or start talking, talking to ourselves, through
ourselves, beyond ourselves. "I never pity saints who suffer," wrote
Thérèse in a letter. "I know they have the grace to endure, and that
they give glory to God; but I pity those who are not holy and who
waste their sufferings."[12] In Chekhov's *Three Sisters* and *The Cherry
Orchard* and *Uncle Vanya*, nothing is wasted, even if at first the lives
looked in upon seem empty and without resource. They are not
tragedies; Chekhov himself insisted upon calling them comedies,
and they are that, comedies in the medieval sense, dramas that end
positively. They end in hope, a realistic hope, no matter how much
colored by the language and images of fantasy. The hope is not the
one openly expressed—to save the old home and land of *The Cherry
Orchard*, to return to Moscow as the Three Sisters and their brother
never cease planning to do, to make a life of mere hanging on into
something grandly significant as Uncle Vanya schemes to do. The
hope is hope itself, hope made into a faith, hope anatomized at the
edge of despair and all the more convincing for being seen for what
it is and how and where it may turn up. There is realism here, what
might be called Thérèsian realism. It is never sentimental. It has an
Augustinian grace of form, presenting its substance indissolubly
caught up in form, the substance of faith hoped for, of love
guessed at.

It is such substance, less easily defined but unmistakably present,
that we get so often in the best painting of our time, which for much
too long devout people have pushed aside from their viewing, as if
it were irrelevant to them, indecent even one might conclude from
their captious dismissals. The fact that it is the painting of genius is
not enough, apparently. But where there is genius, there is love,
and where there is love there must be attention. Where the love of
the painters contemporary with this great central lover of our

time, Thérèse, is so close in intensity of devotion to their art to her intensity of devotion to her calling, we had better pay attention. The parallels are instructive. What did painters like Picasso and Matisse do with their devotion? Where did they take their intensity? They anatomized their world, took it apart, its lines and colors and textures, its spatial dimensions, to see what made it work or not work. Picasso and Braque and their cubist confrères brought everything that caught their attention as material for painting into a two-dimensional picture plane. What would it be like, they asked themselves, to see everything flattened to the surface dimensions of canvas and board and paper, stripped of the conventions of third-dimensional perspective. What would it be like to see everything in those two dimensions, every scrap of visible surface in a given area, even if we must see through some scraps to see others? Held to those flat surfaces, we see more, not less, in a greatly enlarged visual field which, even as it dwells on the surface, takes us well below the surface. We become conscious of seeing, of the act of seeing, of the art of seeing, of what seeing brings to consciousness, as a result of the cubist revolution. And everybody's viewing has been changed by the cubists, whether they know it or not, even when they shrug it off or fight fiercely against it.

The cubist vision is pervasive. It has been with us more and more strongly since well before World War I. It may come through a comic strip, a television commercial, a flamboyant holy card. Much that we see, we see in two-dimensional terms—two eyes on the same side of a cartoon face, a transparent set of table legs in which all four legs occupy the same flattened space, bits of all-over design from a dress fabric, a newspaper or magazine, wallpaper, a chair, a couch. And what Picasso and the cubists do with the picture plane, reducing and enlarging simultaneously, Matisse does with color and line, finding in the rhythms of color and in incomplete, insinuating outline a whole new modality of being. That is what such attention to the constituents of an art can bring. That is what such anatomization means.

When we hear music intensely proclaiming its essentials in Schoenberg and Stravinsky, the one in terms of the basic half-tone relationships of Western music, the other pursuing its possibilities for rhythmic invention, we are at the center of another majestic anatomizing. All who anatomize this way work toward centers, trying to discover how form slips into content, how color, line, rhythm, sound, dimensions of space and time and human relationship reveal some inexorable principle. It is a world of successes and defeats they bring us, with definition by persuasive example rather than any miracle of reductive verbalization. They are wonderfully concentrated and they lead us to a similar fixation on central points of being and becoming as their work narrates for us their concern and their experience. When Thérèse anatomizes love, she reflects the same sort of concentration, never forgetting the defeats. "I have not always been so enraptured by practising charity," she tells us, recording in her anatomization of love all that comes with the movement of the soul toward God or neighbor, the negative with the positive.[13]

The point of so many of these figures is always to understand more, to appropriate more, through their psyches, through their souls, through their materials, through their methods. Theirs is a holy greed to know more about what it is that they are gifted to do with words or pigments or sounds or the postures of prayer, what it is that draws them, takes them so strongly at the core of their being, gathers them in. The central text of the Song of Songs for Thérèse says it simply, eloquently: "Draw me: we will run after Thee to the odor of thy ointments." She meditates with this text on the task given to her to pray for two missionary priests. They are spiritual brothers for her, replacements as she sees them for her own little brothers who died in childhood. The words "Draw me" lead her to say that the Lord, in drawing her in, gathering her in, will also take to himself the souls she loves. But it is enough, she says, to say "Draw me." She need not fill in all the lines. She can flatten the dimensions of the text to the two words that suggest all the rest. This is her modernity, the reduction to fundamentals. This is her kind of anatomizing. Just say "Draw me"; the rest will be understood where it must be understood: "When a soul has been captivated by the intoxicating odor of your ointments, she cannot run alone. Every soul she loves is drawn after her—a natural consequence of her being drawn to you."[14]

After this passage in Thérèse, there is a rapturous explosion of the fires of love. She is at once erotic and chaste, not as startling or self-contradictory a combination as some may think. All she loves, she loves in Jesus. In Jesus, she loves all. Hers is not a merely dutiful love, nor even a dutifully rhetorical love. It is rather a superb example of willing execution of the duties of love, of happy use of the rhetoric of love, handsomely shaped by her exercises as a religious and by her restlessly anatomizing spirituality. It is worthy in its way to be set beside the work of other great votaries of the Song, the earlier Teresa, John of the Cross, Bernard of Clairvaux, William of Saint-Thierry, Origen, Gregory of Nyssa. We are required to put Thérèse in this exalted category, I think, for what she offers us in her bursts of poeticized theology is an eschatology in brief. The Song as she understands it, love as she understands it, will take us where we must go, even if we do not realize very clearly that that is where we must go. She explains that she does not fly in such great confidence to God because she has been preserved from mortal sin; she would be equally sure, absolutely confident, if she were weighed down with every possible sin. If that were so, she would throw herself into the arms of Jesus, remembering his love of the prodigal son, imitating the Magdalene's "astonishing—or rather her loving—brazenness which charmed the heart of Jesus,"[15] and has altogether won her own—Thérèse's—heart. What she is offering here is just that wholeness of being that a metaphysic should present. But her handsomely crafted, late nineteenth-century outpouring is even more than that. She is offering us a psychology and an esthetic as well.

Hers is a gathering of being in which thought and feeling and practise are seamlessly joined. And all are focused on that abandonment which, she understood with her canny spiritual insight, one does not have to have graces of her kind to imitate. One must simply understand that graces somewhere in that order of being are what really matter and be persuaded that one can correspond with those graces, at whatever level they are offered. One must be willing to follow along with one's own littleness. "O Jesus," Thérèse exclaims, "if only I could tell all little souls . . ." What follows, in French, is "combien ta condescendance est ineffable."[16] Using cognates, in a literal translation, this becomes "how ineffable your condescension is." One translation makes it "how immeasurable is your condescension." But surely she is saying how impossible it is to make the ineffable—the unutterable—effable; it is not simply im-measurable, it is beyond words, unspeakable. And so it is with "condescendance"; "condescension" will not do; what Thérèse means is "submission." She is talking in this remarkable document, written just a year before her death, in the language of the theology of kenosis, of Jesus' self-abasement. He is not being condescending —affable to his inferiors—but submissive, putting himself alongside, at the same level as, the rest of humankind. But, Thérèse is saying, for all the unspeakable nature of this submission, its reach beyond natural understanding and the vocabulary of natural understanding, it is something that happens in nature, in our world, and can happen at any time to anyone, especially to little ones, to those like herself, feeble souls, though she is sure none more feeble than herself could be found.

Because this unspeakable submission of the Lord is true, it must be spoken about, even if one must say after having spoken, "I cannot speak about it." And so she says that every great favor would be heaped upon feeble souls if only they abandoned themselves to the Lord with utter confidence, and so she ends her letter, tracing the secrets entrusted to her by Jesus, with a prayer to him to choose a horde of such victims, little ones, feeble ones, worthy of his love. That is her way of giving voice somehow to the unspeakable. She cannot keep quiet.

It is customary even among those zealous in their devotion to Thérèse to make apologies for this sort of outpouring. One of her better translators, John Beevers, in his introduction to his version of the autobiography, tells us that "As literature it cannot be com-pared with St Augustine's *Confessions,* with St Teresa's autobiog-raphy, or with St Francis de Sales's *Introduction to a Devout Life.*" Frequently, he says, somebody reading Thérèse's work "for the first time will be quite unimpressed and may even find it distasteful because it is written in the idiom of an age which, though near us in time, is emotionally far distant from us." There is hope, however: "Once read, it cannot be forgotten." And, he assures us, it does have a remarkable "range of appeal," from the simple and "ill-educated" to "great scholars."[17] I have a different assurance. I say *The Story of a Soul* can be compared with precisely those volumes Beevers says it does not match. It is one of the great spiritual narratives, fervent in a modern way as Teresa of Avila's autobiography is in a sixteenth-century mode. It is honest as Augustine is in his *Confessions,* if more brief, in revealing the pulse of love in the most hidden depths in a saint's interiority. And it is, I suspect, more useful for moderns than Francis de Sales in the cultivation of the life of devotion. What is there is to be drawn from Thérèse and to be shared with her—a knowing, joining, fulfilling modern spirituality. What she makes accessible to us is what is caught up in two German words—*Innerlichkeit,* inwardness, profundity, warmth; and *Innigkeit,* tenderness, ardor, intimacy—an inspired subjectivity completely given over to what she knows to be objective truth.

What those miss who feel in spite of their devotion to Thérèse there is something they must apologize for—stylistic limitations, an old and discredited idiom—is exactly that which makes her modern, alive to us, clear, winning. She is an anatomizer of the materials of her art as the great moderns are of theirs. As Joyce took apart the languages of daytime fantasy and nighttime dream to make new sense of the novel and of everyman in his modern setting, as Schoenberg looked to apply what he thought the essential arithmetic of Western music to contents as large as the relationship of Moses and Aaron, as Matisse worked out a vastly simplified grammar of color and syntax of line for the Chapel of the Rosary of the Domincans in Vence, as Eliot joined the cadences of modern verse form and ancient patterns, personal experience and mystical tradition, in the *Quartets,* so Thérèse addressed sanctity.

Thérèse's is a double anatomization, to compare God's love for us and ours for God, and to discover, by constant probing, especially of her own experience, what our love for God might become, what development is open to it. It is a comparative method not unlike that used in that valuable pairing of selections from *The Imitation of Christ* and the works of Thérèse which is called *Just for Today.* There, in a work much larger than its unassuming title suggests, we see how approaches to a love-centered life of the spirit more than four hundred years apart in time can come together. Bringing them together does not make Thérèse a contemporary of Thomas à Kempis or whoever wrote the *Imitation,* nor does it make the *Imitation* into a modern work. But it is fair to follow the suggestion of Ronald Knox in his finely made little introduction, to put a holy card of Thérèse in a copy of the *Imitation*. It will then no longer be anonymous: "she did not write it, but much more importantly, she lived it."

Msgr Knox knows exactly what this modern spiritual writer has accomplished. "Our minds tend to confuse what is simple with what is easy," he reminds us. Then he proposes a demonstration of Thérèse's tough-minded performance. Look up any day in this volume, which is arranged by days to cover a full year's spiritual reading: "you will find something which is so simple that you could have thought of it for yourself; so far from easy, that you have spent a lifetime not doing it." Here, in Thérèse and the *Imitation,* he tells us, are two witnesses, "faithful as those of the Apocalypse, to brush away our feeble excuses with their pitiless realism. The phrases may be well enough known, but they have been fixed in place "in laborious copperplate by a fifteenth-century ascetic, and retraced, God knows how laboriously, by a childish hand, contemporary with ourselves."[18]

Thérèse's is a childish hand; one sees that in the copybooks and letters in which she incised her wisdom. It is the hand of a young girl, of an adolescent nun, of a young woman, finally, just barely beyond girlhood.[19] But the words reveal a grownup in the spiritual life, one of a maturity that few of us many years older than she can even begin to approach. It is the way she lives the pulses of love that makes her book entirely worthy of comparison with the *Imitation,* with Augustine or the Spanish Teresa or Francis de Sales. Her anatomization of sanctity comes to us, in word and act, in the accents and rhythms of our time. She is indeed our contemporary, very much a modern, something she herself recognized. In this age of inventions, she tells us, she has an immediate aid for her spiritual life — elevators. No need any longer to walk up endless stairs. She is too small, she has noticed, to climb the rough, steep stairs of perfection. She has her elevator in Scripture. From Proverbs 9:4, she takes "Whosoever is a little one, let him come to me"; from Isaiah 66:12-13, "You shall be carried at the breasts and upon the knees; as one whom the mother caresses, so will I comfort you."[20] Her vehicle is Scripture, but Scripture reduced, economized, made accessible to us in pithy extracts. Hers is an economy of salvation which has room for even the most minuscule forms of love. Her anatomization of the life of the spirit makes its hallowed paths small enough for the least of us.

It is not enough to say of Thérèse's little way that it is accessible to the least of us; it is specifically directed to the least of us. We must remember here, too, that this is not because her spirituality is a reduction to the lowest common denominator, but because she is herself, in every way that she could make herself, one with the least among us. That does not mean making herself more small or humble; she is in essence one of the small and humble. What she had to do was to learn what that meant. The learning became her prophetic wisdom, forecasting what may be the most considerable achievement of the twentieth century.

In a time of genocide, of terrorism, of cruelty that so far outstrips anything known or practised in the past that it is a mockery to speak of medieval torture chambers, we have nonetheless distinguished ourselves with an enlargement of compassion that is very new indeed. We have come to see the value of the least of us, of the most deformed and disadvantaged. Nobody is to be discarded. All are wanted, by somebody, somewhere. By our insistence on the worth of the hitherto spurned, the very least of us, we have demonstrated in the midst of the horrors of our time an understanding of Thérèsian wisdom and a desire to follow it where it leads. To be handicapped, physically, mentally, or psychically, we have begun to recognize, is not necessarily to be a candidate for rejection. It may in fact be an opening to a new set of acts of love. Mind you, we do not do this by saying we—they—whoever—are anything different from what we—or they—are. If we are handicapped, in any way, if our mental or psychic structures are not quite right, we must accept that as fact and deal with it as fact. But we must also see that in our bumbling, stumbling, awkward ways we bring something of value with us—a different consciousness of things, a different mode of being. This is surely one of the great achievements of our time, to see this value, to proclaim it, to protect it. This is what Thérèse discovered in her anatomy of love, the little way of the little people, the way, as she understood it, to the inner courts above. "Une petite voie," she calls it, "bien droite, bien courte, une petite voie nouvelle"—a little way, unmistakably direct, short, and altogether new.[21]

Does this seem like a discredited idiom, the product of an age emotionally distant from us? Thérèse uses no euphemisms and makes herself one with the least, the most feeble, as those most commendable to the incarnate God. Is that a dated spirituality or a clumsy one, something left over from the dark observances of an obscure Norman Carmel of a hundred years ago? Can we speak in such terms of one whose skill is to turn surface limitations into inner achievements, of a modernist who anatomizes of all things, not sounds, not words, or colors, or lines, but love? She is—it must be repeated—our contemporary, who shows us in her almost every act how to go beyond surfaces to find the pulse of ancient rhythms beneath modern stresses, to discover again the knowledge that is an end in itself, the love that makes us one with being itself.

Still, we remain perplexed by Thérèse, almost all of us who are apparently not endowed with the mystical graces, or if we are do not see that we are, or if we see that we may be so graced do not know what to do about it. She is so sure of herself in her love. In a time of such massive self-doubt, her certainties baffle us even as they please us. They need not do so any more than those of the great moderns in the arts. What we find in her, as in them, is a willing probing after the truth, which she is certain is to be found at the end of the contemplative journey which all of us are called to take—but not only at the end. She reminds us many times of that ancient truth that the journeying is in itself a form of the truth.

Thérèse, this most modern of saints, has shown us here, now, in this time, the way. This is what her anatomy of love offers us to understand and take up here, now, in this time—a work, a set of words, a way of life. The least of us can understand it; so can the largest. She spoke—she speaks—to everyone. One does not have to be locked away in a remote religious community to imitate Thérèse or to live in any other kind of religious community, but equally, one does not have to deny oneself a full Thérèsian understanding because one lives in a religious community. Nor can we say of ourselves that the imitation of Thérèse is absolutely beyond us, that we cannot even attempt it, because we do not possess her kind of heroic virtue. How would we know? How would anyone know? It was not until the full process of examination for canonization was well under way that anybody was willing to attempt to calibrate Thérèse's heroic virtue and to measure it against some kind of scale, in numbers and words. Littleness is enough and all of us can boast of that. Feebleness may be better, and who of us is not skilled at being feeble in something? That is enough—to remind ourselves of our feebleness, not to be proud of it, not to use it as an inverted rhetoric of sanctity, as a negative capability, to make sure that we are seen as small enough to be big enough. It is enough to be just what we are and to acknowledge with appreciation the graces of a form of life in which the truth that is love has its own peculiar compelling being. It is what makes Thérèse for me the special doctor of the spiritual life of the modern world.[22] It is what makes her, I think, somebody to celebrate, not simply in a religious setting, but in the special setting of modernity where her genius can be compared—and better understood for being compared—with anyone else distinguished for the anatomization of some central part of being.

THÉRÈSE OF LISIEUX:
A CHALLENGE FOR
DOCTRINE AND THEOLOGY—
FORERUNNER OF VATICAN III

William M. Thompson

William Thompson is a professor of theology at Duquesne University in Pittsburgh. In the past decade he has had several books published by Paulist Press.

What are her theological credentials? By what right is she a challenge to the Church's teaching and doctrinal function? By virtue of what might she be a forerunner of a council to come? The "Thérèse" event" is so rich and so complex, with so many contours, that one must hesitate to say. But perhaps she herself gives us a decisive clue in her Manuscript C when, speaking of her great ordeal, she says of God: ". . . he was giving me even the experience of *years*" (S:210). A theology which wants to view itself as critical reflection upon Christian experience (which is the intersection between human openness and divine initiative), and a view of doctrine as a pastorally needed intensification of aspects of Christian experience, will find in Thérèse the credentials of experience, an experience whose attractive form compels and challenges even while it invites.

André Combes, Hans Urs von Balthasar, and René Laurentin have written book-length theological treatments of Thérèse, and Combes has even taught an entire course on her at the Lateran, so there can be no question here of developing anything like the full theological response which Thérèse deserves. At first I had planned to review these theologians' perspectives in a summary way, but even that has proven impossible within the limits of this presentation. More modestly, then, let me say that I have been guided by these studies, and I'm sure that partly through them, partly through my own contemplation of Thérèse, and partly through some other helpful studies, I've noticed something like a glowing center, or at least a significant focus, within our great saint. And it is with an eye upon this center or focus that I would like to look at doctrine, theology, and even the question of a future ecumenical council.

A particularly fine example of this glowing center comes toward the end of Manuscript A, as Thérèse imaginatively writes up her "wedding invitation" to her coming profession:

> God Almighty, Creator of Heaven and Earth, Sovereign Ruler of the Universe, and the Most Glorious Virgin Mary, Queen of the Heavenly Court, announce to you the Spiritual Espousals of Their August Son, Jesus, King of kings, and Lord of lords, with little Thérèse Martin, now Princess and Lady of His Kingdoms of the Holy Childhood and the Passion, assigned to her in dowry by her Divine Spouse, from which Kingdoms she holds her titles of nobility—of the Child Jesus and the Holy Face (S:168).

Here we glimpse the creative and tension-filled interplay between devotion to Jesus the Child and Jesus the broken-humiliated-suffering one, or, rather than projecting outward onto Jesus but introjecting inwards, into Thérèse, the creative tension between the joyful child, who knows herself especially loved, and the somewhat withdrawn, hurting and vulnerable one, who has lived through her own passions of continuous separations, the near-breakdown of "St Vitus' dance" (or some serious psychosomatic malady), the rejection by schoolmates, and the seemingly endless series of dark nights. Without pretending that she always experienced this "devotion" to the child and to the passion at an equal pitch, still I think the two dimensions together reveal, with growing, intersecting, and spiraling magnitude, something of the center of the Thérèsian *attrait.*

It is this back and forth, to-and-fro movement between infancy and passion, the child and suffering, Jesus' infancy and Jesus' cross, that I would like to probe in this essay. Interestingly, if we follow the lead of literary critics, paying attention to the subtle interrelation between form and content, this child-passion interplay somewhat characterizes the very form and structure of Thérèse's literary remains themselves. Is there not a playful, childlike, carefree structuring to the autobiography, a rough and unfinished feel to it, and maybe even something of the child's feeling that one's own world is the very center of the universe itself? And what about the playfulness of her rich world of metaphors? Yet, something of the suffering and the passion comes through too, in the autobiography's unpolished, jagged, even bumpy form, its rough, "notebook" character, and perhaps especially in its radical distancing from its author. For there is something of a separation between every author and her or his book, but in Thérèse's case this was radical: a complete giving over of the text to others, even to the point of letting it be destroyed or retouched or restored, as the case may be. Surely this is a kind of passion for the self, and one experiences it almost mimetically by reading the work itself: the Thérèse we read is the Thérèse "delivered over" to those who have restored the text for us. One experiences this "delivered over Thérèse"—the evangelical "handed over" (?)—even more emphatically if one has first read the earlier even more touched up version.

What did Thérèse mean by "the child" and by "the passion" (of the "Holy Face")? The latter is perhaps the easier to speak about (although surely not the easier to do!): passion is passion, suffering, *in forma Christi.* Again, Manuscript A:

> The little flower transplanted to Mount Carmel was to expand under the shadow of the cross. The tears and blood of Jesus were to be her dew, and her Sun was his adorable Face veiled with tears . . . Ah! I desired that, like the Face of Jesus, "my face be truly hidden, and that no one on earth would know me." I thirsted after suffering and I longed to be forgotten (S:151-52).[1]

And what about the child? This seems more difficult, and surely Thérèse grew in her awareness of what it means, as she most surely grew in her awareness of what the passion means.[2] Patricia O'Connor surely sounds correct when she says that "To Thérèse the word 'child' meant something distinct from the dependent, naive behavior suggested by the word 'childish.'"[3] This is something all the Thérèsian scholars are at pains to point out. And most recently Monica Furlong's *Thérèse of Lisieux* tries to do this again emphatically. But what, then? For the time being, I find rather helpful Thérèse's statement (in LC, 139):

> To be little is not attributing to oneself the virtues that one practices, believing oneself capable of anything, but to recognize that God places this treasure in the hands of his little child to be used when necessary; but it remains always God's treasure. Finally, it is not to become discouraged over one's faults, for children fall often, but they are too little to hurt themselves very much.[4]

If we follow the lead of this text, the child seems to symbolize a healthy sense of dependence, a lack of pretentiousness, but also a gladsome sense of being cared for, as well as an optimistic openness that comes from this kind of deep security. Here childhood wears a rather more positive face. Interestingly Thérèse seems to combine something of the negativities of childhood (children are, after all, weak, untutored, etc.) with a somewhat modern-sounding appreciation of the dignity of childhood: littleness becomes strength, smallness is dignity, and so on.[5] Not surprisingly for Thérèse, we meet the Gospel theme of kenosis: emptiness as fulness, weakness as strength, etc.

With all of this as preface, let me come back to the dimension of the to-and-fro movement between these two, childhood and passion. If you will, there is for Thérèse "this marvellous play of gazing and turning away" from the Holy Face, as Von Balthasar suggests. Remember, too, the wedding or espousal context of the profession invitation above, a context which highlights the interrelational, to-and-fro, playful and serious, present and absent, attuned and withdrawing nature of this experience. Here Von Balthasar shows how the game of the child moves along with a sensitivity to the humiliated Holy Face, and after thinking about this, he goes on to comment:

> Her secret intercourse with the Holy Face should not be seen as separate from the devotion which inspired her first title of the Child Jesus. If the depth of her childishness is only revealed to those who also take into account her adoration of the head covered with blood, the boldness of this later devotion needs to be seen in terms of her childishness if it is to be properly understood.[6]

Following this lead, might we say that the Thérèsian childhood —in the main—is the principle of novelty, creativity, openness, exploration, wonder, while the Thérèsian passion—in the main—is the principle of self-critique, purgation, watchfulness against narcissism, etc.? If you will, the child remains critically open, rather than naively accepting of all, through the purgative fires of the lived out devotion to the Holy Face. And the Thérèse who is made self-critical through her passional purging of the ego is freed from crippling fear, closure, and brooding stasis through the free play of the child. This is a movement, a back and forth, to-and-fro experience, and not a once for all achievment. Just as one must move through the narrative of the autobiography, so one must move through this experience. And as the autobiographical experience seems repetitive, a return and yet a movement ahead, a to-and-fro, so childhood and holy face constitute a similar spiral in the world of our saint.

It seems to me, now, that this rather potent "child-passion dialectic" led Thérèse toward some remarkable challenges for the Church's doctrine and theology, and may still continue to do so. Let me use the word "doctrine" in its ample sense as referring to the Church's function of guiding primarily the mind. In this sense, the doctrinal function is an aspect of the Church's larger ministry of pastoral guidance. I will concern myself with theology only in the sense in which it, too, can draw fruitful lessons from what Thérèse can teach us about doctrine. In what follows, let us ask ourselves what clues the sanctified experience of St Thérèse might offer us for the future exercise of the Church's doctrinal function and for the future of a theology at least partly in service to that doctrinal ministry. At the end, I will come back to the theme of "Vatican III."

First, Thérèse's experience suggests that the Church's doctrinal ministry must surely continue.[7] This may seem rather obvious, but I think there are pressures, felt continuously through the ages, and now again in our own time, which make it seem less obvious. It has always been the temptation of the elite, the privileged, the learned (the gnostics) to think that they transcend the needs of the untutored rabble. Perhaps the latter still need the Church's official guidance, but they surely do not. Now as the possibility of education becomes more fully democratized, if you will, at least here in the West, surely one of its shadows is this constant "neo-gnostic" temptation.

During her final passion, Thérèse, on the other hand, says that she offers "up these very great pains to obtain the light of faith for poor unbelievers, for all those who separate themselves from the Church's beliefs" (LC:258). She has a sense of needing to adhere to those beliefs. And I've often thought that one aspect of her final great trial of faith (about believing the Church's teachings on the life-after) was to bring her to a profound sense of the danger of gnosticism in her own life, a sense of her own need to walk humbly by faith, not simply by knowledge (*gnosis*). Pure faith, perhaps the gift of this trial, is a faith purged from gnostic arrogance.

In any case, I would suggest that our continual need for the guidance of the Church's doctrinal ministry is a corollary of both the Thérèsian devotion to the child, and that to the passion. Despite the element of boldness in the child, there is also that of littleness, dependence, humility, nonpretentiousness. Thérèse is quite aware of the danger of trying to measure the "divine power" in terms of one's own "narrow" mind (S:209). Mystery humbles, and humility opens one to guidance. That's one of the reasons for becoming a Carmelite, joining a community, the *ecclesiola in loco parentis*. Learning to deal with Mystery doesn't seem to be like learning to drive a car. In the latter case, there usually comes a point where one is on one's own, without the teacher. In the former, one can always learn more, and the Church's doctrinal ministry sacramentalizes that "always-more-to-be-learned" dimension.

The child's littleness creates a space for the other, as her playful metaphor of herself as the "little zero" hauntingly illustrates. Writing to her "priest-friend," she says:

. . . Let us work together for the salvation of souls; I of course can do very little, absolutely nothing, in fact, alone; what encourages me is the thought that by your side I can be of *some* use; after all, zero, by itself has no value, but put alongside *one* it becomes potent, always provided it is put on the *proper side,* after and not before! . . . So please, Brother, be good enough to send your blessing to the *little zero* the good God has put beside you.[8]

Thérèse's anthropology is ecclesial and social through and through: "I want to be a daughter of the Church," she said, like the great St Teresa of Avila (S:253).

The Thérèsian devotion to the suffering Holy face also involves, as corollary, serious commitment to the Church's doctrinal guidance, I think. Thérèse learned, not only the child's playful sense of solidarity, but also the sense of our brokenness, our sinfulness. Not a little of her attractiveness stems from her own brokenness itself: the little girl who suffered from what some have thought to be St Vitus' dance is a girl destined to know much about the shadow dimension of existence. Again, I would just mention the not unimportant connection between Thérèse's last great trial of faith and her subtle development in appreciation of the Church's doctrine, in this case, the doctrine of the life-after. As she grows in her living out of the passion—as the Holy Face becomes the mirror of her own—she comes to an awareness of her own real fragility and ability to be tempted, even intellectually. And thus she comes, may I suggest, to a deepened appreciation of doctrinal guidance through the cross.

"At this time I was enjoying such a living faith, such a *clear* faith," Thérèse says, "that the thought of heaven made up all my happiness, and I was unable to believe there were really impious people who had no faith." Here Thérèse is very sure, but perhaps rather too sure, of her doctrinal orthodoxy. But then came the great ordeal, and the important awareness of our underside: ". . . Jesus made me feel that there really were souls who have no faith, and who, through the abuse of grace, lost this precious treasure . . ." Thérèse is not just speaking of others: "He permitted my soul to be invaded by the thickest darkness, and that the thought of heaven, up until then so sweet to me, be no longer anything but the cause of struggle and torment" (S:211). *Per Crucem ad Lucem,* through the cross to the Light of Faith, the great theologian of mysticism Von Hügel would say.[9] Theologies which stay in touch with our cruciform kind of existence understand these things!

My second corollary for doctrine from the Thérèsian experience is a bit more difficult to express. Much as she is a daughter of the Church, both the child's boldness and the critical insight which comes from the passional Holy Face combine in her to create a certain "relativization," humbling, purifying, perhaps even critique of the Church's doctrinal guidance. This is the side of Thérèse which bothers Von Balthasar in his great theological study of the saint, for he feels that at times Thérèse manifests a lack of appreciation for the fullness of the Church's tradition, a tendency to shrink God's ways to the ways she knows only through her own experience, all of which probably stems from "the lack of contact between her and the Church's ministry."[10] While it will become apparant that I see Thérèse somewhat differently in this respect, still I think Von Balthasar is enormously helpful in characterizing Thérèse's theology as "existential": this highlights the attentiveness to her experience, which is the source of her boldness and her mature wisdom.[11]

There seems to be in Thérèse a heightened sense of the personal self (not individualistic self!), of the irreplaceability and irreducibility of the unique self, which may well be one of her most important contributions to our understanding of the Church's doctrinal function, surprisingly enough. Sr Geneviève of St Teresa (Thérèse's sister Céline) seems to surface this "intensified self," in her beatification testimony for her sister, when she tells us that "she had no spiritual director," in the strict sense. For she "saw what she had to do so clearly that she never felt the need to ask."[12] And perhaps it is this somewhat "precocious" self that lies behind her bold statement that her little way is "very straight, very short, and totally new" (S:207). And was Thérèse thinking of herself in her little story about Sr Marie of the Eucharist who, in wanting to light candles for a procession, found herself lacking matches, and so turned to the little lamp burning in front of the relics? With it she succeeded in lighting her own, and those of the entire community.

It was . . . the half-extinguished little lamp which had produced all these beautiful flames which, in their turn, could produce an infinity of others and even light the whole universe. Nevertheless, it would always be the little lamp which would be first cause of all this light.

Yes, a very little spark will be capable of giving birth to great lights in the Church . . . (LC:99-100)

In many ways, Thérèse seems to be a woman of the modern age (Von Balthasar sees her as the Catholic answer to the Protestant Reformation[13]): her little way is a kind of Catholic form of the priesthood of the people in the Church. Perhaps, then, her sense of the person's dignity (the little one, without titles, without a *"de"* in one's name [S:121]) owes something to this modern sense. And surely, too, to the evangelical teaching on God's love for us, so celebrated by Thérèse in Manuscripts B and C. And these two sources are not necessarily incompatible. The God who can speak to us in our modern age is a God who can help us, through that age, recover as yet deeper truths in the Scriptures (and vice versa!).

In any case, I would like to suggest that Thérèse's sense of the personal[14] is not simply a now antiquated, embarrassing residue of her "modern temperament," but an enduringly true appropriation of Jesus' revelation of love, which has an especial importance in our "post-modern" atmosphere. If the mark of the latter is to rehabilitate the social and the ecclesial (tradition in that sense), the mark of the former is to attune us to the unique person as never able to be swallowed up in the collective, even the collective of the Church; to attune us to the originating sources of personal experience as the ground for God's fresh beginnings in history and the Church; to attune us to the never-fully-conceptualizable unique person's experience as the ground for ongoing renewal and critique in the Church.[15]

It may well be the case that the modern spirit, perhaps particularly in the "developed" West, must continue to wrestle with the demon of an exaggerated individualism-tending-to-slide-into-narcissism. But it seems also true that the final source which will enable us to do this, to rise above this kind of cultural conditioning, is not a new form of ecclesial fascism (itself a form of cultural conditioning) but a Church which is the custodian of the irreplaceable person, whose unique heart is the source of both corruption and renewal (cf. Mk. 7:17-23). Part of the appeal of Thérèse, I think, is her attempt to carve out an inhabitable space between just such an individualism (the typical "Catholic" perception of the Protestantism and Modernism of her time) and the ecclesial fascism which was rather powerful in her own Catholic world. Her Little Way was, surely, a "Catholic" form of the Protestant priesthood of all believers, a radical critique of all ecclesial elitism. And precisely because she always refused to sanction the crushing of anyone, no matter how small, she became an expert in the "science of love," contributing one of the most original "love models" of the Church in the entire history of theology.[16]

So we must struggle through to a new, post-modern rehabilitation of the social and the ecclesial. But under Thérèse's guidance, it must not occur by bypassing the sovereign and irreplaceable person, but through the renewed sense of the person. It is the "little candle" which lights up the others, let us remember.

Again, I would suggest that the Thérèsian discovery of the irreplaceable self is rooted in her two-in-once commitment to Jesus' infancy and his passion (Holy Face). The infant/child expresses her sense of freedom, her personal interiority, the sacred space which frees her from institutional smothering; her "attic world," to use O'Connor's phrase for her early "breathing" space.[17] Or, as expressed in a literary way, Thérèse tends to think in metaphors/images. This is a more primal, originary form of attending to experience than analytic thought, more humble, suggestive, open to deeper nuances—in a word, creative or fresh. This is where Thérèse starts. And theology and Church teaching should start here too, and return here.

The Holy Face expresses her growing maturity, her struggle against narcissism, her awareness, too, of the sinister forces which put Jesus down, the darkside of existence. She could be quite bold, like the child: in her critique of an exaggerated and distorted view of Jesus' divinity (LC:159), of a distorted Mariology (LC:161), of ecclesial and social elitism, even of the senseless exclusion of women from positions of authority, especially the priesthood.[18] In her ability to illuminate the shadows, there was something of the hunting dog in her:

I am a "little hunting dog," I am the one who runs after the game all day. You know, the hunters (novice-mistresses and prioresses) are too big to hide in the bushes; but a little dog . . . well, it has a sharp nose, and naturally it can slip in anywhere! So I keep a close watch, and the hunters are not dissatisfied with their little dog.[19]

But what keeps the dog, if not simply tame, at least not wild? Surely it is the maturity of the cross, the Holy Face whose mirror image which Thérèse is enables her to boldly propose modulations in the Church's guidance which truly are for the Church, not for her own to-be-pampered ego. And, of course, here we have, applied to doctrine, the reality of Thérèse's missionary apostolate, I think.

I think we may discern yet a third corollary from the Thérèsian experience for the Church's doctrinal ministry in all that we have just said. Is there not embedded in the Little Way something of a new intimation and even celebration of a Catholic form of the "democratic principle" (or, because the term "democracy" is open to such a variety of meanings, perhaps we should say "collegial principle") which may have important implications for the Church's exercise of its magisterial function? We often confine Thérèse's little way to the area of the spiritual life, understanding the latter in rather narrow, personalistic terms. In this way, perhaps we circumscribe the explosion which Thérèse is too much, taming her and failing to bring out the fuller theological and doctrinal implications of her life and work. But can her celebration of the small, the non-elite, be so easily confined? The answer must be no, for a theology and doctrine which wants to root itself in the experience of the saints and mystics.

Surely, on one of its registers, the Little Way is an exaltation of the common, the lowly, and in that sense a critique of all elitism. Clearly her great elevator metaphor (S:207) is the "classic" expression of her way, but maybe one more expression of it might help.

. . . how this difference that exists here on earth between masters and servants proves so well that there is a heaven where each one will be placed according to his interior merit, where all will be seated at the heavenly Father's banquet. But, then, what a Servant we shall have, since Jesus has said: "He will come and serve them!" [Lk. 12:37] This will be the moment for the poor, and especially for the little ones to be recompensed amply for their humiliations (LC:142).

In some sense, Thérèse seems to be wishing here for what some would call the empowerment of the little. She universalizes the "precocious self" that she is. And is this not in some sense collegialization, an intimation of the collegiality finally given greater attention at Vatican II? Only with Thérèse it seems somewhat wider: not only an episcopal and papal collegiality, but one which seems to find expression throughout the Church (see *Lumen Gentium* III: 22-23). There is even an urgency in Thérèse about this: she feels that her mission is one of "giving my little way to souls" (LC:102) in a quite general way.

One senses that we Catholics will go slowly with this one, and rightly so. We are in some sense a hierarchical Church, and we would want to resist the notion that Christian truth comes from a kind of mob majority. One the other hand, one senses that the lessons about the lowly being raised up which Thérèse draws from her experience, after great testing, are an important part of the thrust of history, and of the Church. In some form, democracy is a goal of many if not most nations. And, ecclesially, many churches have adopted "democratic" structures, while the Orthodox have their synodal forms of governance, and we have seen Vatican II resurface the notion of collegiality and communion as Church structures, not clarifying how far to extend them.

Perhaps we Catholics are waiting for the "tested experience" of our saints, like Thérèse's. For we sense dangers here, and yet also an almost irresistible tug. A tug which perhaps comes, not from a desire to be up to date, but from a genuinely evangelical intuition. Perhaps Thérèse's "way" can give us some helpful clues. Could we say that the infancy principle suggests that the little are to be in some sense "empowered" in the Church, and that the principle of the cross suggests that this must not be done naively, but critically, carefully, in a tested way? The little do not create Christian truth (only God does that), but are in touch with it precisely through their littleness. That is the source of their ecclesial empowerment, on Thérèsian grounds. And that is precisely why they must be listened to, not only when it is convenient, but *de jure*. There is a sort of "magisterium" of the saints, the *sensus sanctorum* (or *sensus fidelium* in its proper sense), which deserves greater ecclesial and perhaps even juridical (canonical) recognition. But that littleness must be constantly purified, through the cross of struggling against the narcissism, narrow self-interest, mob-rulism, relativism, and anarchism often associated with certain forms of democratic governance. And this is why there is a certain legitimate hesitation about using the language of democracy in ecclesial matters, with a consequent turning to other, less "dangerous" terms (viz., collegiality, communion). Although surely no words are perfect, all can be misleading and contaminated, and even "communion" and "collegiality" can be given quite secular, non-biblical meanings, and don't only originate from divine revelation. What words in Scripture, for example, stem only from revelation? Even *agape* is a Greek, secular term. Whichever term we use, we must try to "baptize" it, giving it something of a new, Christian meaning.

And perhaps here we have a kind of Thérèsian thinking through of the hierarchy, now in the light of the two devotions of infancy and passion.[20] For surely on a Catholic view of it, and on a Thérèsian view of it too, a collegialism of the faithful as a whole will not replace the hierarchy. As we have seen, the Thérèsian "child" is open to guidance and direction, seeking that kind of ecclesial welfare which is for us the mission of our pastors in the Church. And the Thérèsian principle of the cross alerts us to the egotistical and sinful tendencies in our lives, and so the need for a pastoral guidance and sifting once again.

Thus we have seen the Thérèsian experience confirm the Church's teaching ministry, limit and balance it, and perhaps guide it toward a new development of the Church's structure. In this way, Thérèse, like all the great saints, experientially exemplifies and develops in some way the Church's faith-heritage. Even while she exemplifies the heritage already in possession, she does so in a very fresh way, for she burrows down to the attractive experiential love-ground of that heritage.[21] And the way in which we have seen her possibly "develop" doctrine is through a fresh appropriation of the "old" biblical teaching about the little, the last. This is but a smattering of the possible implications we can draw for the Church's exercise of its doctrinal ministry in the works of Thérèse. But these are perhaps central lessons, still only partially appreciated, and perhaps even in danger of being ignored. They are surely enough to show us that Thérèse is definitely a challenge for today's doctrine and theology. I would have liked to have said something about Thérèse's heightened sense of the life-after too, for this surely is a significant doctrinal tendency in her, which both seems to fill her with hope even while it keeps her realistic, avoiding a utopianism which is really a form of human arrogance. Especially when one has the heightened sense of the child's boldness, like Thérèse, one seems to need a similarly heightened sense of the fragile nature of this world we inhabit. Perhaps the dimension of littleness in the child, as well as the devotion to the Holy Face, will to some extent compensate for our not pursuing this theme any further here. Especially with respect to the Thérèsian "intimations" about a greater expansion in the Church's "collegialism," I would suggest that we must keep her "non-utopian" (in the negative sense) realism in mind. If you will, we are the "Church militant," not the "Church triumphant."

Is St Thérèse a forerunner of Vatican III? There can be no doubt that she was a forerunner of Vatican II. It is as if she worked through many of the great issues the Church needed to confront in our modern period already in her own experience. She was, as it were, a Vatican II in miniature. And this is one of the roles of the great saints, their mission: to sift through, in their own purifying experiences, the great issues and struggles to which the rest of us are called. At Vatican II, the Church was trying to catch up with Thérèse, and it was able to do so partly, perhaps greatly, through her making assimilable to Catholics the issues that council had to confront: a Church more centered on love, on the person's dignity, on the Gospels, less elitist in its structures and spiritual teaching, less Jansenistic, less self-focused and more mission-oriented, etc.

But I'm not so sure that Vatican II was sufficient to "catch up" with Thérèse. Implied, at least as corollary, in the Thérèsian event is a summons to the Church to find a way to embody the struggle against elitism which her bold but critical Little Way teaches. Is there not an affinity between that Little Way, properly understood, and a future council at which not simply an elite preside and vote, but the little too, in some structured way, participate, and that *de jure*: women, religious of all types, humble priests, the "doctors" of theology, as well as the episcopal leadership in the Church? Would this go beyond the legitimate limits of Catholic hierarchicalism, or would it represent a Thérèsian-inspired modulation of the hierarchical structure? To paraphrase Thérèse, can the saint that she is be a fulcrum which might "lift" yet further the Church she is called to serve? (S:258)

NOTES

SONG OF SONGS AND THÉRÈSE

1. In what follows I am summarizing the commonly accepted results of current biblical scholarship. Not all would accept the dialogical unity which I recognize in the Song. For details see the (forthcoming) *New Jerome Biblical Commentary*, and also Roland E. Murphy, "Towards a Commentary on the Song of Songs," *Catholic Biblical Quarterly* 39 (1977):482-96, and "The Unity of the Song of Songs," *Vetus Testamentum* 29 (1979): 436-443.

2. For a fuller discussion, see Roland E. Murphy, "Patristic and Medieval Exegesis Help or Hindrance?" *Catholic Biblical Quarterly* 43 (1981): 505-16.

3. S, 179.

4. For another example of Sanjuanista influence, see S, 195. The text has "O Jesus, I know it, love is repaid by love alone . . ." and the note to this refers to John's comment on the *Spiritual Canticle*, stanza 9, 7.

5. At the same time, we are not to think of her as naive: "It's only in heaven that we'll see the whole truth about everything. This is impossible on earth. Thus, even regarding Holy Scripture, isn't it sad to see so many different translations! Had I been a priest, I would have learned Hebrew and Greek, and wouldn't have been satisfied with Latin. In this way, I would have known the real text dictated by the Holy Spirit." — see LC, 132.

6. A good example of the way the Divine Office influenced Thérèse, precisely in her use of the Song, can be seen in one of her letters to Céline; she uses lines from Sg. 1:12, 11, 16, as these are in the Office for the feast of the Sorrows of the Blessed Virgin; see L1:634, n. 16.

   Guy Gaucher has counted many references to the Song in thirty-five of her letters, twelve poems and five plays, and he makes the significant remark: "She does not seem to have had a complete text at hand, but knew the Song of Songs through the liturgy, St John of the Cross, and so on"; cf. Guy Gaucher, *The Story of a Life: St Thérèse of Lisieux* (San Francisco: Harper & Row, 1987), 141, n. 1. Gaucher, *Story of a Life*, 139 notes that Thérèse did not have an Old Testament book, but used Céline's notebooks in which several passages had been copied out (among them Prv. 9:4, which seems to be the seed of the "little" way). She also got from Céline the Gospels and St Paul's Epistles, bound into a single volume. (Gaucher, *Story of a Life*, 122)

7. S, 254-59; the quotations are from 257 and 258.
8. LT 144, Thérèse to Céline, 23 July 1893, GC2:711 [=L2:804].
9. LT 201, Thérèse to P. Roulland, 1 Nov. 1896, GC2:911 [=L2:1017].
10. LT 141, Thérèse to Céline, 25 April 1893, GC2:692 [=L2:785]; see also GC2:644 [=L2:732].
11. LT 165, Thérèse to Céline, 7 July 1894, GC2:765-66 [=L2:861-62].
12. For more details on "Aminadab," see *The Song of Songs,* trans./ed. Marvin H. Pope, Anchor Bible 7c (Garden City: Doubleday, 1977), 587-89.
13. LT 108, Thérèse to Céline, 18 July 1890, L1:629-32.
14. LT 149, Thérèse to Céline, 20(?) Oct. 1893, GC2:731-32 [=L2:827].
15. Quoted in Gaucher, *Story of a Life,* 141. From comments on "Thérèse et le Cantique des Cantiques," *Annales de Sainte Thérèse de Lisieux* no. 662 (Nov. 1987): 6-7 we learn that Thérèse revealed this to a young Carmelite novice, Marie of the Trinity.
16. *Sermon* 79, 1.

THE WORLD OF THÉRÈSE

1. ED's NOTE: The author offers the following books as a bibliography of collateral reading.

Daniel-Rops, Henri. *A Fight for God, 1870-1939.* London: Dutton, 1966.

Gaucher, Guy. *The Story of a Life; St Thérèse of Lisieux.* San Franciso: Harper & Row, 1982.

Magraw, Roger. *France 1815-1914: The Bourgeois Century.* Oxford: Oxford University Press, 1986.

McManners, John. *Church and State in France, 1870-1914.* London: S.P.C.K., 1972.

Moser, Mary Theresa. *The Evolution of the Option for the Poor in France, 1880-1965.* Lanham, MD: University Press of America, 1985.

Plongeron, Bernard. *Les réguliers de Paris devant le serment constitutionel.* Paris: J. Vrin, 1964.

Rich, Norman. *The Age of Nationalism and Reform, 1850-1890.* New York: W.W. Norton and Company, 1977.

Rohrbach, Peter-Thomas. *Journey to Carith.* Garden City, New York: Doubleday and Company, Inc., 1966.

Shirer, William L. *The Collapse of the Third Republic.* New York: Simon and Schuster, 1969.

Smet, Joachim. *The Carmelits: A History of the Brothers of our Lady of Mount Carmel, Vol. 4.* Darien, IL: Carmelite Spiritual Center, 1985.

AN ARTIST AND A SAINT

1. Ben Maddow, *Edward Weston: His Life and Photographs*, rev. ed. (Millerton, NY: Aperture, 1979).

2. Any Conger, *Edward Weston in Mexico, 1923-1926* (Albuquerque: Univ. of New Mexico Press, 1983).

3. Beaumont Newhall and Amy Conger, eds., *Edward Weston Omnibus: A Critical Anthology* (Salt Lake City: Peregrine Smith, 1984).

4. Charis Wilson and Edward Wilson, *California and the West* (New York: Duell, Sloane & Pearce, 1940).

5. Amy Conger, *The Monterey Photographic Tradition: The Weston Years—Essays by Dr Amy Conger* (Monterey: Monterey Museum of Art, 1986).

6. S, 97.

7. Guy Gaucher, *The Story of a Life: St Thérèse of Lisieux*, trans. Anne Marie Brennan (San Francisco: Harper & Row, 1987), 139.

8. S, 180.

9. S, 210.

10. LC, 205.

11. S, 197.

12. L1:353.

13. LC, 77.

14. *Poems of Sr Teresa, Carmelite of Lisieux*, trans. S.L. Emery (Boston: Carmelite Monastery, 1907), 50; LC, 264.

15. LC, 181.

16. LC, 141.

17. LC, 58.

18. LC, 134.

19. LC, 105.

20. *Photo Album of St Thérèse of Lisieux*, trans. Peter-Thomas Rohrbach (New York: P.J. Kenedy & Sons, 1962), 186.

21. *Poems*, 141.

22. LC, 197.

23. LC, 200.

24. LC, 173.

194   *Notes to "Religious Plays of St Thérèse"*

25. LC, 195.
26. LC, 224.
27. LC, 108.
28. LC, 175.
29. *Poems*, 105.
30. I recommend using the excellent indices of the ICS Publications volumes on Thérèse to see the amount and the variety of images used.
31. S, 213.
32. S, 259.
33. LC, 215.
34. LT 110, Thérèse to Sr Agnes, 30-31 Aug. 1890, L1:652.
35. LC, 138.
36. S, 1-9.
37. LC, 60.
38. LT 230, Thérèse to Mother Agnes, 28 May 1897, L2:1100-01.
39. LC, 57.
40. LC, 253.
41. LC, 45.
42. LC, 155, 165 and 241.
43. LT 89, Thérèse to Céline, 26 April 1889, L1:558.
44. S, 277.
45. *Poems*, 1.
46. LC, 228.
47. S, 179.
48. S, 194.
49. LC, 206.
50. S, 99.
51. S, 266; LC, 157.
52. LT 221, Thérèse to P. Roulland, 19 March 1897, L2:1073.
53. LC, 47 and 93.
54. Letter to the author, 26 August 1988.

RELIGIOUS PLAYS OF ST THÉRÈSE

1. The recent French editions, which include her correspondence, her final conversations, her poetry and recreational pieces, are available from Éditions du Cerf — Desclée de Brouwer in Paris.
2. Patricia O'Connor, *Thérèse of Lisieux: A Biography* (Huntington, IN: Our Sunday Visitor, Inc., 1983) and *In Searth of Thérèse* (Wilmington, DE: Michael Glazier, 1987).

3. Monica Furlong, *Thérèse of Lisieux* (New York: Virago/Pantheon Books, 1987).
4. See, for example, Joann Wolski Conn, "Conversion in Thérèse of Lisieux," *Spiritual Life* 24 (Fall 1978):154-63 and "Thérèse of Lisieux from a Feminist Perspective," *Spiritual Life* 28 (Winter 1982):233-39. Also William M. Thompson, "Reflecting on Ministry with St Francis of Assisi and St Thérèse of Lisieux," in his *Fire and Light: The Saints and Theology* (New York: Paulist Press, 1987). Special mention should be made of the recent work of Guy Gaucher in English translation by Sr Anne Marie Brennan, *The Story of a Life: St Thérèse of Lisieux* (San Francisco: Harper & Row, 1987). The journal *Carmelus* (Institutum Carmelitanum, Via Sforza Pallavicini, 10, 00193 Rome, Italy) has produced extensive reviews of the critical editions of St Thérèse's writings, especially in 1978, 1983 and 1987.
5. Sainte Thérèse de L'Enfant Jésus et de la Sainte-Face, *Théâtre au Carmel: "récréations pieuses"* (Paris: Éditions du Cerf — Desclée de Brouwer, 1985), 439 pp. This critical edition was edited by Sr Cécile of the Carmel of Lisieux and Guy Gaucher, along with a team of scholars. Cf. John F. Russell, "Théâtre au Carmel: a Review Article," *Carmelus* 34 (1987):67-77. Throughout this article references to this edition will be abbreviated "T" followed by the page number for reference.
6. Russell, "Review Article," 69.
7. The critical edition offers titles for each of the plays which were created by Fr François de Sainte-Marie, writing in 1956. The plays are entitled "The Mission of Joan of Arc or the Shepherd of Domremy listening to Voices," "Angels at the Manger of Jesus," "Joan of Arc Accomplishing her Mission," "Jesus at Bethany," "The Small Divine Beggar at Christmas," "The Flight into Egypt," "The Triumph of Humility" and "St Stanislaus Kostka." Since the first play or "récréation pieuse" is "The Mission of Joan of Arc . . ." it is known in the critical edition as RP 1. The second play chronologically is "Angels at the Manger . . ." and thus is is recorded as RP 2 and so on until the last play, "St Stanislaus Kostka", which is RP 8.
8. Gaucher, *Story of a Life*, 131.
9. See L1:450 and 588.
10. St Teresa of Avila, *Collected Works: Volume Two* (Washington, D.C.: Institute of Carmelite Studies, 1980), 420.
11. Russell, "Review Article," 71-76.
12. Ibid., 72.
13. Hans Urs von Balthasar, "The Timeliness of Lisieux," *Carmelite Studies* 1 (1980): 112-13.
14. Elizabeth Johnson, "Christology and Social Justice: John Paul II and the American Bishops," *Chicago Studies* 26 (August 1987):164.
15. Most Rev John Malley, O.Carm., "Father General's Letter for the Marian Year," Rome: Curia Generalizia dei Carmelitani, 1988. Xeroxed letter, p. 11.
16. P, 246.
17. Simon Tugwell, "Thérèse of Lisieux," chap. 18, *Ways of Imperfection* (Springfield, IL: Templegate Publishers, 1985), 225.
18. S, 221.

THÉRÈSE'S APPROACH TO GOSPEL LIVING

1. *Autobiography of St Thérèse of Lisieux*, trans. Ronald Knox (Fontana Books, n.d.), 27-28. [U.S. ed. New York: P.J. Kenedy, 1958, 36-37]

2. LT 96, Thérèse to Céline, 15 Oct. 1889, CG1:504 [=L1:587 and 588].

3. LT 142, Thérèse to Céline, 6 July 1893, CG2:701 [=L2:795].

4. DE, 231 [=LC, 67].

5. DE, 214-15 [=LC, 50-51].

6. DE, 584.

7. LT 201, Thérèse to P. Roulland, 1 Nov. 1896, CG2:909 [=L2:1015].

8. Knox, *Autobiography of Thérèse*, U.S. ed., 308-09 [=S, 256].

9. DE, 376 [=LC, 200].

10. LT 141, Thérèse to Céline, 25 April 1893, CG2:693 [=L2:785].

11. Cf. S, 195.

12. Knox, *Autobiography of Thérèse*, U.S. ed., 106 [=S, 77].

13. LT 142, Thérèse to Céline, 6 July 1893, L2:794-95.

14. DE, 788-89 [=LC, 268].

15. DE, 203 [=LC, 38].

16. DE, 273-74 (*Novissima Verba* substitutes "m'éblouisse" – "may dazzle me") [=LC, 105].

17. Cf. CG2:668, Preparatory Notes for the Apostolic Process, "Virtue of Fortitude" [=L2:758].

18. DE, 203-04 [=LC, 38-39].

19. DE, 313 [=LC, 142-43].

20. Cf. CG2:1002, n. f [=L2:1113, n. 6].

21. LT 167, Thérèse to Céline, 18 July 1894, CG2:776-77 [=L2:872].

22. LD, Mother Agnes to Mr & Mrs Guérin, 6 Dec. 1896, CG2:924 [=L2:1031]

23. Cf. CG2:728, n. h, Preparatory Notes for the Bishop's Process [=L2:823, n. 8].

24. Cf. P, 72, PN 10.

25. *St Thérèse of Lisieux by Those who knew Her*, ed. and trans. Christopher O'Mahony (Huntington, IN: OSV, 1975), 262.

26. DE, 201-02 [=LC, 36].

27. DE, 307 [=LC, 137].

28. LD, From Céline to Pauline Romet, 18 Feb. 1889, L1:532-34, esp. n. 6.

29. LC, 51.

30. Prayer 14 – see Ste Thérèse, *Prières: l'Offrande à l'Amour Miséricordieux* (Paris: Éditions du Cerf – Desclée de Brouwer, 1988), 49.

31. P, 210, PN 45, st. 6.

32. LC, 51.

33. P, 210, PN 45, st. 7.

34. P, 222, PN 45, st. 5.

35. S, 108.

36. T, 92.

37. S, 15.
38. P, 177, PN 34, st. 1.
39. Ibid., Refrain 1.
40. S, 196-97.
41. P, 177, PN 34, st. 2.
42. Ibid., Refrain 2.
43. P, 227, PN 51, v. 1.
44. Ibid., st. 2.
45. Ibid., st. 3.
46. Ibid., st. 4.
47. Ibid., st. 5.

THÉRÈSE AND THE MOTHER OF GOD

1. LC, 161. The important poem, 'Why I love you, Mary,' has not yet been published in English translation from the critical edition. Cf. P, 238-48 (where it is PN 54): "Pourquoi je t'aime, O Marie!" The translation is mainly my own, with no attempt to put it in verse.
2. LC, 162.
3. S, 40-41.
4. S, 64-66.
5. S, 246.
6. LT, 161, Thérèse to Céline, 26 April 1894, L2:851. *The Collected Letters of St Thérèse of Lisieux*, ed. A. Combes and trans. F.J. Sheed (Sheed and Ward, N.Y., 1949) had 238 entries, while the 266 items in the Clarke edition follow a new numbering pattern. The concordance of the two numberings promised for the end of Clarke's vol. 2 (p. 61, n. 3) is missing. ED's NOTE: Cf. L2:697 for an *In Memoriam* notice in honor of Fr John Clarke (d. 1985).
7. LC, 88.
8. See Louis Guillet, "La Sainte Vierge et Thérèse de l'Enfant Jésus," *Vie Thérèsienne* 23, no. 3 (1983): "Sous la voile de la Sainte Vierge."
9. S, 13.
10. LT 137, Thérèse to Céline, 19 Oct. 1892, L2: 761.
11. LT 92, Thérèse to Marie Guérin, 30 May 1889, L1:567-69.
12. As reported in L1:569, n. 4.
13. LC, 182-183.
14. S, 196: "Jesus, then enlighten me, for you know I am seeking only the truth."
15. See S, 108.
16. L1:61, n. 2 indicates that this item will appear not in the letters volume but in an additional book containing several of Thérèse's prayers—see Ste Thérèse, *Prières,*

(Paris: Éditions du Cerf—Desclée de Brouwer, 1988), 55 where it is Prayer 21. I take the translation here from F.J. Sheed, *Letters*, 370 where it is the very last entry, no. 238.

17. See the listing in n. 39 below.

18. Gaucher, *Story of a Life*, 185.

19. LC, 166.

20. LC, 235.

21. S, 82.

22. Gaucher, *Story of a Life*, 185.

23. Ibid., 184.

24. According to François de Ste Marie, in the article cited in n. 39 below.

25. S, 214 (capitalization by Thérèse in the original).

26. LC, 44.

27. Gaucher, *Story of a Life*, 141, n.1.

28. S, 142.

29. LC, 158.

30. LC, 63.

31. LC, 87.

32. LC, 164.

33. S, 180.

34. S, 276.

35. See the R. Valabek reference in n. 39 below.

36. S, 123.

37. LT 159, Thérèse to Céline Maudelonde, 26 March 1894, L2:846-47.

38. LT 166, Thérèse to Mme. Céline Maudelonde Pottier, 16 July 1894, L2:865-66.

39. Among the many studies consulted in preparing this paper the following deserve special notice:

Redemptus Valabek, the chapter, "More Mother than Queen: Our Lady of Mt Carmel and St Thérèse of Lisieux," *Mary Mother of Carmel. Our Lady and the Saints of Carmel*, vol. 2, (Rome: Carmel in the World Paperbacks, 1988), 75-100;

R. Valabek, "St. Thérèse of Lisieux seen through her Poetry," *Carmelus* 30 (1983): 3-57;

[Bishop] Guy Gaucher, *The Story of a Life: St Thérèse of Lisieux*;

L. Guillet, "La Sainte Vierge et Thérèse de l'Enfant Jésus," *Vie Thérésienne* 23 (1983) issue no. 3;

Abbé André Combes, "Marie pour Sainte Thérèse de Lisieux," *Divinitas* 14 (1970): 75-124;

François de Sainte Marie, "*La dévotion Mariale de Sainte Thérèse de l'Enfant Jésus 'Marie plus Mère que Reine,'*" *La maternité spirituelle de Marie*, from the 8th

national French Marian Congress, July, 1961, with a facsimile of the auto-
graph of the poem "Why I love you, Mary";

Marie-Joseph Nicolas, "The Virgin Mary in the Gospel and in the Church according to Saint Thérèse of Lisieux," trans. Warren Carlin, *The Sword* 19
(1956):250-263, 363-370; originally in *Revue thomiste* 52 (1952):508-527.

The interest in Europe in analyzing handwriting is much greater than in America,
and various studies have been done on the writing of St Thérèse. A recent
American example by a master graphanalyst is "St Thérèse's Handwriting," by
Norman Werling, M.G.A., *Carmelite Digest* 3 (Summer, 1988):3-11.

THÉRÈSE AND JOHN OF THE CROSS

1. Spiritual Canticle, Prol. 2. ED's NOTE: for the works of St John of the Cross we
will use the following abbreviations, found in previous volumes of CARMELITE
STUDIES:

A = Ascent of Mount Carmel   C = Spritual Canticle
N – Dark Night   F = Living Flame of Love

The page number following the reference indicates the I.C.S. ed. of *The Complete
Works of John of the Cross.*

2. C, Prol. 3; 409.
3. S, 179.
4. S, 14-15.
5. S, 15.
6. S, 189.
7. A, Prol. 3; 70. Underlining mine.
8. S, 27.
9. A, 2, 5, 4; 116.
10. LC, 251.
11. S, 91.
12. LC, 73-74.
13. S, 97.
14. Mt. 5:48.
15. LC, 138-39.
16. Other Counsels, 5; 681.
17. A, 1, 4, 5; 79.
18. S, 196 and 197.
19. A, 1, 22, 6; 98.
20. A, 2, 7, 8; 124.
21. S, 125.

22. A, 1, 5, 9; 82.
23. S, 237.
24. A, 3, 20, 2; 247.
25. LT 142, Thérèse to Céline, 6 July 1893 quoted from *Collected Letters of St Thérèse of Lisieux,* trans. F.J. Sheed (New York: Sheed and Ward, 1949), 167. [=L2:796]
26. A, 1, 14, 2; 105.
27. S, 207.
28. LT 226, Thérèse to P. Roulland, 9 May 1897, L2:1093.
29. Mt. 11:28.
30. S, 72.
31. S, 200.
32. S, 180.
33. LC, 77.
34. F, 2, 5 and 12; 597 and 599.
35. LC, 77.
36. S, 157.
37. S, 172 and 173.
38. N, 2, 9, 4; 347.
39. N, 2, 9, 5; 348.
40. Ibid.
41. LC, 88.
42. S, 179.
43. S, 254.
44. S, 242.
45. S, 214.
46. L, 30, 11 and 12; 198 and 199 (I.C.S. ed.).
47. N, 2, 9, 8; 349.
48. S, 211.
49. N, 2, 7, 1; 340.
50. S, 212.
51. S, 99.
52. LT 82, Thérèse to Céline, 28 Feb. 1889, L1:537.
53. LT 89, Thérèse to Céline, 26 April 1889, L1:558.
54. LT 85, Thérèse to Céline, 12 March 1889, L1:546.
55. LC, 72.
56. LC, 205.
57. S, 193.
58. S, 178.
59. C, 28; 413.
60. C, 29; 523.
61. LC, 177.
62. C, 39, 14; 562.

63. LC, 56 and 73.
64. LC, 243.
65. LT 254, Thérèse to P. Roulland, 14 July 1897, L2:1142.
66. S, 259.

A FEMINIST VIEW OF THÉRÈSE

1. This phrase is a theme in Elisabeth Schüssler Fiorenza, *In Memory of Her* (New York: Crossroad, 1983).
2. For a detailed account of Thérèse's life and culture see Guy Gaucher, *The Story of a Life*. For an original and provocative biography see Monica Furlong, *Thérèse of Lisieux* (New York: Virago/Pantheon Pioneers, 1987) and my review of Furlong in *Spiritual Life* 34 (Summer 1988):116-118.
3. Sandra Harding, "The Instability of the Analytical Categories of Feminist Theory," *Signs* 11 (Summer 1986):645-664.
4. Joann Wolski Conn, ed. *Women's Spirituality* (New York: Paulist, 1986).
5. Karl Rahner, *The Christian Commitment* (New York: Sheed and Ward, 1963). See also George Vandervelde, "The Grammar of Grace: Karl Rahner as a Watershed in Contemporary Theology." *Theological Studies* 49 (September 1988):445-459.
6. Joann Wolski Conn, "Spirituality and Human Maturity," in R. Wicks, R. Parsons, and D. Capps eds. *Clinical Handbook of Pastoral Counseling* (New York: Paulist, 1985).
7. Robert Kegan, *The Evolving Self* (Cambridge, MA: Harvard, 1982). My reasons for preferring Kegan to Carol Gilligan, *In a Different Voice* (Cambridge, MA: Harvard, 1982) are explained in Joann Wolski Conn, *Spirituality and Personal Maturity* (New York: Paulist, 1989).
8. Patricia O'Connor, *In Search of Thérèse* (Wilmington, DE: Michael Glazier, 1987).
9. See S.
10. See L1 and L2.
11. Joann Wolski Conn, "Review of *St Thérèse of Lisieux, Her Last Conversations,*" *Horizons* 6 (Fall 1979):308-309.
12. *Thérèse de Lisieux: Dialogue entre René Laurentin et Jean-François Six* (Paris: Beauchesne, 1973).
13. Joann Wolski Conn, "Thérèse of Lisieux From a Feminist Perspective," *Spiritual Life* 28/4 (Winter 1982):233-239.
14. Bernard Lonergan, *Method in Theology* (New York: Herder & Herder, 1972).
15. Joann Wolski Conn, "Conversion in Thérèse of Lisieux," *Spiritual Life* 24 (Fall 1978):154-163.
16. S, 97-99.

17. Ibid., 97.
18. Ibid.
19. Jean-François Six, *La Véritable Enfance de Thérèse de Lisieux* (Paris: Éditions du Seuil, 1972), 218.
20. *Dialogue entre René Laurentin et Jean-François Six,* 85-86.
21. LT 201, Thérèse to P. Roulland, 1 Nov. 1896, L2:1016-17.
22. "Thérèse From a Feminist Perspective."
23. Ibid.
24. LT 142, Thérèse to Céline, 6 July 1893, L2:796. See note 17 to this letter for an example of Thérèse's mature self-sacrifice regarding this practice.
25. LT 191, Thérèse to Léonie, 12 July 1896, L2:965-67.
26. Jean-François Six, *Thérèse de Lisieux au Carmel* (Paris, Éditions du Seuil, 1973).
27. LT 191, Thérèse to Léonie, 12 July 1896, L2:966.
28. S, 192.
29. S, 250.
30. S, 224.
31. S, 208.
32. S, 219-220.
33. S, 236.
34. LT 190, Thérèse to Mo. Marie de Gonzague, 29 June 1896, L2:958-62.
35. S, 193-194.
36. Constance FitzGerald, O.C.D., "Contemplative Life as Charismatic Presence," *Spiritual Life* 29/1 (Spring 1983):25-26.
37. Ibid., 28.
38. S, 211-214.
39. S, 214.
40. S, 211.
41. S, 99.
42. Six, *Thérèse au Carmel,* 251. See also Jean-François Six, *Thérèse de Lisieux et les incroyants,* Les Nouvelles de l'Institut Catholique de Paris, Numéro Spécial-Mai, 1973: 156-59.
43. S, 212.
44. S, 150.
45. S, 212.
46. Sebastian Moore, *The Inner Loneliness* (New York: Crossroad, 1982).
47. S, 189.
48. LT 191, Thérèse to Léonie, 12 July 1896, L2:966.
49. On the cultural interpretation of Thérèse, see Barbara Corrado Pope, "A Heroine Without Heroics: The Little Flower of Jesus and Her Times," *Church History* 57 (March 1988):46-60.

50. These effects of mutuality are developed by Jean Baker Miller, "What Do We Mean By Relationships?" *Work in Progress, No. 22* (Wellesley, MA: Stone Center Working Paper Series, 1986).

A PSYCHOANALYST LOOKS AT THÉRÈSE

1. Barry Ulanov, *The Making of a Modern Saint* (New York: Doubleday, 1966), 116.

2. Ibid., 118.

3. Ibid., 119.

4. See S. Freud, *Beyond the Pleasure Principle*, vol. 18, and also "Mourning and Melancholia," vol. 14, and also The Economic Problem of Masochism," vol. 19, in *The Standard Edition of The Complete Psychological Works of Sigmund Freud*, trans. James Strachey (London: Hogarth Press, 1955, 1957, 1961). See also M. Klein, *Envy and Gratitude and Other Works 1946-1963* (New York: Delacorte/Seymour Lawrence, 1975), 28.

5. See Esther Menaker, *Masochism and the Emergent Ego* (New York: Human Sciences Press, 1979), 61-63. See also Karen Horney, *New Ways in Psychoanalysis* (New York: Norton, 1959), chapter 15.

6. D. Erasmus, *The Praise of Folly*, trans. Hoyt Hopewell Hudson (New York: Modern Library, Random House, 1941), 87.

7. See M. Masud R. Khan, *Alienation in Perversions* (New York: International Universities Press, 1979), 148, 217.

8. C. G. Jung, *Psychology and Alchemy, Collected Works*, vol. 12, trans. R.F.C. Hull (New York: Pantheon, 1953), 10. For discussion of religious instinct, see also Ann Belford Ulanov, *The Feminine in Jungian Psychology and in Christian Theology* (Evanston: Northwestern University Press, 1971), 85-96.

9. Rosemary Gordon also writes about this view. See her, "Masochism: the shadow side of the archetypal need to venerate and worship." *The Journal of Analytical Psychology* 32, No. 3, 1987.

10. See Lyn Cowan, *Masochism: A Jungian View* (Dallas: Spring, 1982), 5-6, 11-12, 36-37, 41-42, 61, 98.

11. See Ann and Barry Ulanov, *Religion and the Unconscious* (Philadelphia: Westminister, 1975), chap. 9, "Moral Masochism and Religious Submission" for additional discussion.

12. For discussion of the anxiety of being and nonbeing, see Ann Belford Ulanov, "The Anxiety of Being," in *The Thought of Paul Tillich*, eds. James Luther Adams, Wilhelm Pauck, Roger Lincoln Shinn (San Francisco: Harper & Row, 1985).

13. Barry Ulanov, *Modern Saint*, 103.

14. Ibid., 104.

15. Ibid., 135.
16. My husband and I experienced this in writing about envy and about the witch.
    See Ann and Barry Ulanov, *Cinderella and Her Sisters: The Envied and the Envying*
    (Philadelphia: Westminster, 1983); Ann and Barry Ulanov, *The Witch and the
    Clown: Two Archetypes of Human Sexuality* (Wilmette: Chiron, 1987).
17. See Ann Belford Ulanov, *The Wisdom of the Psyche* (Cambridge: Cowley, 1987),
    38-46 for a discussion of the false cross.
18. Barry Ulanov, *Modern Saint*, 268 and 316.
19. Ibid., 225. See also 125.
20. Ibid., 324.

THÉRÈSE AND THE MODERN TEMPERAMENT

1. In my biographical study of Thérèse, I began by speaking about her "genius . . .
   for accurate observation of the world around her and all the people in it . . ."
   That, I suggested, was her realism. That is her modernity. See Barry Ulanov,
   The Making of a Modern Saint (Garden City: Doubleday, 1966), v.
2. Pranzini had killed two women and a child in the course of a robbery in the spring
   of 1887. Thérèse thought she might be able to intervene for his soul in some way,
   with a special mass and prayers. Just before he was guillotined, Pranzini grabbed
   the crucifix a priest was offering him and kissed it three times. "It was a true
   exchange of love," Thérèse said. See *The Making of a Modern Saint*, 118-119
   [=S, 101].
3. These words are addressed to Mary; they conclude:
       To love and suffer is our joy,
           As thine was, here below.
   The translation appears in *Just for Today* (Springfield: Templegate, 1950), 49
   [=PN 54, st. 16 "Pourquoi je t'aime, O Marie!"].
4. The variations on HCE, and more particularly on Humphrey and Earwicker, are
   endless in *Finnegans Wake*. Humphrey yields, among other things, hump, hunfree,
   and trihump; Earwicker yields its source, the insect called earwig, and by ancient
   association, secret communications received through the ear, thoughts wiggled
   into the head.
5. See *Just for Today*, 48. [=LT 191, Thérèse to Léonie, 12 July 1896, L2:966].
6. See James Joyce, *Finnegans Wake* (New York: Viking Press, 1939), 194. This is
   within a page of the end of chap. 7, which is essentially a portrait of the artist.
   Joyce himself, or in his major persona in the *Wake*, Shem the Penman. The words
   that follow this quotation are significant: "when day's woe, and lo, you're doomed,
   joyday dawns and, la, you dominate . . ." Circular, cyclical sentiments, woe and
   joy inextricably joined together.

7. Joyce would not have called his work an Act of Oblation, using capital letters as Thérèse did for her offering to God's "merciful love," but his sentiments, especially where he appears as Shem the Penman in *Finnegans Wake*, are not far removed from Thérèse's great cry, "O my God, is your despised love doomed to remain imprisoned in your heart?" See chap. 7 of the *Wake* (169-195) and *The Making of a Modern Saint*, 211-212.

8. See T.S. Eliot, "Burnt Norton" (first of the *Four Quartets*) in *The Complete Poems and Plays: 1909-1950* (New York: Harcourt, Brace, 1952), 117.

9. See "Burnt Norton," ibid., 119.

10. See especially "East Coker," second of the *Quartets*, ibid., 127, from "You say I am repeating" to the end of the passage, "And where you are is where you are not." It is an almost exact quotation from John of the Cross, *The Ascent of Mount Carmel*, 1, 13, 11, cadenced to fit Eliot's verse scheme, but only barely reworded.

11. The best translation into English is by Michael Meyer, in *The Plays of Strindberg*, vol. 2 (New York: Vintage Books, 1976).

12. Suffering must come; the question put to us by Thérèse is simply, What will you make of suffering and its graces? Love cannot be found without suffering — wasn't it by suffering that redemption came to the world? Thérèse was splendidly un-sentimental about all of this. See *Just for Today*, 109, 194, 227 and *The Making of a Modern Saint*, 351-59 [compare with LT 89, L1:557-59].

13. That is the beginning of the reminiscence about her "neighbor" in prayer "who did nothing but rattle her rosary, or make some other slight noise the whole time." I have quoted from two different sources in this footnote, chap. 10 of the *Autobiography* in the John Beevers translation (Garden City: Image Books, 1957), 142, and *Just For Today*, 109 [=S, 249].

14. See the Beevers version of the *Autobiography*, 145 [=S, 254].

15. See the St Thérèse, *Manuscrits autobiographiques* (Paris: Livre de Vie, 1957) 301. The French reads, "mais surtout j'imite la conduite de Madeleine, son étonnante ou plutôt son amoureuse audace qui charme le Coeur de Jésus, séduit le mien." This is in the great tradition of the devotees of the Song of Songs [=S, 258-59].

16. See the *Manuscrits autobiographiques*, 233 [=S, 200].

17. See the Beevers edition, 15.

18. *Just for Today*, v-vi.

19. Let us not be condescending about Thérèse's hand. She writes neatly, clearly, with a studied serif-filled elegance which, perhaps, only the young could accomplish so evenly, so insistently. If it is a childish hand, working "laboriously" at its task, it is a gifted hand, too, and admirable in its several determinations to be clear, with just enough changes of slant and variations of ornamentation to reflect at least some of the passion that is in the content.

20. See the *Manuscrits autobiographiques*, 240-241; Beevers, 114 [=S, 208].

21. Ibid.

22. "Ah!" Thérèse exclaims in one of her most touching passages, "malgré ma petitesse, je voudrais éclairer les âmes comme *les Prophètes, les Docteurs* . . ." (Her

italics)·"In spite of my smallness," she says, "I should like to enlighten souls as the prophets and the Doctors of the Church did." She has done just that. The title should be hers; it would confer honor on those who might be responsible for making it official. See the *Manuscrits,* 224 [=S, 192].

THÉRÈSE, CHALLENGE FOR DOCTRINE AND THEOLOGY

1. Thérèse is referring to the theme of suffering in *The Imitation of Christ,* I,2:3; III, 49:7; and Is. 53:3. We recall the importance that Guy Gaucher gives to this theme in his *La Passion de Thérèse de Lisieux* (Paris: Éditions du Cerf — Desclée de Brouwer, 1972), and we know that Mother Agnes (Pauline) testified, at the beatification process, that "Devotion to the Holy Face was the Servant of God's special attraction. As tender as was her devotion to the Child Jesus, it cannot be compared to her devotion to the Holy Face." (LC, 13) Note Thérèse's statement, while dying, recorded in LC, 135: "These words of Isaiah: 'Who has believed our report? . . . There is no beauty in him, no comeliness, etc.,' [Is. 53:1-2] have made the whole foundation of my devotion to the Holy Face, or, to express it better, the foundation of all my piety. I, too, have desired to be without beauty, alone in treading the winepress, unknown to everyone."

2. One of the major themes of both Von Balthasar and O'Connor is the notion that Thérèse moves from a desire to always want to suffer and die, to a stance of simply being open to God's Will, whatever it may be. The latter stance seems a greater selflessness, and thus a greater participation in the kind of passion charac- teristic of Jesus: egoless love. Again, note LC, 183: [Pauline] *"asked 'You prefer to die rather than to live?'* "O little Mother, I don't love one thing more than another; I could not say like our holy Mother St Teresa: "I die because I do not die." What God prefers and chooses for me, that is what pleases me more.'" See Patricia O'Connor's chap. 4, "The Romantic — The Martyr," *In Search of Thérèse,* 65-82; and Hans Urs von Balthasar's chapter "Indifference," *Thérèse of Lisieux: The Story of a Mission,* trans. Donald Nicholl (New York: Sheed and Ward, 1954), 225-41. Of course, the "great" St Teresa of·Avila knew and lived the kind of utterly selfless love of which the "little" St Thérèse speaks: cf. the former's ". . . Lord, either to die or to suffer; I don't ask anything else for myself." (*The Book of Her Life* 40, 20, 283]; cf. *Spiritual Testimonies* 9: "This surrender to the will of God is so powerful that the soul wants neither death nor life . . ." [*ibid.,* 365]).

3. O'Connor, *In Search,* 90; see, too, 83-99. See also Joann Wolski Conn, ed. "Thérèse of Lisieux from a Feminist Perspective," *Women's Spirituality* (New York: Paulist, 1986), 317-25.

4. Surely Thérèse grew in what it means to be a child, as the biographies indicate.

5. Henri Bremond has made much, we recall, of the shift in seventeenth-century French piety from thinking of Jesus the child as symbolic of suffering (children are weak and easily die) to thinking of him rather more positively, as comely and dignified. Marguerite de Beaune (du Saint-Sacrament) is the crucial figure for Bremond. Perhaps, too, the evolution of the way we have come to think of children comes into play here. My impression is that childhood was a mix of positivities and negativities in seventeenth-century French piety, but the positive side does seem to sublimate the negative in Thérèse. Sublimate does not mean erase. See Bremond's *A Literary History of Religious Thought in France*, 3, *The Triumph of Mysticism*, trans. K. L. Montgomery (London: SPCK, 1936), Part 3/ Chap. 1, "The Spirit of Childhood and the Devotion of the Seventeenth Century to the Child Jesus," 435-96. Also helpful: Lloyd de Mause, ed., *The History of Childhood* (New York: Harper Torchbooks, 1975). A helpful "liberationist" reading of childhood is provided by Gustavo Gutierrez, who has tried to bring out the social "power" implied in spiritual childhood, for entry into the world of poverty requires a child's humility. He also appreciatively refers to St Thérèse in the same book. See *We Drink from Our Own Wells*, trans. Matthew J O'Connell (Maryknoll, NY: Orbis, 1984), 122-27, 88, 111.

6. Von Balthasar, *Mission*, 160 and 163. See S, 151, 155 and 200. Also helpful: Mary E. Peters, "Christological Symbolism in the Writings of St Thérèse of Lisieux: Synthesis and Mimesis," Ph.D. Dissertation, Florida State Univ., 1986, vii + 231.

7. In what follows, I have been stimulated, at least catalytically, sometimes even rather more explicitly, by Karl Rahner's many writings on doctrine, esp. "Yesterday's History of Dogma and Theology for Tomorrow," *Theological Investigations* 18, trans. Edward Quinn (New York: Crossroad, 1983), 3-34.

8. The text is from one of her letters: LT 226, Thérèse to P. Roulland, 9 May 1897, *Collected Letters* ed. Sheed, 333-34 [I.2:1095].

9. See *Letters from Baron Friedrich von Hügel to a Niece*, ed. Gwendolen Greene (Chicago: Henry Regnery, 1955), 119.

10. Von Balthasar, *Mission*, 62; one needs to read Von Balthasar's whole work to catch his critique of the saint, although, of course, he is enormously careful, respectful, and overwhelmingly positive about her. Laurentin tries convincingly to correct the notion that Thérèse thought she was not a sinner, as well as the idea that she was not a great mystic (both views of Von Balthasar) in *Thérèse de Lisieux: Mythes et réalité*, 2nd ed. (Paris: Beauchesne, 1972), 165-88.

11. Von Balthasar titles an entire chapter "Existential Theology," *Mission*, 13-36. Remember that he wrote this book in 1950. While he seems to appreciate the role of experience, he tends, so far as I can tell, to highlight its subjective dangers, even tracing this, for Thérèse, back to her Order's beginnings: "We may also detect here a certain weakness in the tradition of Carmel which is traceable to those masters in psychology and self-analysis, Teresa of Avila and John of the Cross" (p. 117). We can accept his view of the dangers of the experiential, without

always agreeing to the specific conclusions he draws. See, for example, his "Experience God?," *New Elucidations* (San Franciso: Ignatius Press, 1986), 20-45.

12. *St. Thérèse of Lisieux by Those who knew Her: Testimonies from the Process of Beatification*, ed. and trans. Christopher O'Mahony, (Huntington, IN: Our Sunday Visitor, 1976), 117. Listen to Baron Friedrich von Hügel's report of Cardinal Bourne's comments about her (the Baron died in Jan., 1925; she was canonized in May of the same year; interestingly, one of the Baron's daughters was a Carmelite): ". . . she had marked an epoch in his own spiritual life; . . . she had specially taught him two things, how little human direction certain souls need—God is their Director; and how hidden is the life of most holy souls, since we know of her holiness only thro' the accident of having been ordered to write down her experiences and by the favours granted thro' her after her death" (as reported in Michael de la Bedoyère, *The Life of Baron Von Hügel* [London: J. M. Dent & Sons, 1951], 349-50).

13. Von Balthaser, *Mission*, 209: her little way is a Catholic formulation of justification by faith.

14. Please note that I speak of the "personal," rather than the "individual," to emphasize that Thérèse is not individualistic in the pejorative, narcissistic sense. Her ego went through too many purifying dark nights to have been egotistical. A very suggestive essay on this theme would be Karl Rahner, "On the Significance in Redemptive History of the Individual Member of the Church," *Mission and Grace*, 1, trans. Cecily Hastings (New York: Sheed and Ward, 1963), 114-71.

15. See Karl Rahner, "Modern Piety and the Experience of Retreats," *Theological Investigations* 16, trans. David Morland (New York: Seabury, 1979), 135-55, for this theme of the modern sense of the person (which Rahner sees markedly in St Ignatius Loyola) and the post-modern sense of community, together with the need to keep the two in tension.

16. Joann Wolski Conn has pointed this out very helpfully, and anyone studying the theological manuals of Thérèse's own time will quickly catch the profound difference between the Church viewed as a "perfect society" and the Church whose "heart is love." Thérèse here drinks more fully from the mystical tradition of ecclesiology, perhaps that of the French School, whose thinking is quite similar. Bérulle, Madeleine de St Joseph, Olier, St John Eudes, St Louis-Marie Grignion de Montfort, and St John Baptist de La Salle all have ecclesiologies of love. See Ida F. Goerres, *The Hidden Face: The Life of Thérèse of Lisieux*, trans. Richard and Clara Winston (New York: Pantheon, 1959), 258-71, for the suggestion of the French School as a source, at least orally. Cf. *Bérulle and the French School*, Classics of Western Spirituality, ed. William M. Thompson, trans. Lowell M. Glendon (New York: Paulist, 1989).

17. Patricia O'Connor, *Thérèse of Lisieux: A Biography*, 26; cf. S, 90.

18. S, 140, 192-200. "The sacrifice of not being able to be a priest was something she always felt deeply," said Geneviève, *Those who knew Her*, 155-56. See O'Connor,

In Search, 118-39, and my *Fire and Light: The Saints and Theology* (New York: Paulist, 1987), 164-77.

19. Geneviève's testimony, *Those who knew Her*, 134.

20. To the common charge that Catholicism cannot be a democracy because truth comes from God, not from the people, while the intent of the charge needs to be appreciated (the fear of reducing revelation to simply a human-made reality), surely there is room for a distinction between truth and the mode through which truth comes to us. Truth is of God, and in fact, God; but we come to truth through historically-mediated sources: hierarchy, the faithful, etc. The issue of some form of Thérèsian-inspired collegialism or democratization seems but a thinking through of these things more carefully. Still, perhaps the possible misunderstandings of the term "democracy," even when taken over and "baptized" by Christianity, outweigh the advantages, given the current cultural climate.

21. "Few theologians have shown the same skill as Thérèse in mapping out the realm of love; she has sketched a sort of map of the spirit on which certain hills and rivers are noted for the first time," says Von Balthasar, 210. Perhaps not since Fénelon has someone contributed as remarkable a phenomenology of love as has Thérèse. It was, early on among Thérèsian scholars, a special quality of André Combes to have emphasized Thérèse's contribution to a theology of love; cf, among others, his *Saint Thérèse and Her Mission: The Basic Principles of Thérèsian Spirituality*, trans. Alastair Guinan (New York: P. J. Kenedy & Sons, 1955), esp. chap. 2, "Love's Essential Nature," 27-55.